The

AMAZING

Story of How I

CURED

my

BIPOLAR

DISORDER

How I Cured

my

Bipolar Disorder

by

Charles Shelton

December 2025 Printing

ISBN: 978-1-7336235-5-1

Dedication

I would like to dedicate this book to anyone who suffers from depression or bipolar disorder or any other type of mental illness.

.

CONTENTS

Acknowledgments

I would like to thank God, the Almighty, the Creator of all things, for giving me the knowledge, wisdom, strength, and ability to cure myself of bipolar disorder, which is something that He deserves the full credit for. For it is something that I would not have been able to accomplish or do, hadn't it been for the God-given brain, innate talents, reasoning, thinking abilities, and other amazing gifts and things that He so generously equipped and supplied me with.

Preface

The reason this book was written is to tell my inspiring, true story, about how I cured myself of depression and bipolar disorder. And, also to provide comfort and encouragement to other victims of the disorders, and to their families and love ones as well—showing that there is genuine hope that they too (the victim of mental illness) may someday be cured of their illness too!

Also, in addition to being an encouragement to other victims of mental illness, this book can also prove to be a real source of inspiration and hope to anyone and everyone, even to people without depression and bipolar disorder, for it shows how an ordinary person can muster up an incredible amount of strength and courage to fight and overcome great odds to defeat any foe that they may face in life, even major illnesses like chronic depression and bipolar disorder!

What is most encouraging and helpful about this book, is that, it contains a comprehensive, step-by-step narrative, showing and explaining how I progressively, over a relatively short period of time, completely healed myself, once and for all time of the distressing and often debilitating illness—bipolar disorder, along with the painful episodes of depression that it produces.

I, the author and writer of this printed publication, who, in the past, had been a bipolar disorder patient for over 10 years, but, now, no longer have or show any signs or symptoms of the illness, hope that this amazing medical breakthrough that I experienced, as well as the exciting groundbreaking information presented within the pages of this book, can offer inspiration and hope, as well as shed some valuable insight into perhaps providing a cure for others too.[1]

In this book you will learn how I rose above and out of depression and bipolar disorder—fighting against all odds. For just think, some years ago, I personally believed that there was absolutely no hope for my mental health condition—that there was simply no chance of ever being cured—at least, not in my lifetime. How sad! Especially, because, at that time (that is, up until the time that I cured myself of bipolar disorder), in the medical community and elsewhere, according to psychiatrists, doctors, psychologists, mental health organizations, professionals, experts, specialists, etc., (throughout the entire world), there was no known cure for bipolar disorder. For according to them, bipolar disorder is a chronic, incurable, lifelong condition. However, look at me now! I proved all of them to be wrong. For I am now 100%, completely healed of my mental illness! What an amazing turnaround I have made in my mental health! This makes me extremely happy! For one of the greatest assets or gifts that a person can possess in life, is to have a measure of good health, including mental health, which is something that I am extremely grateful for, especially, now that I have been totally healed and cured of my illness—bipolar disorder. This priceless gift is more valuable than any material possessions or anything else that one might come to have or possess!

Charles Shelton

3 May 2021

---

[1] This book is not a substitute for therapy. Also, it is not a medical book that is intended to provide medical advice or to take the place of medical advice and treatment from your personal healthcare professional, physician, etc. See full disclaimer in the back of book.

BIPOLAR DISORDER

FINDING A CURE

From the early beginnings of time man has been diligently and unceasingly searching for a cure for various illnesses and diseases. Unfortunately, he hasn't had much success, not even as far as finding a cure for the simple, common cold. So for me to suggest or say that I've found a cure for my bipolar disorder, which is a much more serious, severe, and long term illness than a mere viral infection such as a cold, is quite a statement or claim. Nevertheless, truth is, I did find a cure for my illness. And now I am eager to share this exciting and valuable information with others, especially those who are suffering from the same malady or illness.[2]

---

[2] Note: I do not recommend that anyone else do this. But, eventually (after having been on them for quite some time), I had my mental health professional (psychiatrist) wean me off of my bipolar medications. The primary reason why I did this is because I felt that I didn't need them anymore. Also, a secondary reason why is because I wanted to prove to myself and others that my medications had nothing to do with curing me of bipolar disorder, but, rather, that I accomplished this completely on my own, without the help of anyone or anything. I'm not saying that prescribed medications are not good or beneficial to take, or that they are necessarily bad—because they're not. Many of them do

1

For those who may not be thoroughly familiar with the life altering illness that painfully inflicts so many people throughout the world (no matter their race, gender, nationality, age, etc), Bipolar Disorder, formerly known as "Manic Depression," is clinical depression, a mental illness. This type of depression is much different and more severe than the ordinary, common or garden variety depression; the regular, normal ups and downs of life. One prominent characteristic or feature of bipolar disorder is that it involves two separate phases of extreme mood swings that alternate or go from (1) depressive lows, to (2) manic or euphoric highs. In other words, with bipolar disorder illness you display only two prominent moods—one at a time (either you're very happy, or you're very sad). Because the internal gravitational forces of the illness that takes place from within you, pulls your moods in the direction of either up or down. There is no middle ground.

An interesting fact to note is that, the two extreme mood swings associated with bipolar disorder, are not like a light switch that quickly turns on, and then off again. These episodes or phases may last for weeks or even months at a time.

Speaking from personal experience, I can honestly say that bipolar disorder is one of the worst, if not the most difficult and painful thing to have to cope and live with in life. Often, in regards to my personal case (prior to being healed of bipolar disorder illness), whenever I happened to be in the bipolar *depressive phase,* it would often generate an extremely sad and hopeless type of condition or feeling in me—a sort of deep, gnawing, emotionally painful sadness that would eat at, consume, and overwhelm my soul. At times, it was so extremely anguishing, distressing, and miserably

---

help people and serve their purpose in regards to certain needs and objectives. However, personally, I just felt that they were no longer needed in regards to my individual situation or case. The good thing is, in the end, it turned out that I was right. Disclaimer: I do not endorse or recommend that anyone stop taking their prescribed medications. Readers are advised to consult their own doctors or other qualified health professionals regarding the treatment of medical conditions such as depression and bipolar disorder and their prescribed medications.

intense, that it made me groan, and even weep and cry. During this time, I felt like my heart was shattered or broken, or that I was mourning the death of a loved one, but only ten times worse! The effects can be so physically, mentally, and emotionally draining, that you don't even have the energy, strength, or desire to go anywhere or to do anything. Often, all you want to do is lie down, bury your head in a pillow and go to sleep.

Due to the unrelentingly sad and overwhelming degree of mental and emotional pain that is often associated with bipolar disorder, it can cause feelings of hopelessness—that perhaps your heart will never ever feel true joy and happiness again. You look for comfort and seek relief, but these things seem to have vanished from off the face of the earth. At times, things can get so bad, that you loathe your life, and you wish that you had never been born. You feel like the man of ancient times in the Bible, named, Job, who, because of the severity of his unceasing misery, pain, and sufferings, cursed the day he was born.—Job 3:1-26.[3] (See footnote)

Fortunately, for me — occurring not a moment too soon — early in the year 2021, my Psychiatrist, and also my Mental Health Psychologist, both informed me that my bipolar disorder is in the remissive stage. In other words, I am no longer showing any signs or symptoms of the disease. Interestingly, although this was welcoming, happy, and good news, it wasn't something that was totally surprising to me. Why not? Because, for quite some time (over a relative lengthy and progressive period of time), I had personally been working hard to heal myself of the distressing and debilitating illness.

Sometime later, after a significantly long period of additional time had passed; once again, to her utter surprise, my psychiatrist confirmed and stated that I had made a complete, 100% turnaround in my mental health. And due to the fact that I am now completely cured of depression and bipolar disorder (as she, herself, fully

---

[3] Note: In addition to what I have already highlighted above, for a fuller description of Bipolar Disorder, along with more of its symptoms, see the information *"Bipolar Disorder,"* in the appendix, on pages 182-197.

confirmed and stated), she, in congratulations to me, for my dramatically improved and sustained, vibrant, mental health and success, totally released me from her care, and all mental healthcare—both present and future. What an amazing reversal I have made in my mental health! which is something that I accomplished all on my own, without the help of anyone, including psychiatrists, doctors, etc.[4] As a result, today, I am finally at peace with myself and happy and healthy in all respects!

Interestingly, when I initially began working towards a cure, I did not know for certain that an actual cure for bipolar disorder was even remotely possible and, especially, that I would be the one to actually find it. Especially, because, at that time (that is, up until the time that I cured myself of bipolar disorder), in the medical community and elsewhere, according to psychiatrists, doctors, psychologists, mental health organizations, professionals, experts, specialists, etc., (throughout the entire world), there was no known cure for bipolar disorder. For according to them, bipolar disorder is a chronic, incurable, lifelong condition. Nevertheless, I still worked hard towards this goal anyways. The wonderful thing is, in the end, all of the persistence, hard work and efforts that I put forth eventually paid off! For look at me now! I am 100%, completely healed of my mental illness! What an amazing turnaround I have made in my mental health! which makes me extremely happy!

Personally, I am absolutely thrilled to have accomplished this amazing phenomena or feat, overcoming and defeating a major

---

[4] Note: My psychiatrist was absolutely fascinated and amazed that I had completely cured myself of bipolar disorder. She asked me what I did to cure myself. However, I didn't say. I was reluctant to tell her, because I had written this book (something that she was unaware of at the time). Interestingly, a couple of years prior to me being cured of bipolar disorder — during various stages of my psych appointments and visits with them — my Psychiatrist and also my Mental Health Psychologist (both of whom are mental health professionals), informed me several times (during the time period leading up to me being declared cured of my mental illness), that I am not showing any signs or symptoms of depression and bipolar disorder anymore. However, it wasn't until the year 2021 that my psychiatrist finally fully confirmed it and released me from her care.

illness—bipolar disorder, which has distressed and plagued so many people and victims for so long, including myself. It is the greatest achievement and victory that I have ever won or experienced in my entire life! But, not only that, I am honored and excited to share my encouraging story and this extremely important and valuable information with others as well.

Not All Appreciative of the Good News

Hearing the amazing news that someone has actually been cured of bipolar disorder can be very exciting and encouraging, especially to others who are suffering from the same illness, and also to their family and loved ones as well. Because it offers hope that they (the victim of mental illness) might be cured someday too!

Sad to say, however, not all are appreciative of the good news. For example, one uninformed person (a non-medical professional) wrongly asserted or implied that I didn't really cure myself of bipolar disorder. But rather, they said that it is a symptom or case of *grandiose* thinking that I am having or experiencing.[5] However, this is farthest from the truth! Because according to the dictionary, the definition of the word *grandiose,* in regards to Psychiatry, means "Having an exaggerated belief in one's importance, sometimes reaching delusional proportions, and occurring as a common symptom of mental illness, as *manic* disorder."

Notice that it says that *grandiose* thinking is a symptom of *"manic"* disorder. In other words, for me to be exhibiting grandiose thinking (as the person had implied above), I would have to be undergoing or experiencing a *manic* episode, which I am not. For one thing, *manic* episodes are a symptom of and occur *only* in people with "Bipolar Disorder I." This is not a symptom of "Bipolar Disorder II."

---

[5] *Grandiose* thinking, in regards to mental health, is a symptom experienced by people with "Bipolar Disorder I," during *manic* episodes, which are often characterized by fantastical beliefs that one is famous, omnipotent, wealthy, or otherwise very powerful.

Personally, I don't currently have, nor have I ever had Bipolar "Disorder I." Both, initially (when I first became ill), and thereafter, I was diagnosed and treated for Bipolar Disorder II. Interestingly, with Bipolar Disorder II, a person may experience *hypomania* (a milder version of mania), but it never reaches full blown mania, as it does in people with "Bipolar Disorder I," who might experience and exhibit *grandiose* thinking—one of the possible symptoms of "Bipolar Disorder I," only!

Another important point to note about *manic* episodes (that occur only in people with "Bipolar Disorder I"), is that these episodes last just a relatively short period of time. Depending on the individual, a *manic* episode could last for days or a week or more, but not much longer than this. Interestingly, due to the short time frame or nature of *manic* episodes, my supposed manic episode (that is, if I were in fact having one—which I am not), would never have lasted for as long a time as my bipolar disorder has been in a state of total remission (which has now been years), where I am not experiencing any signs or symptoms of the illness or disorder anymore.

In summation, we have learned some interesting things about the subject of *grandiose* thinking, along with its symptom, *manic* episodes. One: Grandiose thinking is a symptom of *manic* disorder only. Two: Grandiose thinking is exhibited only during manic episodes. Three: Manic episodes are symptoms of "Bipolar Disorder I," only. And finally: Manic episodes don't last forever, but, rather, they are relatively short-lived in duration.

From the above information, we can clearly see that my case or claim of being cured of bipolar disorder is truly *not* a matter or case of *grandiose* thinking, as was wrongly asserted by the misinformed person mentioned above.

Another person erroneously said that they don't believe that my bipolar disorder was actually cured, but, rather, that perhaps, I am in a state of *denial*—not wanting to accept or face the fact that I have the dreaded illness. However, I know this also to be totally untrue. One reason why is because denial usually happens or takes place early in the process—when one is initially given the results or bad news that they are bipolar, which may be very difficult for some people to personally acknowledge and accept at first. Nonetheless, as time progresses, one usually begins to accept the diagnoses, along with recommended medical treatment, which is something that I personally did many years ago![6]

Expelling Doubts

Sometimes, in order for a person to be able to accept something new or that is hard to believe, such as the idea or notion that a patient has been cured of a major illness such as bipolar disorder, they (the non-believing person), needs to be educated or given more knowledge or information on the subject first. Then, afterwards, they can go on to make a well informed and educated decision on the matter.

In other words, it is best for a tentative or skeptical person to get to know or acquire accurate knowledge first, of what the illness (bipolar disorder) really is, along with its various symptoms. Then, they can look at or examine the cured patient's life and health condition, as to what it was *prior* to the cure, in comparison to later, *after* the healing took place. Subsequently, if the end results show that the patient is no longer showing any signs or symptoms of the illness, then they can rightly assume or conclude that his illness is either in a state of remission or that he has been completely cured.

Personally, I know for certainty that I have been completely healed and cured of my bipolar disorder illness, for not only did my psychiatrist fully confirm it, but, also, I am perfectly in tune with and know my own mind and body very well. In other words, I know if I am healed or not. In addition, sufficient time has elapsed, thereby confirming it to be true. And as future time goes by, it will only add even more concrete evidence. Also, the very content of this book will go on to undeniably show that "the proof is in the pudding"—

---

[6] Note: Just because a person has bipolar disorder, clinical depression, or any other mental illness, it doesn't make them a bad person or anything. Nor is it something to be ashamed of. These things can happen to anyone.

meaning that, the truth, that I have been cured of my bipolar disorder, is proven, based on the results.

However, it's not important for me at this time to be concerned about what other people think. For there will always be negative people, naysayers, skeptics, and even jealous and hateful people that try to discount something credible, true, factual, or good. The important thing is for me to continue to truly believe in my heart and mind that I am cured of my bipolar disorder, otherwise, what good is it if I don't? This would only work negatively against me. When you think about it, my believing and having confidence that I am cured, is just like anything else important in life, in which we as humans, must have strong faith or belief in. Having this *positive* thinking, viewpoint, outlook, and assurance is not only good and healthy for us as individuals, but it also helps us to be more confident and successful in achieving our personal goals and endeavors in life.

When I look back at and reflect on the remarkable progress that I've made, concerning my recovery from bipolar disorder and gaining improved health, one thing about me now, that is truly amazing (than it was previously in the past when I was ill), is how much my mindset, thinking, and moods have changed for the better. For I no longer think, behave, and feel the way that I use to when I was sick. For one, my moods have stabilized to where I no longer have or experience the dark moods that are associated with bipolar disorder. Nor do I have the ups and downs of severe mood swings— the two separate and distinct phases of prolonged episodes of bipolar, that alternate or cycle in an out, which are: (1) the *Depressive Phase*, that produces an overwhelming sad state of depressive lows and, (2) the *Mania Phase* that generates manic (or hypomanic) highs. Mania meaning: euphoric or great excitement, marked by hyperactivity.

Personally, I am absolutely ecstatic! For how truly wonderful it is to finally be cured of bipolar disorder! to have all of the mentally and emotionally painful, stressful, and often debilitating symptoms of the illness behind me now, so that I can go on to live a peaceful, happy, and normal life.

Before revealing the healing process or explaining how the cure for my illness took place, I would first like to point out that in my individual situation or case, that I don't believe that my bipolar disorder was due to genetics or something that I was born with—like it may have been for some people who are bipolar. But, rather, I sincerely believe that *environment* was the primary factor or cause of my sickness, and that my illness was something that developed or happened over a lengthy period of time.[7]

In my previously published book *'Bipolar Disorder, A Patient's Story,'* I stated in Chapter #3, on page 48, paragraph 1: "After having thoroughly examined and considered all of the facts and circumstances associated with my individual case of bipolar disorder, I personally have come to discover and believe that my illness developed over an extended period of time, through a series of stages, which were: (1) *bouts of depression* that, (2) gradually and progressively escalated to *chronic depression or mental illness,* which, in turn, (3) led to an *emotional trauma* that finally triggered *bipolar disorder*.[8] Although I didn't fully realize and appreciate it at the time of the discovery, this was very valuable and important information for me to have figured out, as the future would go on to clearly show.

Because I prefer in this book to focus primarily on the *cure*, and not the *cause*, I won't go into detail at this time by rehashing and explaining what the *environment* was that caused my illness, or the

---

[7] "Environment," meaning: All of the external factors that have a formative influence on a person's physical, mental, emotional, and moral development. The environments that I'm referring to are *long-term environments*—those that we spend a considerable amount of time in, such as at school, at work, or in our neighborhood, etc.

[8] An important thing to note, in regards to bipolar disorder that might be caused by *environment,* is that, whatever it is or may be in the environment that creates or causes mental illness or bipolar disorder in one person (although others might be exposed to the exact, same environmental conditions or situations)—it may not necessarily cause it (bipolar disorder) in someone else. The reason why is because we are all separate and unique individuals with different internal makeups and characteristics. Hence, whatever affects one person a certain way, may affect someone else completely different, or perhaps, not at all.

entire *series of stages* that led to my bipolar disorder—which I extensively wrote about in my previously published and released book *"Bipolar Disorder, A Patient's Story."* However, for comprehensive purposes, I think that it would be helpful if I provided you with a little bit of background information on what I believe caused and triggered it, so as to help you to better understand how I contracted bipolar disorder.[9]

Essential Background Information

My full legal name that I was born with is Charles Leonard Shelton Jr. I was born in the year 1956, in the northern state of Minnesota—a Midwestern U.S. state bordering Canada and Lake Superior. Generally speaking, I had a relatively happy childhood. Growing up as a youth, my interest was primarily in sports, in particular, basketball. I loved it so much! I couldn't get enough of it. Obviously, this love and passion for the game, along with a strong desire and drive to improve and excel, helped me to eventually become very skilled and successful. For later, I went on to become a high school basketball star, earning All City, All State, and All American honors. Later, after I finished school, I entered the workforce or employment field, where I also had a very successful career.

Although, overall, I had a pretty good and happy life in general, all was not rosy or peachy however. For later, there were times when I battled bouts of depression, which eventually led to chronic depression and, finally, bipolar disorder.

Prior to being diagnosed with bipolar disorder, I suffered a mental breakdown. It occurred in the year 2010-11. Interestingly, after having a breakdown, it left me feeling mentally paralyzed and disabled to a large degree. Mentally, I felt like I had reverted back to my childhood. It was as though I had to start out all over again, learning from the beginning. When I think back as to why this

---

[9] Note: For a detailed explanation of the *environment* and *series of stages* that lead to my bipolar disorder illness, see my book *"Bipolar Disorder, A Patient's Story."* It is available at Amazon.com

occurred, I can now somewhat understand. Personally, I believe the reason why this happened is because, even though the human mind is an amazing thing that is highly resilient and extremely adaptable, in reality, it can only take so much pain and abuse. Subsequently, after a while, due to an extreme overload of suffering and pain that life and other things might put or bring upon us as an individual, sometimes the brain shuts down, so to speak, to protect itself, in order to prevent further trauma, damage, and pain.

The fact is, I have experienced and gone through many things throughout my life, both good and bad. However, in my case, the bad or negative things that I experienced overshadowed or outweighed the good. And, as time progressed, the buildup from all of these things together, became too heavy and great of a weight and load to carry, until the last problem or situation became the final straw that broke the camel's back, so to speak.

How My Bipolar Disorder Was Triggered

Someone once told me that they think that my mental illness—bipolar disorder, is something that I was born with. In other words, it is hereditary—something that is part of my genetic makeup that was passed down through a parent or family genes. However, I know this to be totally untrue in my personal situation or case. Because, if bipolar disorder disease is part of my genetic makeup, then it would be something that would be incurable. However, in my case, it was completely cured. So the principle factor or root cause of my mental illness had to be due to something else, other than genetics.

When it comes to the structure and functions of the amazing human body and brain, some things are just too complex or difficult to be understood or explained. With this in mind, I will go on to attempt to explain how I believe that I came to have bipolar disorder—how it developed or was triggered.

Upon personal, thorough examination of my individual, situation or case and how I came to have bipolar disorder, I believe that in my brain, the area that controls emotions was broken or

11

damaged in some way, perhaps gradually over an extended period of time, but especially when I suffered my mental breakdown (which I explained in my previous book *Bipolar Disorder, A Patient's Story*)—that perhaps a severance or break, or some type of disconnection or damage occurred within the link or connection between the thinking *mind,* and the *heart* (the seat of human emotion). Why did this occur? I believe that my mind and body did this in order to protect itself from any further or additional suffering and pain. In other words, I believe that the many bad and negative things that I experienced in life, along with a final traumatic blow (a traumatic or stressful, emotional experience) that I later suffered in the year 2010-11, caused serious injury or damages to my brain's regulatory system, in particular, the area that regulates *emotions*— hence manic depression or bipolar disorder was triggered or set in. The end result (from that time going forward), was that my brain was no longer able to regulate emotions such as joy, sadness, etc., in the way that or to the degree that a "normal," healthy person might function or feel. Don't get me wrong, it's not that I didn't feel and display any emotions or have a certain measure of these things after the break occurred. It's just that my brain could no longer regulate the proper degree or level of emotions that a mentally and emotionally healthy person might experience or feel in life. However, the important question at that time was: "Can this damage be reversed, repaired, or cured?" Only time would tell.

Interestingly, in regards to being bipolar, I personally think that for some people, that it is not caused by genetics, as it may be for others. Nor do I believe that it is necessarily triggered by just *one* thing alone, such as undergoing or suffering a traumatic or stressful experience. But, rather, for some people, I believe that it is possibly brought on by several or many, different factors, all working together in unison at the same time — underlying issues or problems that we either knowingly or unknowingly go though in life — things that we experience and are exposed to within our environment — stressful and harmful things that gradually and progressively accumulate and build up over an extended period of time. Like the *"Snowball Effect."* Subsequently, the end result can be that the crushing weight from all of these weighty problems or things — accumulated or added together — winds up taking its toll upon a person's mind and emotions and, eventually, they mentally snap from the sheer force and gravity of the heavy burden and weight. In analogy, it's like placing too much weight or stress on a literal bridge. The overwhelming, heavy load can cause it to suffer a severe structural collapse. Like what happened to the Minnesota, I-35W Mississippi River Bridge on August 1, 2007—the horrible tragedy that ended up taking precious lives. True, the human mind can be amazingly resilient, adaptable, and extremely strong in many ways. And it can often withstand a lot of suffering and pain. And yet, at the same time, it can also be very fragile too![10]

So, in a nutshell, the above scenario is what I believe caused my bipolar disorder.

And lastly, before I go into explaining how I cured myself of depression and bipolar disorder, I feel that it is important for me to say, that from trial and experience, I personally have found that there is no "one thing" that will cure a person of bipolar disorder. In other words, there is no magic bullet, pill, or cure. What I personally have discovered along my amazing journey in quest for a cure for my bipolar disorder, is that, my being healed and cured of my illness involved many things. I also discovered that I had to treat, not just the mental health part of my disease alone, but, also, the emotional, physical, and spiritual aspects as well—the *complete* person. And, in addition to treating the *entire* person, I also had to be willing to put in the time and effort (each and every day) working towards healing and curing myself of depression and bipolar disorder; otherwise, I believe that I would not eventually have been cured. Because, to be honest with you, from personal experience, I've found that it takes a certain amount of time, commitment, and consistent effort to heal oneself of the illness. However, the wonderful and encouraging thing is that it can be done, as my inspiring, true story, so clearly proves!

With all of this having been said, let me now go on to explain each of the progressive steps (step-by-step) that I personally

---

[10] For a full and detailed explanation of what caused my bipolar disorder, see my book "Bipolar Disorder, A Patient's Story."

devised, put into place, and took that led to me being completely healed and cured of depression and bipolar disorder illness, once and for all time!

Step 1

FINDING YOURSELF

You might find this to be a little odd, or even somewhat surprising. But the *first step* within the healing process that I took on the road leading to being cured of my depression and bipolar disorder (although during the time I was unaware that the healing process had begun), was that I began to make a diligent and thorough search to find myself, that is, my true character or identity — the real man or person that I am inside — that special and unique individual that sometimes lies hidden deep within a person (that, not only myself, but many people long to find and get to know about themselves), that lies undiscovered, lost, or is hard to be found. Interestingly, now that I am cured of my illness, and I look back at the past and how the healing process took place, I can see that this was a very important step (*finding myself*), in a series of progressive stages that I took, that would eventually lead to me being completely healed and cured of my depression and bipolar disorder. As a matter of fact, this first step formed the very foundation and support for the next steps that were to follow.

The odd or strange thing, is that, prior to making a search for my true identity, I never even realize that I was lost. As a youth growing up in the northern state of Minnesota, and well into my adult and later years, I never felt lost, or even questioned who I was. Because, I had confidence in myself, and I felt that I already knew who I was. But, apparently, this wasn't the case, as my life later revealed. Now, in retrospect, when I think of the concept that I would have an identity crisis later in life, it seems a bit puzzling and strange to me, especially, because I didn't seem to have any struggle or problems with identity issues in my past. However, it later became apparent, at the right time, that there was an empty space or void in my soul that needed to be filled. And so I took the necessary steps to fill it by finding myself. This of course was not an easy thing to do. It was a very difficult and relatively long journey. Nonetheless, there was a compelling force or something inside of me that was driving me… that felt that this was something that was absolutely necessary and essential for me to accomplish. Why? I believe it was because, somewhere, deep down inside of me, I realized that my overall health and well-being depended on it—in order for me to be able to eventually find and acquire true inner peace, joy, contentment, and happiness in my life.[11]

Often in life, when a person fails to truly find their self, it can lead to or cause a certain degree of mental and emotional anguish, distress, anxiety, and pain. For they can begin to feel empty, unfulfilled, or even lost, which can trigger feelings of frustration, sadness, and even deep depression. The unfortunate thing is that some people never really find themselves in life. Fortunately, for me, I eventually did. True, it took a little while, for it didn't happen until later in my life, that is, until after I began the search. Then, at that point, it happened relatively fast. The important thing is that I made the search and found myself (the true inner person), for it has deeply influenced and enriched my life for good.

You might ask: How does one find his or herself? Well, one way is by thoroughly scrutinizing or taking a serious look at yourself—at both your past and present life, as to what kind of person you were

---

[11] Note: I am not implying or saying that everyone who suffers from depression or bipolar disorder is lost or has an identity crisis. I'm just relating to you what happened to me.

back then, and the kind of person you have evolved into today—by thoroughly examining yourself, by means of deep thought, meditation, and soul searching. Interestingly, one *good* thing, if you can call it that, that often comes with depression or emotional suffering and pain, is that, it can cause or make a person delve deep inside themselves, where they can often discover and uncover unknown truths and things about themselves (both good and bad)—things that sometimes lie hidden in secret, which they may not have known or realized about themselves. But, also, it can reveal fascinating and amazing things about them too—things that can be a real source of encouragement and inspiration to them individually—wonderful things that can bring them a sense of real comfort and wellbeing, and also add true happiness, value, and depth to their life.

Personally, upon finding myself (which involved periods of solitude and isolation), I felt a great sense of comfort and relief, along with a tremendous amount of peace, satisfaction, and joy. I was so happy! It made me feel as though my mind, heart, and soul, were finally released from the dungeon of a dark and horrible prison where I had been held captive for many years. And because I had found something that was so immensely gratifying, special and valuable to me (my true identity), from that time going forward, I determinately resolved in my mind and heart, that I would never allow anyone or anything to ever mislead, capture, and imprison me again. For now, like a caged bird that has been finally set free from the confines of its restrictive cage, my mind, heart, and soul are forever free to move about, to develop and grow (to whatever extent I choose and want to), to explore and discover an endless variety of wonderful and exciting things in the vastly large, amazingly beautiful world and universe that surrounds me. Yes, poetically speaking: "I am finally free! to spread my wings and fly; to soar up to the highest of heights! with the greatest of ease, joy, excitement, and true heart's delight!"

Out of all of the many benefits and things that I have gained from finding myself, perhaps the greatest gift that came from it, is that, now, for the first time in my life, I truly love and appreciate who I am as an individual and person. Interestingly, in looking back at this amazing uncovering, discovery, and wonderful time period in my life, I can see that this was an important factor and turning point in helping me to get on the road of the healing process that would eventually lead to me being cured of my depression and bipolar disorder illness.

To help you (the reader) to better understand the arduous journey that I went through and the process of how I searched for and found myself, in addition to some of the thinking, feelings, and things that I experienced during that particularly difficult and challenging time period in my life, please consider my short story concerning this that I wrote. The story is entitled *"Finding The Lost Man That Lies Within—Me."* It is located in the Appendix, on pages 244-248. I'm sure you will find it to be a most interesting, encouraging, and enjoyable read.

Although finding or getting to know myself (the real me) was an important factor and accomplishment in the bipolar disorder healing process, which was imperative to my overall health and wellbeing, including my mental and emotional health—more was required in helping to rid and cure myself of bipolar disorder, as the next step clearly shows.

Step 2

OPEN YOUR HEART TO

PEACE, JOY, AND LOVE

The *second,* vitally important step or phase that I went through on the curative road of the bipolar disorder healing process, involved acquiring or obtaining three special qualities—valuable, key features or healthy characteristics, that to a certain degree I was lacking to some extent. What were these qualities? And why is it so important for one to possess them?

Out of the few essential qualities that humans need most in life, nothing is more important than having a good measure of inner *peace, joy,* and *love.* These three amazing attributes are absolutely vital elements that are needed for one's overall health, including their mental and emotional wellbeing. But also, they make our life more satisfying and enjoyable too. Unfortunately, sometimes, there are certain distressing and difficult issues or problems that we may personally experience or go through in our life that happens to get in the way—things that wind up robbing us of one or more of these valuable qualities. And, depending on the degree or severity of the challenging issue(s) or problem(s) that we may be facing or undergoing, it can often lead to one suffering from feelings of anxiety, stress, and even sadness, which, if not addressed, corrected, or controlled, can lead to more serious issues such as clinical depression, and so forth. Fact is, we as humans, require a certain measure of *peace*, *joy*, and *love* to feel secure, to be happy, and healthy. What the exact amount, percentage, or healthy measure of these things is, that a person needs or is lacking, that causes them to fall into a state of deep depression, I don't know. However, I'm sure that it is different for different people, because everyone is not the same. For each of us are distinct and unique individuals with specific needs.

When it comes to life, everyone has their own set of unique issues and problems that they have to face and deal with, sometimes even serious ones. As for me, personally, in regards to my past (prior to coming down mentally ill), it was the problem of having to cope and deal with an overly critical and negative environment that was causing me issues and difficulties—a brutally unjust and discouraging environment that wound up dragging me into a state of clinical depression, which eventually led to bipolar disorder illness.

Sad to say, the world has a long and bad reputation of being cold and cruel, especially to certain individuals or people that it can bully or take advantage of in some way. As a result (based on the frequency of how often this may be happening, or how unbearable and horrible the treatment is that one is receiving), some people, who are targeted victims and recipients of such insensitivities, cruelties, and injustices, sometimes wind up becoming hesitant, wary, and even distrustful of others in life, which may result in them turning inwards, isolating or shutting themselves off (psychologically, or physically—or both) from society and people to a certain degree, in hopes that the hurtful, unbearable, tormenting things that they are going through will stop; or if not entirely eliminated, that perhaps in some way they will somehow lessen the frequency or intensity of the attacks.

On the other hand, sometimes, becoming a victim of the world's unjust, cruel treatment and behavior has nothing to do with being bullied, or its exploitation of a person (wanting to take advantage of them in some way for personal or greedy gain). Instead, it might have to do with something in particular that they (the victim) individually possesses—something that is perhaps good or valuable about them that the jealous antagonist covets or envy's. Things such as: innate abilities, talents, intelligence, or even outward beauty—things that make the assailant angry, and envious of them. And, therefore, as a direct result, they attack or persecute them for it. Like what happened to the young, fair maiden, Snow White, in the fascinating fairytale and yet, often relatable story of *"Snow White and the Seven Dwarfs,"* where, because of Snow White's beauty, the wicked queen schemes to have her done away with.

True, in real life, it's not that someone would necessary go as far as the wicked queen went in the story, *Snow White,* to harm someone *physically*. But, nevertheless, having an envious and jealous spirit can cause an antagonist to view and treat the one that they are jealous of in a negative, mean, unjust, cruel, and bad way—thereby inflicting mental and emotional harm and torment on them, which sometimes can be worse than being subjected to physical abuse.

Other possible reasons for people being victims of cruel treatment and abuse by others, is that, some people are just downright evil and mean; whereas other antagonists may be acting out of pure ignorance.

Today, in observing the overall structure, health and condition of society and the world in general (from both observation and personal experience), I've noticed that although there are good and beneficial things happening in the world, that there often seems to be a battle taking place (almost on a daily basis) between good and evil; with evil being the antagonist and aggressor. Looking even closer, I've noticed that for some strange reason, the world doesn't seem to like goodness, truth, and true beauty much. As a result, at times, it will vehemently (without any remorse or mercy) battle and fight against these things. One example of this, is that, it is not uncommon to find people that are outwardly *physically* beautiful, suffering from low self-esteem, which is often hard for others to comprehend. For how can someone that is very attractive have low self-worth? Well, often the reason why is because from a very early age onward, the world mentally and emotionally attacks and beats up on people like this, with the intent or purpose to mentally and emotionally crush and destroy these ones, perhaps so that they—the opposers and haters of their victims—who are not content or satisfied with their own personal, outward appearance, will feel good and better about themselves. Or maybe, it could be, so that they can eliminate the competition or feel better or superior to the attractive person in some way. Interesting, and perhaps even more so, this same battle of *evil* against *beauty* also holds true for people who have beautiful inward qualities and personalities too.

Unfortunately, many who happen to be victims of the world's injustices and cruelties (inside or outside of the home), especially at a very young age, often begin to look down on themselves in a negative way, perhaps feeling that it is their fault that these things are happening to them—that they are a bad person, or that there is something wrong with them personally, and that is why they are being targeted and attacked. Often, as a direct result of the bad treatment they are receiving, they begin to view themselves in a negative, unhealthy, discouraging, and worthless way—thereby causing them to develop low self-worth or low self-esteem—something that they may wind up struggling with the rest of their lives. Sad to say, for some of these ill-fated, poor souls, it becomes so hard for them to cope with and recover from a lifetime of mental and emotional abuse, that, in the end, it winds up completely ruining their lives.

During the time that I was growing up — in the 1960s and 1970s — life was a little different than it is today, especially for a mixed-race kid like me. We had our own set of problems and things to deal with. I talk about this extensively in my book *"Bipolar Disorder, A Patient's Story,"* which I won't go into at this time. However, I would like to say that, in my case, just like a lot of people today, I too was a victim of the world's injustices and cruelties in the past, which started when I was growing up as a young boy. As a result, I began to distrust and distance myself—sometimes psychologically, other times physically (not completely, but in a selective way) from people in general to a certain extent. Because I didn't know who I could trust. You could say that this served as sort of a protection (at least, so I thought). The reason being is because I didn't want to suffer anymore abuse—to continue to get my feelings crushed and hurt, repeatedly, over and over again, which was something that was happening on a pretty regular basis. To me this was a way to perhaps minimize the damage and pain. Regrettably though, I believe that because I started doing this at a very young age, it became part of my personality to be autonomous and a bit of a loner. Although, I did have selected, close friends throughout my life, and a regular group of buddies whom I hung out and socialized with (played basketball, went to movies, and did a lot of fun things with, etc). Interestingly, the friends that I chose to hang out with when I was growing up, particularly during my teen years, were usually older than I was (about 4 or 5 years). The reason why is because, at the time, I felt that kids my own age were too mentally and emotionally immature. But also, the older kids that I hung with were good kids with admirable qualities.[12] Today, I still thank one of the guys (my mentor), in particular, for helping me, and taking me under his wings.

Truth is, sometimes (if it is feasible or possible), there are times and specific circumstances when there are certain difficult people in life that it is best for one to avoid or steer clear of. However, it is not good to fall into a thinking pattern or habit of treating everyone and everything this way. It would not be good and healthy for us individually. Because, as humans, we were not meant to isolate ourselves from one another, but instead, we were designed and created to be social creatures that can feed and thrive off of others.

In looking back at my past, I can see that, although I did what I thought was good, right, and best for me at the time; in certain ways, this sort of self isolation (limited, not total)—shutting myself off

---

[12] Another thing that contributes to my autonomous nature is being a poet, writer, music composer/arranger, and artist/painter, etc. Although I like people and enjoy associating with them, like many artists, I am somewhat of a loner at times. The reason being is because I am a creative person that needs quiet time, to be able to reflect, think, process my thoughts, and exercise my imagination and creativity. For when you are around people who are talking a lot or on different thought processes or wavelengths, it can be very distractive.

from people in general, with hopes of protecting my emotions and feelings from getting hurt—had a negative and detrimental effect upon me personally. In particular, it robbed me, to a considerable degree, of my inner peace, joy, and love—the good, essential, and beneficial qualities that are needed to be emotionally balanced, happy, and healthy. The end result was that I eventually fell into a state of depression that grew and, over time, progressively led to clinical depression, as well as bipolar disorder.[13] True, I believe that there was still some measure of these qualities (peace, joy, and love) in me, even when I was dealing with depression and bipolar disorder. For, without having any measure of these characteristics (something that perhaps totally ceases to exist in some people, that possibly causes them to completely give up on life), I don't think I would have survived. But, apparently, a significant portion of these useful and healthy qualities, that I at one time possessed to a larger degree in the past (prior to coming down sick), progressively diminished over time—a portion large or extensive enough to cause me to fall into a state of misery, despair, and depression, that eventually led to bipolar disorder.[14]

The fact is, we as humans, need a certain measure of inner peace, joy, and love to be happy and healthy. Interestingly, somewhere in the stream of time (during the bipolar disorder healing process), while I was on the road to recovery from my illness, which would eventually lead to me being completely healed and cured of my bipolar disorder, my mind (either consciously or unconsciously) came to realize the importance and value of having the good, helpful, and beneficial qualities of *peace*, *joy*, and *love*, and it took the necessary steps to acquire them—in large measure! because, without them, the pathway towards acquiring good emotional and

---

[13] Note: Certain people were not the only thing that caused or contributed to my depression or bipolar disorder. Although they were a significant part of the problem that robbed me of a measure of peace, joy, and love, there were other things that contributed to my illness as well, as I highlighted in my previous book *"Bipolar Disorder, A Patient's Story."*

[14] Note: I am not insinuating or implying that everyone who suffers from depression or bipolar disorder lacks peace, joy, and love. I'm just relating to you what happened to me.

mental health would be virtually impossible to achieve.

The wonderful thing, is that, now that I have fully recovered and healed from depression and bipolar disorder, and I am healthy mentally and emotionally in all respects, I no longer have bad or hard feelings towards those who treated me negatively or badly in the past, or even those that might treat me unjustly today. For I have let go of any and all resentment and hate—things that can so easily grow and develop in us (consciously or unconsciously), when we are badly mistreated or abused in some way. Instead, I have developed a blanket type of *agape love* for the world in general, which is a love that is based on principle—a love that covers everyone, no matter who or what they are, or where they come from, including those that might even view me as their enemy. But also, I've come to recognize and see that we need other people. This is how we as humans are internally built or made—that we were designed and programmed from birth onwards to be social creatures. You could say that it's in our DNA (Deoxyribonucleic Acid), for having healthy associations and interactions with other people on a regular basis is good and beneficial for us as a group, and also individually. And yet, although it's important to have people and associates in our lives, the key is to invite and have good and positive people that appreciate, respect, encourage, and love us for who we are.

In regards to the quality of *love*, it cannot be overstated and emphasized how highly important this amazing and beautiful quality is for each and every one of us to have and display in our lives. Not only do we need to love ourselves as individuals (a properly balanced love of course). But also, it is important that we love others, and also that we be and feel loved by them too. To note the importance and need for love in our life, see the information *"The Importance of Love"* in the Appendix, on page 266.

Unfortunately, truth is, there is a real shortage of love in the world today. However, I've come to realize that just because the world may be this way; it doesn't mean that I have to be that way also. Personally, my thinking and resolve has come to be—instead of allowing myself to be influenced and infected by an unloving spirit that can so easily rub off on and create problems for me—I prefer and choose to love both myself and others. For I have found that it is truly a beautiful and healthy way to live and be!

One interesting thing that I recognize now (that I didn't completely realize when it was taking place), which ended up being an important aspect of the healing process on the road leading to being cured of depression and bipolar disorder, is that, in order for me to heal certain wounds and bad things that happened to me in the past, it *required* that I must *first* sincerely *forgive* others from the heart, and show love for them, in particular, to those whom I felt did me wrong—which I eventually did. I simply had no other choice but to forgive and love them, that is, if I wanted my mind, heart, and spirit to be at peace, and to completely heal and be healthy.

Of course, my being both forgiving and loving to people; in particular, to the ones that treated me badly, was not something that was forced upon me. But rather, I did it of my own free will, because, not only was it the humanely just and right thing to do, but also, because this is something that I personally reasoned upon, decided, and wanted to do from my heart. In other words, I had developed a willing and voluntary spirit to forgive others.

What does it mean to be forgiving? To be forgiving means: to *completely pardon* or let go of a wrong that a person committed against us (whether it was done intentionally or unintentionally). To cease from feeling resentment and anger towards them, and not wanting, desiring, or seeking retaliation or revenge.

In looking back at the remarkable adjustments and positive changes that I have made in my thinking, attitude, and outlook of life and concerning people in general (while on the road to recovery and being cured of bipolar disorder), I have found, through putting it into practice, that this overall, new thinking, mindset, outlook, and behavior that I have developed, is good and healthy for me. Because it brings me a lot of *peace, joy,* and *love*—things that to a considerable degree I was lacking or missing in the past. In other words, it makes my mind and heart feel very good!

Although, it took me years to learn how to cope and deal with the world and people in general in a much better, balanced, effective, and healthier way, than I did in the past, I'm glad that I finally figured it out. As a result, my life is so much more peaceful, joyful, and happier now. But also, it, along with other things, helped to lift me up and out of depression, and eventually helped to cure me of my bipolar disorder illness.

To give you (the reader) a clearer picture and understanding of the extremely difficult and challenging things that I went through in life, and how I eventually came out of them, see Short Story #2 that I wrote, entitled *"No Vacancy Here,"* in the Appendix, on pages 249-253.

Yes, as is shown in the information above, *peace*, *joy*, and *love* are vitally important and essential qualities that were needed for me to regain my mental and emotional health. However, this was just part of the recovery and healing process that I went through. For I would soon discover that more things were required for me to eventually be completely healed and cured of bipolar disorder, along with the painful episodes of depression it produces, as the next step shows.

Step 3

RESPECT YOURSELF

The *third,* essential step that I took on the road leading to being healed and cured of my bipolar disorder involved acquiring *self-esteem.* Interestingly, although I had gained a certain measure of confidence and self-esteem during the first phase — Step #1 *"Finding Yourself"* — of the bipolar disorder healing process, which was instrumental in helping me to find myself or my true identity, future time, during Step #3, would go on to reveal that more adjustments and developments were required in my life, in order for me to be able to acquire the proper amount or degree of self-esteem that would fortify and strengthen me to the extent that was needed to make me *solid* and *complete* in ways that I hadn't been in the past—things that I believe were necessary to the recovery and healing process.

What is self-esteem? And why is having it so important? According to the dictionary, *self-esteem* means: confidence in one's own worth or abilities; self-respect.

Having self-esteem or self-respect is extremely important for each and everyone to have. Because, having low self-worth or being without self-esteem can make it hard for us to feel confident and good about ourselves as individuals, which can lead to behavior and feelings of insecurity, self-doubt, inadequacy, fear, disbelief, discontentment, self-deprecation, and sometimes even a sort of self-hatred, that can cause frustrations, irritability, anger, anxiety, and even *depression*.[15]

What can cause a person to have low self-esteem? Some adults have low self-esteem because of the way they were viewed and treated by their parents when they were growing up. Either they failed to meet their parents' expectations, or their parents' were guilty of making unfair comparisons. Others grapple with feelings of inferiority due to their own limitations. And then, there are others who develop low self-esteem from being around people who are high-minded or insulting.

Personally, upon examining my life, I found that the main thing that caused me to have low self-esteem was not my parents, nor was it any personal limitations that I had, but rather, it was the people that I happened to be around or associated with later in life. The problem was, these people thought way too much of themselves! Truth is, they were very high-minded, arrogant, and condescendingly insulting in both speech and behavior. As a result, they not only viewed and treated me with disrespect, but they also placed an extremely low value on me and my importance. Making me feel as though I didn't measure up to them, and that I never could; no matter what I did to improve myself in various ways. Unfortunately, the end result of being in this overly critical and negative environment, was that it left me feeling bad about myself, worthless, frustrated, annoyed, angry, and sad, which not only led to me battling with feelings of low self-esteem, but also suffering from anxiety and depression.

Someone might ask: "How could you have allowed yourself to get in to that kind of bad situation, with horrible people like that?" Interestingly, it's not that I consciously selected or chose to be in

---

[15] Note: I am not saying that everyone who suffers from depression or bipolar disorder lacks self-esteem. I'm just relating to you what happened to me.

that type of condescending and degrading environment or that I chose to be around self-centered, egotistical, and arrogant people like that, it's just that sometimes things like this happen in life.

The interesting thing, is that, although there were negative and troubling things about my previous, bad environment (the environment that I was in prior to being healed of my bipolar disorder) that I did not like — which were things that were causing me anguish, distress and pain — this character degrading and damaging environment that I was in, was not readily apparent or visible to me during the time that it was happening, nor was I aware of the harmful and damaging influences and effects that the ugly environment was having on my mental and emotional health. I simply had no clue! One reason why, is because, I gave the people that I was hanging around or associating with the benefit of the doubt. I felt that since they professed to love me, that they would do nothing to hurt or harm me.

Another reason why the degrading and damaging environment, along with the harmful and bad effects that it was having on me, was not readily apparent or visible to me, is because it was something that was insidious in nature—something that was secretly hidden beneath the surface, so to speak. In other words, these detrimental things were both existing and operating below the threshold of my consciousness. However, the important thing is that I finally woke up… wised up… and made the necessary adjustments and changes in my life to correct the things that were stumbling and hurting me— the unhealthy things that were damaging to my character and self-esteem.

Unfortunately, the sad thing is, it is not just myself only, but there are many people in the world who struggle and suffer with low self-worth or low self-esteem issues. With this being the case, what are some ways that a person can build their self-esteem?

First of all, there is a correct way to go about gaining self-respect, but also, there is a wrong way of trying to obtain it. Unfortunately, sometimes, people with low self-esteem mistakenly try to develop self-worth through other people. For example, some try to project an image of self-esteem by assuming the role or lifestyle of a promiscuous socialite. However, beneath the surface these people still grapple with feelings of inferiority. Others indulge in promiscuity as a means to banish feelings of depression, to increase self-esteem by feeling wanted, to achieve intimacy. However, for many who try to substitute sexual intimacy as a comfort, they end up feeling even more emptiness, loneliness, and depression. How sad it is, for a person to bring this sort of pain on themselves, or even worse, if they were to end up with an unwanted pregnancy, or a Sexually Transmitted Disease (STD).

Yes, people who look to others to make them feel good about themselves or to build their self-worth or self-esteem, in the end, find out that this doesn't work. Because others cannot build self-esteem in us. We are the only ones that can build it in ourselves. That is why it is called *"Self"* esteem.

Rather than resorting to a self-destructive, undermining, and disappointing lifestyle like the above, some of the better ways to boost or build self-esteem are:

- *Acknowledge your positive assets and qualities.* All of us have strong points, good, and positive things about ourselves. Why not concentrate and work on these, rather than focusing on the negative.
- *Avoid Unfair Comparisons.* As Eleanor Roosevelt, wife of the 32nd president of the United States once said: "No one can make you feel inferior without your consent." Does the fact that someone else looks better; has more material things; or is smarter than you make him or her a better person than you are? The answer is, no.
- *Avoid the Snare of Jealousy.* Jealousy breeds insecurity. Learn instead, to rejoice with people who rejoice and be genuinely happy over their accomplishments. If you do, others will be far less prone to make negative remarks about your successes.
- *Get Involved With Other People.* The more you are active and involved with others, the less you will worry about your own feelings of insecurity. The *key* here of course is to surround yourself with people that truly love, respect, and appreciate

you—people who really care about your happiness, health, and welfare.

- *Take Criticism in Stride:* "Do not give your heart to all the words that people may speak," says the Bible at Ecclesiastes 7:21. How true this advice is, especially, when others are simply putting you down. On the other hand, if criticism is legitimate, find ways to apply it. You may fall short in one area, but that hardly makes you a failure as a person. Interestingly, some criticism is meant to help and produce improvements, whereas, there is another type of criticism that does nothing more than destroy and tear down. See the information "Constructive Criticism?" on pages 267-268.

- *Set Realistic Goals:* You do not need to be the class valedictorian to be a fine student, or an Olympic athlete to enjoy sports. And yet, don't set your goals excessively low because of fear of failure. Failure can serve as a means of learning and making adjustments that can lead to making improvements and becoming more successful.

- *Don't Be Afraid to Be Different:* Youths who allow peers to control their speech, dress, and grooming are little more than puppets and slaves.

- *Take up a productive hobby*: Learning to play a musical instrument, mastering a foreign language, or working on some other fun and productive hobby, etc., can also help boost a person's self-esteem. Personally, for me, learning to compose or arrange music on my Roland XP-80 keyboard; artistic painting; being creative in various ways and, becoming a successful author and professional writer helped tremendously!

- *Avoid being around overly critical and insulting people.* Luckily, for me, in time, I wised up and broke away from damaging and discouraging people that dis-esteemed and tore me down. Now, when I choose associates, I pick friends and people that value and appreciate me for who I am as a person. People who are truly interested in my personal welfare and success—friends that love me, encourage me, and build me up.

- *Being content with yourself and life.* Having a certain amount of contentment can be good for self-confidence and self-esteem. Because you don't feel like you have to measure up to others or unreasonable goals or demands.

- *Making good use of positive affirmations.* This is another thing that can help to build self-esteem. Affirmations are positive statements that a person can either repeat to themselves or write down—that can help them to overcome self-sabotaging and negative thoughts. When they repeat them often enough, and believe them, they can start to make positive changes in their life. Personally, I find positive affirmations to be very encouraging, uplifting, and effective mental exercises that help to build confidence and self-esteem, especially when written down repeatedly. I speak more about positive affirmations later, on pages 103, 104, 112, and 113.

- *Physical cleanliness, dress and grooming.* There is something about being physically clean and being dressed and groomed well, that has a positive effect on us personally—that picks us up and makes us feel good about ourselves. Interestingly — not to compare ourselves with animals of course — but, of the canines that my family owned, whenever we would take them to the local pet groomer to get bathed and groomed, afterwards, they would proudly prance and strut around like they were the stuff! It's almost as though you could see the confidence and joy on their faces. It was pretty cute! Well, the same is true of humans too. We feel so much better and good about ourselves when we are clean, properly groomed, and dressed well. But, not only that, you'll find that people will often view and treat you differently and more positively too. It really works!

From the above information we can see that having or gaining self-esteem stems a lot from feeling good and confident about ourselves, our abilities, and our accomplishments.

Helpful Note. The suggestions above can no doubt help a person to gain self-worth. However, don't expect self-esteem to develop overnight. Be patient. Expect setbacks, and try not to indulge in self-pity. For in due time, you will find yourself feeling more confident and secure than ever!

Word of Caution. Although it is important to have self-esteem, it is also important not to think too highly of ourselves either—to the point of being arrogant or a narcissist. To help us in this endeavor we must strive to have a balanced view of our true value as a person.

An interesting thing, is that, somewhere along the stream of time — during the time when I had and was suffering from depression and bipolar disorder — my mind came to realize and figure out the importance of having self-esteem or self-respect (something that I lacked to a certain degree at the time), and it took the necessary steps to acquire it. This was yet another important movement, factor, and step that would play an essential role and part in helping me to eventually be healed and cured of depression and later, bipolar disorder illness. For more information on how I came to realize my worth, value, and to appreciate who I am as an individual and gain self-esteem, see Short Story #3 that I wrote, entitled *"Old Man Zuckerman and His Noisy Ole Cane,"* in the Appendix, on pages 254-257.

Yes, thanks to the extremely helpful and beneficial phase of Step #3 *"Respect Yourself,"* that I went through along the journey and road to recovery from my mental illness, I no longer suffer from a lack of self-esteem. However, as good as acquiring self-esteem or self-respect was to my personal growth, development, happiness, and health—both mental and emotional, the next step goes on to clearly show that more was required for me to eventually be healed and cured of my bipolar disorder.

Step 4

MAKE JOY YOUR

CLOSE FRIEND

As was highlighted earlier in Step #2 *"Open Your Heart to Peace, Joy, and Love,"* of the healing process that was leading to me being cured of depression and bipolar disorder, it required that I open my mind and heart to the healthy qualities of peace, joy and love. Interestingly, of these three qualities, two of them, *peace* and *love*, although they have an enormous amount of importance and value—and believe me, I'm not downplaying their worth or importance in any way. Because, individually, they are awesome, beautiful, and wonderful attributes in their own special and unique ways — qualities that turned out to be extremely helpful and beneficial to me. However, sometime later, along the road to recovery, during Step #4 *"Make Joy Your Close Friend,"* of the bipolar disorder healing process, I began to focus more intently on the inner quality of *joy* above peace and love and other things.

While I did not neglect continuing to reach out to obtain the inner qualities of peace and love (because I still needed them), I put greater emphasis on having and obtaining *joy*. Why? Because I came to realize how vitally important, good, and beneficial it is for my emotional and mental health. As far as I'm concerned, *joy* is a lifesaver, a real booster and pick-me-upper, especially during times of sorrow, distress, and special need.

In God's Word, the Bible, at Proverbs 17:22, it says: "A *joyful* heart is good *medicine*." Interestingly, during the time that I was on the road leading to being healed and cured of my depression and bipolar disorder, I didn't know what the Bible said about the health benefits of *joy*. However, for some unknown reason, while I was struggling with my mental illness, I began to focus on and think more indepthly about the quality of joy. And I came to personally discover and believe that this quality had powerful healing properties that could, perhaps, be of great benefit to me and my health, especially, my mental and emotional health. And I felt that, if I could in some way find and latch onto this quality (joy) in great quantity—capturing and utilizing it in a robust way, that perhaps, it could help to lift me up and out of depression. And that also it could possibly even help to heal and cure me of my bipolar disorder illness as well. Would this ideal and plan work? Only time would tell.

Today, now that I am 100%, completely cured of my mental illness, it confirms that I was totally right about my amazing friend—*joy*! I'm so glad that I turned to and leaned on it, along with other essential things for help at the right time. And then, after having obtained it (joy), going forward, from that day onward, it has become my earnest resolve that, if I have anything to do with it, I vowed that I would never, ever again, leave its (joy's) cheerful and uplifting side. For by means of *joy*, my weeping has turned into rejoicing, and my sadness into a smile!

True, none of us (no matter who we are), are going to be joyous or happy all of the time. That's simply not reasonable or humanly possible. Even the Bible at Ecclesiastes 3:1, 4 says: "There is an appointed time for everything… A time to *weep* and a time to laugh; A time to *wail* and a time to dance." We cannot escape this inevitable reality. For it is a natural part of life that applies to all humans.

The good and encouraging thing, is that, although, we as individuals may experience some hard times, bad days, or tough periods from time to time — as we travel along the often challenging road of life — we can however, to the best of our ability, work to have and invite joy in to our lives as often and as much as we can.

Personally, each and every day, even after I was cured of depression and bipolar disorder, I continued to search for and engage in things that brought me joy and happiness—things that would bring sunshine into my life—many things of which I readily and freely shared with others. Fortunately, for me, I found that there was an endless variety of enjoyable and fun (good, clean, and morally wholesome) things to choose from and do! No matter how small or insignificant they sometimes may have seemed to be.

One of the best ways to find joy that I've found is by helping to bring joy and sunshine into other people's lives too, by helping and encouraging them in various ways to bring out the very best in themselves. For I truly believe the wise, old adage or proverb that says: "There is more happiness in giving than receiving."

Because the quality of *joy* is so vital and precious to us as humans, our individual happiness, and overall health and wellbeing (especially our mental and emotional health), once we have obtained it, it is important for us to safeguard, protect, and hold on to it, so that no one or anything will prematurely rob or snatch it away from us.

Unfortunately, there are many *killjoys* or joy robbers in the world that we have to watch out for — both people and things that can rob us of our joy and happiness, that is, if we allow them to. For example, personally speaking, because I am a minority, it would be so easy for me to get caught up in the topic of injustice or systemic racism (something that I used to get so bent out of shape about in the past), which is a big concern and thing in the news and world these days. True, injustice and racism does exist. There's no doubt about that. However, instead of getting sucked into and involved in these often upsetting and discouraging things, personally, I choose to focus my attention elsewhere—on subjects and things that are more uplifting and positive. Truth is, there will always be injustices and racism in the world, as history has clearly played out and shown. This is the inevitable plight of an imperfect, sinful, divided, and chaotic world. Personally, having come to realize through personal experiences that there is nothing that I can do to change things, I prefer not to focus my attention on and let these negative things rob me of the peace, joy, and happiness that I now possess (something that unfortunately I let happen in the past). And, believe me, it is so much better for my emotional and mental health for me to view and handle things in the positive way that I do now.

Some people may criticize me for choosing not to get involved with fighting for certain causes and things that they are fighting for or wrapped up in. But, oh well. As far as I'm concerned, to each his own. Why? Because, if I don't personally take care of my health, who will? My mental and emotional health is more important to me than anything. But, not only that, I choose to leave certain matters and things in God's hands. For I have full faith, confidence, and trust in Him, that if and when justice is due, He will eventually take care of things according to his perfect timeframe and plan.

The above example is just one instance of a *joy robber*. There are many more.

Yes, when it comes to the quality of *joy*, I've discovered that it is an amazing healer and curer. Fortunately, for me, I was able to find, latch and hold on to it along the road to recovery from my mental illness.

For more information on my personal quest for *joy*, and how I eventually found and came to acquire it, see Short Story #4 that I wrote, entitled *"The Pit of Doom,"* in the Appendix, on pages 258-265.

As we can see from all of the information above, having the inner quality of genuine *joy* is vitally important to our individual happiness, health, and wellbeing. However, for me to be completely healed and cured of my bipolar disorder, more was required, as the next step so aptly shows.

Step 5

FINDING THE ROOT CAUSE
OF MY ILLNESS

Another vitally important and necessary step — *Step #5*, that I took in my quest to find a cure for my illness (although I wasn't necessarily conscious or aware that I was looking for a cure at the time), was that I made a diligent and thorough search to find the source or root cause of my bipolar disorder. Interestingly, at the time of my search, I didn't have a clue as to what it was that caused my illness—whether it was something that was genetic, or if environmental factor and influence played a significant role or part, or if something else caused it. However, I was determined to find its origin. Why? At that time, I really didn't know. Nor did I understand the value, benefit, and impact that discovering the root cause of my illness would eventually play in helping to lead me down the pathway of being healed and cured of my bipolar disorder. All I knew is that a strong and compelling force inside of me was driving me to do this.

Sometimes, it is not an easy thing to look back at and recount one's past, especially, if there happened to be negative experiences and things in it that hurt us, caused us bad feelings, or brought us mental and emotional anguish, sufferings, pain, and so forth. However, sometimes, facing one's demons, so to speak, is what is needed in order to release pent-up or suppressed anger or pain, which can be of great aide in helping one to get onto the roadway of healing and recovery. Also, there are times when we have to look back at the past in order to understand or make sense of the present. Because what happened or took place in the past often lays the foundation for the future, or influences or creates what takes place today, within the present time. In this regard, I feel that doing a personal search for and finding the root cause of one's mental illness can also be tremendously beneficial. This is something that I did. It wasn't that someone suggested or told me to do this. It's just something that I personally thought about and chose to do on my own.

Interestingly, now that I look back, I can see that during the time of my search, that, not only was I eager to find the source of my illness, but also that I had reasonable expectations about what learning the root cause of my illness could do for me. I knew that if I was able to eventually find the cause of my illness (at some point or time), that this knowledge, in itself, would not necessary remove or take away my illness. As a matter of fact, I didn't make the search for that purpose. I just felt that, perhaps, if I were to find out what the root cause of my bipolar disorder was, it would in some way be beneficial and useful to help me to get to know myself better, and that it could also possibly help me to better cope with my illness or disorder. Little did I realize though that finding the root cause of my illness would go on to have an even greater impact for good than I could have ever imagined!

As it turned out, in order for me to be able to find the root cause of my bipolar disorder, I not only had to take a good look at myself and my past, and everything in the world and society surrounding me, but I also had to travel or go back in history, so to speak—to a time period long before I was born. I spoke about this most fascinating and enlightening search in my book *"Bipolar Disorder, A Patient's Story."* If you haven't already done so, I would encourage you to get a copy and read about it. I think you will find it to be most interesting!

Initially, during the time when I was searching diligently for the root cause of my mental illness, I was not looking for a cure for bipolar disorder—at least, not consciously. My main goal or purpose in reflecting on and delving into things, including examining or taking a comprehensive look at the past, was to try to figure out and understand the reason for my medical condition or mental illness, so that I could better understand and cope with my bipolar disorder. Also, in addition to this, it was my hope that, perhaps, I could find a workable solution that could help me to make possible changes or improvements in my life, so that my illness would not be as debilitating and crippling to me—so that I could possibly go on to lead and live a much better and more productive life.

Interestingly, one additional, beneficial thing that came out of all of this (besides eventually finding a cure for my depression and bipolar disorder illness), is that, with the valuable insight and knowledge that I have gained along the way, I can now utilize this valuable information to help and encourage others too, especially those who are undergoing similar problems or issues in their lives.

In retrospect, looking back at the past, if I had known back then, what I know today, I could have spared myself a whole lot of heartache, suffering, grief, and pain. But, as it is in life, that's not necessary how things work. In reality, life is our tutor or teacher. And we must learn valuable lessons and experience many things along the way—both good and bad. There's no getting around this inevitable and truthful fact. However, on the flipside of things, along with the negative or bad experiences that I've had, life has also taught me many good and valuable things too, which, not only has been beneficial to me, but also are things that can be used to encourage and help others too.

So, with all of the above having been said, at the end of my search, what did I find to be the root cause of my bipolar disorder? Interestingly, I found that *environment* was the primary culprit or thing that caused my illness.[16] This is something that I thoroughly explained and talked about in more detail in my previously released book *"Bipolar Disorder, A Patient's Story."*

What did learning the source of my mental illness do for me personally? For one, it brought me a tremendous amount of peace of mind, and heart. In what ways? In that I am no longer suffering and groping in darkness mentally, wondering why I have bipolar disorder. Nor am I puzzled about where my illness originated or came from.[17]

Another positive thing that discovering the source of my bipolar disorder did for me, is that, now, from the moment that the amazing revelation or enlightenment occurred, going forward, I could now figure out, put together, and take the necessary steps to eliminate the things in my environment that were causing me mental and emotional anguish, suffering, and pain—at least, so I thought. For unfortunately, I later came to realize that, although the goal of transforming or altering my environment into one that better suits my needs (mentally and emotionally), seemed to be something that was possible or somewhat doable at first, in reality, truth was, the structure of the harmful and detrimental environment that I was in was *"set in stone"* (meaning that it is fixed and unchangeable), and therefore, there was not much that I could personally do about it, no matter how hard I tried. Because I lacked both the ability and power to change or improve anything about it. Therefore, as an alternative solution, I chose to do the next best thing instead, as the next step in the bipolar disorder healing process goes on to show.

---

[16] Note: "Environment," meaning: All of the external factors that have a formative influence on a person's physical, mental, emotional, and moral development. The environments that I'm referring to are *long-term environments*—those that we spend a considerable amount of time in, such as at school, at work, or in our neighborhood, etc.

[17] Note: Although I found that *environment* was the root cause of my bipolar disorder illness, for someone else who is bipolar, the root cause of their illness might have been something else entirely different. The reason being is because each and every one of us are distinct and unique individuals with different internal makeup's, personalities, and circumstances, etc.

Step 6

FINDING THE RIGHT
ENVIRONMENT

When it comes to possessing and growing indoor houseplants, sometimes they can start to develop problems, where perhaps they are no longer thriving or fairing well. They may even start to look like they are somewhat struggling to survive, or that they are downright sick and dying. Personally, during one particular time period in my life, I had several houseplants that were like this—all during the same period or timeframe. The strange thing is, for some unknown reason they were all beginning to look sick—like they were dying. So I decided to try to help them out by completely changing their *soil*. To my surprise, after I did this, within a relatively short period of time, they started to pick up, grow, and look healthier. As a matter of fact, they started to grow so fast and large, and look so vibrant and robust, that I was totally amazed by their vastly improved, good health condition! For just think, it only took a change of soil for them to make a complete turnaround in their growth, vigor, and health.

Why do I bring up the subject of plants? Well, the same is true with respect to us as humans too, in regards to the *environment* or *soil,* so to speak, that we are growing or planted in, because, depending on the type or quality of our soil or environment, it can cause us to either fair well or struggle.

Taking the comparison of plants and humans one step further, another important and valuable thing that we learn from this, is that, if we, personally, are one that is presently struggling with or doing poorly in our present soil or environment (for one reason or another), then, perhaps, what we need to do, in order to recover, fair well, and flourish, is to change our environment to one that will be more favorable, beneficial, and healthy for us individually.

As was disclosed in the previous step (Step #5 *"Finding the Root Cause of My Illness"*), by means of a long and thorough examination of myself, my surroundings, my past, and other necessary things, I came to discover that it was my *environment* that was making me sick—that it was the main culprit that caused my depression and bipolar disorder illness.[18] Yes, my environment was that bad! It was extremely harmful and damaging to my health, in particular, to my mental and emotional health.

After I discovered (without the help of anyone) the root cause of my illness, I also eventually came to discover and realize (also on my own, without the help of anyone), that in order for me to heal and be cured of my depression and bipolar disorder, that it was imperative that I change my environment. Why? Because, like the analogy of the houseplants above, that were faring poorly until after I changed their soil—likewise, the unhealthy, bad environment that I was in was causing serious mental health issues for me and, if I wanted to recover and get better, I had no other recourse but to take myself out of it, and plant myself in a new one—a good and positive environment that would be beneficial and healthy for me (mentally

---

[18] "Environment" meaning: All of the external factors that have a formative influence on a person's physical, mental, emotional, and moral development. The environments that I'm referring to are *long-term environments*—those that we spend a considerable amount of time in, such as at school, at work, or in our neighborhood, etc.

and emotionally)—an environment where I could go on to recover from my illness, heal, grow, and flourish.

Affects of Environment on Health

When it comes to one's physical health and wellbeing, I believe that there is a strong correlation or relationship between one's environment and their health. For example, if one's environment is highly polluted with toxic chemicals, chances are they are eventually going to come down sick. And depending upon the degree or severity of the pollution, it can even wind up being deadly! Well, I believe that the same is true in regards to one's mental health and well-being also—that there is a strong relationship between one's environment and their mental and emotional health. It too can be healthy or harmful to a person (mentally and emotionally); depending on what the environment is like or composed of.

Interestingly, in regards to the latter situation mentioned above—concerning an environment that affects one's mental and emotional wellbeing. If one is regularly being exposed to an unhealthy environment, the damages that may be taking place often go unnoticed, that is, until symptoms of mental illness eventually surface in a person. In other words, the effects of an unhealthy environment may not be instantly realized or visible at first, because they are lying hidden beneath the surface, so to speak, where they are having a gradual, progressive, and detrimental effect on one's health and well-being.

Personally, when it came to my situation and the bad environmental effects on my mental health, I discovered that, not only were the effects that the environment was having on me, not readily apparent, but also, that my subsequent sickness was not something that sprang up or happened overnight. Rather, I believe that it was a sickness or illness that developed slowly and progressively over a long period of time; through a series of stages, which were: (1) *bouts of depression* that, (2) gradually and progressively escalated to *chronic depression or mental illness,* which, in turn, (3) led to an *emotional trauma or stress* that finally triggered *bipolar disorder*.[19] As a matter of fact, I truly believe that, if it wasn't for that bad, overly critical, negative, and harmful environment that I was in—that was crushing my heart and spirit; causing me a tremendous amount of heartache, grief, suffering, and pain—that I would never have even gotten ill in the first place. The good thing, is that, after I came to realize the harmful and detrimental influence and effects that the bad environment was having on me, I was able to take the necessary steps to change things.[20]

Whether we want to accept the truth or not, environments are highly influential (either for good or bad) on us as humans. Therefore, the type of environment that each and every one of us lives and functions in (on a daily basis), is vitally important for us as individuals. Because it can have a powerful influence (both consciously and unconsciously) in shaping who we are and what we become in life, especially, when we are a young child or youth that is highly moldable and impressionable. But it can also have certain molding, character shaping, and psychological effects on us later in life as well, as many examples and peoples life stories (both good and bad) clearly show.

Sometimes, when we personally are in a bad and negative environment that is causing us problems and pain, we might think that we are strong enough to handle and cope with it—that we have the strength of mind to overpower, out will, and overcome it, or anything—that, essentially, all we need to do is *"man up,"* or just hang in there and things will eventually improve and get better.

---

[19] An important thing to note, in regards to bipolar disorder that might be caused by *environment,* is that, whatever it is or may be in the environment that creates or causes mental illness or bipolar disorder in one person (although others might be exposed to the exact, same environmental conditions or situations)—it may not necessarily cause it (bipolar disorder) in someone else. The reason why is because we are all separate and unique individuals with different internal makeups and characteristics. Hence, what affects one person a certain way, may affect someone else completely different, or perhaps, not at all.

[20] Note: I am not insinuating or implying that everyone who suffers from depression or bipolar disorder is in a bad, negative, or the wrong environment. I'm just relating to you what happened to me.

However, as time advances, we soon come to realize or find out, that things really haven't changed for the better after all, and that they most likely never will, but rather, that we are lost in a continuous struggle and battle that will never ever change or end. Personally, for this very reason, I found that it was best for me to take an active role to get up and leave behind my old, negative environment, and the things that were causing me depression and to feel bad about myself and things. Because it was having a negative, harmful, and detrimental effect on my mental and emotional health. In other words, by getting up, moving on, and leaving my old environment behind, I stopped the bleeding, so to speak. Now the healing could finally begin!

Today, when I look back at the vitally important, monumental decision and changes that I have made, by leaving my old environment behind, I can see that it was both the right and healthy thing for me to do. Because I am so much happier and healthier mentally and emotionally now, than I had ever been in the past! However, leaving my *old* environment was just one thing that I needed to do. Another vitally important thing, was that I needed to find and place myself in a *new* environment—a healthy and positive one that would help me to recover from my illness, heal, grow, and become healthy in all respects—especially, mentally and emotionally. However, the question was: Where would I find such an environment?

You might ask: What is a good environment for a person to live and grow in? Well, that all depends on the individual, because just like different types of plants that require different environments to live, grow, and survive (a special environment that is specific to each plant's individual needs—one containing specific soil and conditions for them to flourish and be healthy), likewise, when it comes to humans — what might be a good and healthy environment for one person — may not be good for another. The important thing is to have or be in an environment that encourages and promotes our individual, personal growth and development. Preferably a warm, caring, loving, encouraging, and positive environment that will contribute to our overall health and well-being, as well as our inner peace, joy, and happiness. Currently, if you (the reader) happen to be in or if you find an environment like this, you are doing great! However, in reality, things do not always work out this way. For a good and healthy environment can sometimes be hard to find. The important thing is for a person to know what type of environment suits them and their individual needs best, for them to be happy and healthy, and then, to choose accordingly.

In life, there are good environments, and there are also bad environments. Unfortunately, because the overly critical and negative environment that I lived and functioned in for many years, was crushing, tormenting, and hurting me mentally and emotionally, I had no other alternative or choice (after I discovered the harmful and detrimental effects that it was having on me), but to remove myself from it. The reason why, is because there was no hope that the bad environment would ever change—that it would improve and get better with the passage of time.

Prior to removing myself from my old environment, I had to find a new one—an environment that would be good and healthy for me personally. However, this was easier said than done. Because, when searching for a new environment, I soon discovered that the particular environment that I personally required or needed to recover from my mental illness, to heal, and flourish, could not be found anywhere. So, what I decided to do in my individual case, was to actually custom design, build, and create one of my own making—an environment that would fulfill my personal needs—one that was good, positive, encouraging, beneficial, and healthy (mentally, emotionally, physically, and spiritually) for me individually, which I eventually did.

I know at this time you're probably thinking: What does he mean in saying that he created his own environment? Does this mean that he took himself out of the world and having contact with all people and society, thereby becoming a hermit? No. We (as humans), need to function in the real world, and we also need people and society, for this is good and healthy for us. However, in the process of figuring and working things out (consciously and unconsciously) for myself, in regards to environments, in particular, the one that I personally required, it turned out to be somewhat of a complicated process. Let me go on to explain what happened.

During the process of designing, building, and constructing a new environment for myself, I understood that no environment is going to be totally ideal or perfect. However, if I wanted my mental health to drastically improve, and to eventually be completely healed and cured of my depression and bipolar disorder illness, I first needed to get rid of (as many as I possibly could, if not all) the unhealthy and harmful elements and things that were presently in my life—things that were triggering and feeding my depression and illness—thereby making matters even worse. And then, thereafter, to bring in good, healthy, and beneficial things that would stimulate, promote, and encourage good health, growth, and overall well-being (mentally, emotionally, physically, and spiritually) in me.

Before changing my old environment to a new one, I also had come to realize that there were certain aspects or things about my old environment's structure or makeup; including certain people or individuals (who displayed destructive traits, bad attitudes, and a negative spirit and actions towards me), that, not only contributed to or caused my bipolar disorder illness, but also, that they were often triggering and feeding my depression too, making it even worse![21] However, after I changed my environment from a *negative* one to a *positive* one (including being careful about who I invite into my new life and world), my mental health and medical condition (depression and bipolar disorder) started to gradually and greatly improve from day to day, until I finally reached the amazing level of improvement and good health, both mentally and emotionally, where I am today!

Initially, when I first began creating and constructing a healthy environment for myself, I went to the extremes, by separating myself from anything and everyone that I considered negative and harmful (although I may not have been totally conscious that I was doing this at the time). Now that I look back, I can understand why

---

[21] Personally, I had found that I was best off if I avoided, as much as possible, certain overly critical and negative environments and people that triggered and fed negative feelings and emotions and depression in me. On the other hand, I made sure that I replaced them with good, positive, and encouraging ones.

I did this. I think the reason why, is because I was suffering and hurting really bad! Because many of the people that I was around and had associations and contacts with were a big part of the problem that was creating issues for me.

Perhaps, going to the extremes was a good thing for me to do initially, so that my mind could rest and heal, and also so that I could sort through and get over certain hurtful things that had happened to me in the past—that were extremely troubling to me. However, in time, I came to realize that when it comes to humans and the structure of the world and society in general, that there are certain things in life, including challenging and difficult people, that we have to learn to put up with and tolerate at times. And yet, on the other hand, I also found that this concept and approach does not hold true and work for everything and everyone. Because, unfortunately, there are certain people that we may come into contact with, that have very harmful and destructive personalities (some who are soberly conscious and aware of it, and others that are unknowingly blind to themselves), who can be highly discouraging, harmful, and detrimental to others (individuals with destructive traits), I found it was best for me to keep a safe distance from them, that is, if I wanted to recover from my illness, heal, and to be and stay healthy mentally and emotionally thereafter.

Yes, in life, there are people that have good, encouraging, and upbuilding personalities. And, unfortunately, there are also those that have little to nothing that is good about them. However, the good thing, for the most part, is that we personally have a choice of choosing which ones we want to associate with and invite into our personal lives and space.

Interestingly, the way that we as humans were designed or made, is that, by nature we were meant to be social creatures. Yes, we need other people in our lives. For it is a healthy and beautiful thing! But not just anybody, that is, if we want to be happy and fair well. Ideally, they should be people that love and respect us for who we are. Good and positive people that encourage, support, and build us up.

To be honest with you, custom designing or creating a good and appropriate environment for myself was not an overnight thing. It took some time. But as time progressed, I came to more readily see what type of environment that I personally needed to heal and grow. True, this required both adding and removing certain elements and things from my life, however, in doing this, I had to exercise extreme caution to be careful not to remove *everything* that I considered to be negative or bad (even though I didn't like them). The reason why is because, sometimes, certain things that we might consider or think to be bad for us, may in fact be the exact opposite—they may be helpful and good for us. In other words, if we are not careful we could inadvertently wind up removing the very things from our life that can end up being the healthiest and most beneficial for our personal development and growth in the long run. It's like a child that refuses to eat his vegetables because he doesn't like the taste of them. However, without them (a balanced diet) he will not be properly nourished and grow. On the other hand, the same holds true for things that we might consider to be *good* for us too. Although they rightly may be good in themselves, if we were to be unbalanced or consume or add too much of a good thing, this could be harmful to us also. Again, being reasonable and balanced is the key.

A healthy internal environment: Sometime later, in addition to changing my physical or *external* environment, I also came to discover that I needed to change my *internal* environment as well. What I mean by *internal* environment is the environment that resides internally within the enclosures of the mind, heart, and soul. In other words, to be healthy and fair well, I needed to alter or change this too, in regards to what I allowed, and selectively chose (subject matter and things) to enter and occupy my thinking, mind, and heart.

But wait, you might ask: "Is having a good and healthy *internal* environment really that important? Isn't having a healthy *external* environment sufficient enough?" True, a good and healthy *external* environment can be highly important and beneficial to one's health. But, hypothetically speaking, what good is it if a person has a beautiful and healthy *external* environment and surroundings—even if it's an actual, literal, physical paradise—but, inside themselves, *internally,* they are unstable (mentally and emotionally), a complete mess; totally falling apart, or they are putting and inviting unhealthy and harmful things inside themselves that undermine their own health, well-being, and success. Therefore, because of this (as far as I was personally concerned), it became vitally imperative that I do something, by not only creating a healthy *physical* environment for myself, but also, by providing for and taking care of my *internal* environment (my mind, heart, and soul) as well.[22]

From the information above, we can see how important and valuable having the right or proper environment (*external* and *internal*) is for a person to have and maintain good health. How happy I am that I finally discovered and figured all of this important stuff out. Because, as a result of the healthy, *new environment* that I have now, my life has become so much better! But, not only that, it, along with other essential things, has helped to lift me up and out of depression, and eventually helped to heal and cure me of my bipolar disorder illness, which I am highly grateful for!

Yes, just like the encouraging example of the houseplants that I spoke about earlier — that were faring poorly, that is, until after I changed their soil — so too, the amazing turnaround and transformation of my health (mental and emotional), from being poor to becoming vibrantly healthy, proves what a big difference one's *environment* can have on their health and life for good, if it is a propitious, positive, and robustly healthy one!

Unfortunately, though, sometime later, as time progressed, I soon came to see and realize that my problem was not completely solved. For although I replaced the bad and harmful external environment that I was in with a good, prosperous, and healthy one, something happened that showed me that more was required, that is, if I wanted to improve my mental and emotional health once and for all time. The problem was that, although, initially, I thought that I

---

[22] Note: Although, sometime later, the *internal* environment also came to include the *physical diet* I consumed too, initially, I concentrated on the external environment and also providing the proper and healthy internal environment for my mind, heart, and soul first, by monitoring and censuring the subject matter and things that I permitted to enter and reside there.

could, I was not able to completely get rid of or leave my past, negative environment completely behind. Because, unfortunately, due to circumstances or situations that were beyond my control, there were times when I had to periodically enter back in to it. This was a little hard for me to cope and deal with at first, that is, until I realized that something else, in addition to my environment needed to change too, as the next step goes on to clearly show.

Step 7

PUTTING ON A NEW
PERSONALITY

U p to this point in time, as I traveled along the ever challenging and changing road, that was leading to me being cured of my depression and bipolar disorder, I had personally discovered and incorporated many important and valuable things in to my life—things that were helping me to gradually recover from my mental illness and be healed—although, not knowing at each particular stage in the process, if there would be an additional step or steps to come.

In quick review of the steps that I had taken thus far in my zealous pursuit for good health, especially mental and emotional health, see the list below:

- Step 1: I had to *find myself.*

- Step 2: I had to *open my mind and heart to peace, joy, and love.*

- Step 3: I had to learn to *respect myself.*

- Step 4: I had to *make joy my close friend.*

- Step 5: I had to *find the root cause of my mental illness.*

- Step 6: I had to *find the right environment* that was good, positive, and healthy for me.

Today, as I look back at what had taken place in the healing process, I can see that taking each and every one of these individual steps above were highly important, effective, and beneficial to me and my mental and emotional health—to say the least. However, now, at this particular time and juncture in the bipolar disorder healing process, I had to do something else too, in addition to taking these previous six steps, that is, if I wanted to eventually be completely cured of my bipolar illness. What was it? I had to alter or change my *personality* (not my entire personality, but certain aspects of it). Why did I have to do this? Well, the reason why is because there were things about my personality—certain qualities or traits that I possess that were causing problems, in that they were triggering and stirring up anxiety, depression, etc., in me; in particular, whenever I had to reenter my previous, negative environment. Therefore, I had no other alternative or choice but to change or correct these things (things about my personality), if I wanted my mental and emotional health to continue to improve, and to eventually be healed and cured of depression and bipolar disorder. What was it that I needed to change about myself?[23]

Before I begin to relate what I needed to change about my personality or character, let me tell you a little bit about personalities first—about how they are formed and, how they can be affected and influenced by an environment (for good or bad).

Personalities: There are a number of contributing factors that go into shaping our individual personality. Among them are: our social status, our economic situation, our environment, our culture, our parents, our friends and associates, and also our religious

---

[23] Note: I am not implying or saying that everyone who suffers from depression or bipolar disorder needs to change things about their character or personality. I'm just relating to you what happened to me.

background. Even the television programs and movies we watch, as well as other forms of entertainment, leave their impression and mark. All of these things and more have or play a role in shaping (for good or bad) who we are. Therefore, recognizing situations and things that exercise bad and *negative* influences on us and our personality places us in a better position to minimize their effect. Also, the same holds true regarding things that exercise *positive* influences on our personality or character. In regard to the latter, if we desire and choose, we can use these positive influences in a way to maximize their effects and benefits on us towards good.

A Word of Caution: I have discovered through experience that there are certain aspects or things about us as individuals that we cannot or that it is best for us not to change about ourselves, and that if we were to try to alter or change them, it might eventually lead to or cause us some problems down the line. For example, by nature, I am a *"night person"* (one that often stays up during late hours of the night). The reason why, is because this is when I have the most energy. Also nighttime is usually quieter than daytime, which is more conducive and beneficial to some people, like me, that are writers, artists, or musicians, etc. Personally, I find that because nighttime is generally a more peaceful and quiet time; I can have my thoughts to myself, and be able to reflect, think, focus, and be imaginative, which has been highly productive in producing creative and artistic works. However, because my staying up during the night was a bit disruptive to someone that I live with, I decided to change things by going to bed at night, instead of staying up during late hours. I guess you could say this was a good gesture or thing to do— at least, so I thought. That is, until I soon learned that changing my sleep patterns was not good for me personally. For it completely threw me off. Before I knew it, I was no longer my productive, creative, and happy self. As a result, my productivity and creativity as a writer of literature, poetry, and being artistic in other ways, etc., significantly began to dry up, which left me feeling somewhat sad, useless, and lost.

After realizing the negative effects and consequences that changing my sleep pattern had on me, I decided to go back to doing what I normally have done in the past, which is staying up during the night to get things done. Although I tried to be compromising and accommodating by changing my sleep patterns for a certain individual whom I greatly respect, appreciate, and love;— sometime later, because it became so disruptive and nonproductive to my work, and also harmful to my overall well-being, I just couldn't do it anymore. I guess they (the person that I was trying to accommodate and please) will just have to learn to accept and appreciate me for who I am—a unique and distinct individual— which fortunately they did.

The above example is just one instance that shows that there are certain innate things about ourselves that we cannot or that it is best for us not to change about ourselves. True, it is good to make changes and improvements to ourselves at times. But it is also important to know what and what we cannot change. It is also good to know and appreciate ourselves for who and what we are (as being different and unique individuals), even if society or the world around us doesn't. Well, enough about that! Let me get back to explaining what it was about my personality that needed to change and why.

As human beings, all of us have strengths. But we also have weaknesses too—things that we may not even like about ourselves. Perhaps, there is something that is causing us problems that we personally need to work on to change? It may be that we are a little prone to anger, or being impatient, or prone to abusive speech, or gossip, or something else? Previously, in my distant past, in the initial process of becoming a Christian, there were things about myself that I voluntarily changed that improved my personality for the better. True, the things that I needed to change weren't anything too serious or bad. But they were significant enough to matter to me personally. And so I changed them.

Fortunately for all of us (no matter who we are, or where we come from), when it comes to the matter of making personal changes and improvements in ourselves for good, we have both the option and ability to be able to transform or change things about ourselves and life at any point or time. This is something that is open to anyone who wishes, which is very encouraging and good news, especially for those who may not be happy or satisfied with certain aspects or things about themselves or their life. The amazing thing is, even deeply ingrained things can be changed if we work hard on them.

Interestingly, when it came time for me to change certain aspects or things about my personality, that were causing problems for me in my old environment, the strange thing is, the things that I needed to adjust or change, were not necessarily anything *bad* about me or my character. But rather, it was some of the *good* qualities or traits that I possessed that were causing issues. How so? And what were they?

Through personal observation and experiences, I came to discover and realize that, not only was there certain qualities and traits that I possess that were at odds with my old environment, but, also, that the environment was using them against me in negative ways—to cause and stir up harmful feelings and emotions in me— feelings and emotions that turned out to be damaging to my mental and emotional health. One of these qualities was the attribute of being *nice*. Yes, you read it right! I said *"nice."* I know this sounds a bit odd or strange. Because, how can a wonderful and beautiful quality such as being *nice* work against a person in a negative or harmful way? Well, let me explain.

Although certain qualities that we individually possess may, in themselves, be *good* traits and also beneficial to have; sometimes, having either *'too much'* or *'not enough'* of a particular quality can pose problems for us as individuals. For example, it is good to be *nice* to others. This is a very important, good, noble, and virtuous quality to possess and display. However, from personal experience, I've learned that there is such a thing as being *too nice*! In other words, having and displaying *'too much'* of this quality can sometimes work against us. The reason being is because, rather than appreciating and looking at this and other fine qualities that we might possess as being a strength and good thing in us, sometimes, people view them as a weakness, or something that they can exploit and take advantage of for their own personal benefit or selfish gain.

And then there are those who have no ulterior motives, in regards to taking advantage of a person's niceness. They just simply give the overly nice person a hard time, just to be devilish, spiteful, mean, or difficult. Consequently, for the overly *nice* person, the situation often becomes similar to what we might see comically portrayed or depicted in a theatrical movie or on television, where some geek kid is being kicked in his rear (over and over again) as he walks along a crowded corridor in his high school. Because, unbeknown to him, he is walking around with a *"kick me"* sign pinned to his back. Of course, a person like me, who is often *overly nice* to people, is not a weak person or a geek. But this goes to show how important it is for the qualities that we have and display (whether it is the quality of being nice, or good, or generous, or something else), to be in proper balance.

Unfortunately, today, we live in a "dog-eat-dog" world—a place where people (consciously or unconsciously) are being psychologically programmed to control or dominate others—often engaging in overly aggressive, controlling behaviors; fierce rivalry; and all out competition, etc. It's like being amongst a pack of wild dogs that are fighting to be the dominant alpha male. Personally, I think that, when it comes to humans, that, although sinful human nature is somewhat responsible for this type of overly aggressive thinking and behavior, that the primary contributing factor of this bad attitude, spirit, and behavior is the teaching and byproduct of the 'Darwinian Evolutionary Theory,' that wrongly teaches "survival of the fittest,"—a beastly and animalistic approach to survival and living. The sad thing is, so many have bought in to this idiotic rhetoric and verbal garbage that has encouraged and caused man to dominate man to his injury.

Don't be a pushover: Because of the way that the "dog-eat-dog" world is, there are times when we may personally need to fight back or protect ourselves, otherwise we can be eaten alive! However, in the process, we want to make sure that we don't go too far by adopting the world's animalist aggression and spirit.

Yes, in this "dog-eat-dog" world, sometimes, when it is necessary and appropriate (when it calls for it, without going overboard by being too overly aggressive), a person needs to learn to stand up for themselves and fight back; otherwise, the world will look at you as being a pushover, and it will take advantage of you, by walking all over you. However, when pushing back, so to speak—when we are being inappropriately challenged or bullied—the key here is to be *balanced* in our thinking, viewpoints, and actions. Truth is, everything that we do in life, no matter what it is, needs to be properly balanced. Because, if it isn't balanced, it can work negatively against us.

Another important thing to know, is *when* it may be appropriate or necessary to stand up for ourselves and fight back. Because when dealing with life's negative, challenging, or troubling issues, some things are meant to fight for or against in life, while other things are best to just avoid, or accept, or make personal adjustments for, especially in regards to certain environments, organizational structures, or people, or thinking, or mindsets and things that stubbornly refuse to or simply cannot be changed.

Interestingly, when it comes to the structure or makeup of *environments*, I've noticed that they are a lot like people in certain ways, in that, each and every one of them has its own distinct features or personality within themselves that makes them unique and different from others. For example, some environments are warm and inviting; while others are cold and aloof. Some are encouraging and supportive; while others are extremely picky and overly critical, and so forth. And then, there are those that have a mixture of these things and more. The environments that I'm referring to are *long-term environments*—those that we spend a considerable amount of time in, such as at school, at work, or in our neighborhood, etc.

Another curious and interesting thing about environments, is that, when it comes to the overall structure or makeup of them, it is often virtually impossible to alter or change them. The reason why, is because their characteristics or personality are usually, for the most part, solidly fixed or etched in stone—meaning that they are unchangeable. And because of this, the only three choices that people usually have when it comes to choosing or being in a particular environment are: (1) They can choose to stay within their present environment and adapt and become like it—thereby contributing to its growth and success, and sharing in its failures, and so forth or, (2) They can decide to remove themselves from their current environment, so as to avoid its effects and influences or, (3) They can dislike the environment they're in (groan and complain about it), but decide to stay within it and reap the negative and unhappy consequences.[24]

Interestingly, when it comes to each and every one of us, there are some environments that we might fit into better than others. Also, an environment that works for one person may not be a good fit for another. Truth is, no environment is perfect. And if or when it becomes necessary to choose one, it often comes down to selecting the one that suits us the best—one that we can at least tolerate and function within to a reasonable degree.

Unfortunately, because my previous, old environment was harmful and detrimental to me and my mental and emotional health, I decided that it was best for me to exchange it for another one—one that was better suited for me. However, I later found that it wasn't so easy to just get up and leave the old environment completely behind, because due to situations and circumstances that were beyond my control, I had to periodically reenter it (more than I wanted to)—something that posed a considerable challenge to me at first, that is, until I found a workable solution. This required that I alter or adjust certain aspects or things about myself. Not by compromising who I am, or what I believe in or what I stand for, etc., but instead, by making the necessary adjustments and things within myself to protect myself, so that my environment would have little to no effects on me and my mental and emotional health—so

---

[24] Sometimes there may be an overly challenging and negative environment that we find ourselves in, even though we may not prefer to be there. Because for one reason or another we cannot leave or remove ourselves from it. Or we simply have no other place to go. What do we do then? For help on how to develop, grow, and be productive in an overly challenging and negative environment, see the information "Growing in a Negative Environment," in the Appendix, on page 269.

that it would not cause me anymore suffering or harm.

Prior to adjusting my personality, in regards to adapting to my old, negative environment, I found that, no matter how hard I tried, that there was nothing that I could do in a positive way to influence or change the environment's personality for the good or better. Because it's structure was already solidly fixed or set in stone. As a matter of fact, I soon learned through experiences that being opposed to or going against it in any way (even if it was introducing something positive), made matters even worse for me. Therefore, I had to do the next best thing, which was to alter or change certain aspects of my individual personality that were in conflict with the environment's personality; namely, by balancing out the quality of being *nice*, and other traits that I possess to the proper level or degree—which, after successfully doing, in the end, worked out much better to my benefit. It's not that I wasn't nice anymore, because I was, it's just that I had to monitor the level of niceness that I displayed and showed to certain individuals who would read me the wrong way, or who would try to take advantage of it. The challenging thing was that I had to do this without inhibiting or killing the beautiful qualities that I possess, but also, so that I would continue to develop and grow in positive ways.

Another example of a quality that some people have and display that is good, and yet, may need to be balanced out, is the quality of *generosity*. True, it is important to be generous and share with others. This is something that we learned from kindergarten on. However, there is such a thing as being *too generous*! For example, there are people that are so generous that they will literally give you their last buck or the shirt on their back! Sure, this is a good and noble thing to do. But the problem with this, is that, if we are *too generous* and give too much of ourselves and things to others, we won't have anything left for ourselves. In other words, we will fall in to personal want, need, and hardship. The sad thing is, some people will and do take advantage of overly generous people like this—taking them for everything that they can get out of them. This is yet another good example that shows the importance of having and keeping the good qualities that we possess in proper balance. Because, if we don't, the world will exploit and use these fine qualities to our detriment and harm.

Another important and beautiful quality that is good in itself, but can pose problems and issues for us, that is, if it is misused or not properly balanced, is the quality of *love*. For example, we could develop a strong love and attachment for the wrong things. Like alcohol, illicit drugs, material possessions, money, or even the wrong person. Yes, our love could be misused or misdirected towards something or someone, that, initially, we believed to be good, valuable, and beneficial for us. But, in the end, we may later discover that it or they weren't as good for us as we had imagined they would be. Sad to say, sometimes the things that we attach our heart to brings us a world of hurt and pain!

Another personal quality or trait that I personally possess, that I had to readjust, is the trait of being a *deep thinker* (a person that often has a tendency to over think matters). The reason why I had to adjust this is because this trait was being used against me, by the past, bad environment that I was in, to undermine my peace, joy, and happiness and, to stir up negative feelings and emotions in me that were harmful and detrimental to my mental and emotional health.

How could being a deep thinker be used in a negative and harmful way against me? Well, the way that my mind works, is like a digging tool or shovel that is used to dig into the ground. Whereas some people might use their shovel to break soil and skim along the surface only, I, on the other hand, have the inborn ability and habit of using my shovel, not only to break the ground's surface but, to keep on digging, deeper and deeper, until perhaps you can't dig anymore—where you eventually hit rock bottom!

The matter of me being a deep thinker or intellectual is not necessary a bad thing in itself. However, if this innate gift and ability is not used in the right way, monitored, channeled, or properly balanced out, it can sometimes pose some problems—at least this is what I've found (during certain times), to be the situation in my case.

The problem was, instead of being a person that looks for and focuses on the good and positive in people and things, in the past, I often zeroed in on and focused (consciously or unconsciously) on the bad or negative things about them and things. Interestingly, focusing on negativity was not an innate inclination that I was born with. But rather, I found that it was something that was instigated, triggered, and fueled by the bad environment around me, in particular, by the overly critical and negative way that I was being unjustly viewed and treated by others within my environment. Ironically, you could say that it was a matter or case of *negativity* feeding *negativity*.

One of the reasons why I believe I was being targeted and attacked by my environment, was because it was envious and jealous of the ability that I have to think deeply. It's not that I was showing off or that I was being arrogant or anything, because I wasn't. It's just that by nature, I am a very generous and helpful person, with a big heart, who loves to be of use in assisting others. In essence, I was just freely using the innate gifts that I was born with to encourage and help others, which is a beautiful, generous, and unselfish way to be—at least, so I thought. That is, until I began to be unjustly labeled, persecuted, and attacked. The crazy thing is, I think the ones that were responsible for attacking me, were not even consciously aware that they were doing it. But, apparently, out of pride and jealousy and, the desire to be prominent and shine, they didn't like how I was making them look and feel, which obviously to them was the feeling of being shown up, or being made to feel inferior in some way. The end result was that I became their target—someone to zero in and focus on; to try to find possible weaknesses or faults, so that they could perhaps use these to crush my spirit and elevate themselves and their egos above me. As a matter of fact, they even went so far as to begin to view and treat me as being of little to no value, which, unfortunately, began to gradually undermine the good image and value that I have of myself. In essence, they eventually invalidated my self-worth and who I am.

Unfortunately, this highly caustic, overly critical and negative, soul crushing environment caused a lot of problems for me, because I began to focus and dwell on the bad and negative things that I was experiencing and being exposed to. The sad thing is, is that, in the end, it took a toll on my mental and emotional health and well-being to a large degree. It's not that I intentionally chose to think about and dwell on negative things, because I am not that kind of person at heart. It's just that the brutally unjust and overly critical and negative structure of the environment that I was in (that viewed and treated me so horribly and unjustly), and which was constantly attacking me; often initiated and fed it.[25]

Interestingly, in God's Word, the Bible, it says: "Oppression can drive the wise one into madness."—Ecclesiastes 7:7. It's not that I literally became insane or mad from the unjust treatment and things that I was experiencing. However, the ill effects of my negative environment had a detrimental effect upon my feelings, emotions, moods, and mental health to a large degree. Because it was tormenting my mind, heart, and soul, which generated feelings of irritation, frustration, anxiety, and depression.

Unfortunately, the "two edged sword," as I now call it, (1) my past, overly critical and negative *environment*, along with my (2) *over thinking* matters—focusing and dwelling on the ugly and negative things that were being directed at me personally—stirred up bad and negative feelings and emotions in me, which caused a tremendous amount of hurt and pain. It even went so far as to stir up a certain amount of resentment and anger in me too, because, unwittingly, at the time that it was happening and beyond, I carried things a bit too far, by going too deep, and refusing to let go of the hurt.

To make matters even worse, I also inflicted a certain amount of emotional hurt and pain on myself by focusing too much on my own shortcomings and weaknesses too. Thinking that perhaps my zealous persecutors and fault finders were right—that there were unsightly things about me that needed to be changed or corrected. Later, I came to realize that there was nothing wrong with me per se. The thing that was wrong was the thinking, viewpoints, and

---

[25] This was only part of the problem that I had to deal with in the past, in my previous, bad environment. There was more, as I related in my previously released book "Bipolar Disorder, A Patient's Story."

standards of my overly negative and critical persecutors that were tormenting me, by thoroughly examining me and picking me apart. I'm not saying that I am perfect and that there isn't anything that I have to work on to improve, for I am imperfect just like the next fellow. I'm just saying that the degree of the critical censuring of me that my zealous persecutors were putting me through, exceeded reasonableness, and reality. And it definitely wasn't right, loving, or just.

As a result of the self-censuring, self-debasement, or self-deprecation that I was putting myself through (beating myself up), along with the bad habit of over thinking matters and focusing and dwelling on overly critical and negative people within my old environment; it became so discouraging and depressing that it ended up pulling me downwards into a deep pit of internal suffering and despair. But the good thing is, after I came to the realization of what was happening—little by little, I was finally able to climb up and out of the pit—to finally adjust and balance things out in my life, along with my thinking, so that I was (1) no longer beating myself up, (2) no longer over thinking matters of non-importance and, (3) no longer letting the overly negative thinking and viewpoints of others tear me down—to rob me of my inner peace, joy, self love, and happiness—the extremely important and valuable things that I now possess, and that I refuse to allow anyone or anything to ever rob me of again!

Another vitally important and necessary thing that I did, is that, I made sure that I forgave my jealous persecutors in my heart for the hurt and harm that they caused me. Why? Well, for one, if I hadn't, they would have won. But also, harboring resentment and hatred would have destroyed the beautiful person that I am inside, along with the potential for further self-development, growth, and improvements.

Today, now that I look back at the positive adjustments and progress that I have made, in regards to the things above, along with other essential changes and improvements and things that I have made in my life, I can appreciate how "Old Man Time," and a little bit of wisdom can work wonders! For with a little thought, experience, and passage of time, I was not only able to correct the troubling and damaging things above, but, I was also able to develop a lot more control over my thinking, feelings, and emotions too!

Yes, along the ever enlightening and beneficial road of my amazing journey—that would eventually lead to me being completely healed and cured of my depression and bipolar disorder illness—I have come to discover, understand, and appreciate many things. One thing is that, my qualities or traits of being a *nice* person, and also a *deep thinker*, as well as other fine qualities that I possess, are not bad in themselves, but rather, they are good and positive things, if viewed and used in the right and balanced way. As a matter of fact, they are gifts from God. So, going forward, I am going to try hard to continue to use these in positive and constructive ways. For example, in regard to the matter of being a *deep thinker*, rather than allowing my mind to drift and focus on negative things that discourage and tear me down, which can so easily lead to discouragement, depression, and feelings of low self-esteem, etc., I'm going to use it to focus primarily on good, positive, valuable, and beautiful things that will encourage and build up, both myself and others.

The good thing is, now, that I have successfully altered and balanced out things about my personality and thinking for the better, my former bad environment doesn't have the same harmful effects and influence that it had on me in the past. However, because of the powerful influence that environments can exert and have on people in general, I know that it is best for me (whenever I have to revisit it), not to stay in my former, bad environment too long. Now, rather than spending too much time in it, I keep my necessary visits short-lived and to a minimum. Otherwise, it's strong influence could possibility overtake me again—like it did in the past—causing and reaping havoc and pain on my mental and emotional health, which would be absolutely horrible! And believe me, the last thing that I want to do is to fall back into the same devastating and destructive rut and situation that I was in, in the past—prior to being healed of my depression and bipolar disorder illness.

Yes, as you can see from the information above, Step #7

"Putting On A New Personality," of the recovery and healing process that was leading to me being cured of my illness was highly helpful and beneficial to me, in improving my mental and emotional health. However, as good and important as it was for me to change certain aspects and things about my personality, something else, in addition to this was also required, if I wanted to eventually be completely cured of depression and bipolar disorder illness, as the next step goes on to show.

Step 8

CONTROLLING YOUR FEELINGS
AND EMOTIONS

The *eighth,* vitally important step or stage that I went through on the road leading to being healed and cured of my depression and bipolar disorder illness, involved getting and maintaining control over my feelings and emotions.[26]

As humans, we were created with the amazing ability to be able to express a wide range and variety of feelings and emotions. We can express: love, warmth, affection, goodness, kindness, generosity, thankfulness, joy, peace, mildness, patience, empathy, humility, compassion, and the list goes on.

While *good* feelings and emotions can add color and spice to our lives, making it more pleasant and enjoyable, on the flipside of things, if we are not watchful and careful, certain *bad* feelings and

---

[26] Note: I am not implying that everyone who suffers from depression or bipolar disorder has a problem controlling their feelings and emotions. I'm just relating to you what happened to me.

emotions that we might have or display, can do the exact opposite. They can disrupt our peace, and joy, and bring us sorrow and pain. But even worse than this, they can also be harmful and detrimental to our personal health too. Because our deep feelings and emotions are pillars that support our overall health and well-being— physically, mentally, emotionally, and spiritually.

One example of *bad* feelings and emotions that can be harmful and damaging to one's health, are fits of uncontrolled anger and rage. They can cause high blood pressure, strokes, respiratory issues, digestive troubles, skin diseases, hives, ulcers, and a host of other health problems.

Our *bad* feelings and emotions can also create other problems as well. For example, there's a true story of a restaurant manager, that manages an upscale casual dining restaurant, who, one day, became so upset at one of his employee's (apparently for his lack of work output), that, he (the manager), in a fit of uncontrolled rage, literally hauled off and punched a door with his fist! Only later to discover that he had broke his hand—a serious injury that required immediate surgery, and also that he miss work for the next six weeks. What a shame! All of this from losing his temper and striking a door! What a foolish and painful thing to do! And this was just the physical pain that the restaurant manager put himself through. Not to mention the possible, emotional stress and anxiety that he caused himself, his wife, and also his kids (if he has any) for being out of work, and not being eligible to collect workman's compensation. Because, although the injury happened on the job, he (the manager) made himself ineligible to receive worker's comp benefits, due to being responsible for causing his own accident or injury, which, in reality, was no accident. I'm sure that afterwards, he felt pretty stupid for having done such a dumb thing—losing his temper and punching a door! For just think, all of this drama and pain could have been totally avoided, if only he would have had proper control over his *feelings and emotions*.

In addition to being harmful to our physical health and well-being, our *bad* feelings and emotions can also be detrimental to our mental health as well. Because they can make us sick. For example, *anxiety* can lead to depression, robbing one of their strength and the initiative to act. Says the inspired proverb, "Anxious care in the heart of a man is what will cause it to bow down."—Proverbs 12:25. In other words, worries and anxieties can cause the heart to be weighed down with sadness or depression.

Also, there can be serious physical manifestations from worry too. Observes the book, *How to Master Your Nerves:* "Doctors know how anxiety can affect the body's functions. It can raise (or lower) blood pressure; it can elevate the white blood cell count; it can suddenly affect the blood sugar by the action of adrenalin on the liver. It can even change your electrocardiogram. Dr. Charles Mayo said: 'Worry affects the circulation, the heart, the glands, the whole nervous system.'"—By Drs. P. Steincrohn and D. LaFia, 1970, p. 14.

As we can see from the above examples, our *bad* feelings and emotions can be harmful and damaging to our overall health and well-being. However, on the opposite end of the spectrum, *good* feelings and emotions can do the exact opposite. They can be good and beneficial to our health. Interestingly, in God's Word, the Bible, at Proverbs 14:30, it says: "A calm heart gives life to the body." Meaning, that when we pursue peace, we reap the benefits of a calm heart, which can promote good health. And that's just the good effects that we can possibly gain from the quality of being *peaceful*, not to mention the benefits that can come to us from pursuing other good qualities as well.

Another wonderful quality that promotes good health is the quality of *joy*. For the Bible says: "A heart that is *joyful* does good as a *curer*."—Proverbs 17:22. Also at Proverbs 15:13, it says: "A *joyful* heart makes for a cheerful countenance [face], but heartache crushes the spirit."[27]

Interestingly, prior to me being healed of depression and bipolar

---

[27] *"Countenance"* meaning: appearance, especially the look or expression of the face. Note: The word "heart" in the Bible usually refers to the whole inner person, including his or her emotions.

disorder, I was not previously aware of what the Bible says about the subject of *joy* and its amazing healing properties. However, for some unexplained reason, during Step #4 *"Making Joy Your Close Friend,"* of the bipolar disorder healing process, I began to pursue *joy* above all other things. And believe me; I'm glad that I did. Because in the long run it ended up being a good and beneficial thing that was highly useful to me in the recovery process, in regard to improving my mental and emotional health.

Revealing yet another example of the negative effects that bad feelings and emotions can have on us—but also showing a positive way that this can be remedied or reversed, Proverbs 12:25 says: "Anxiety in a man's heart weighs it down, but a good word cheers it up." Meaning, anxiety causes depression, but kind and compassionate words from others can lift a person's spirits, having a positive effect on their moods and emotions.

Knowing and realizing this, makes me think about myself and how important it is that I be encouraged by others. But also, it shows how important it is for me to reach out and be encouraging and uplifting to others as well, which is something that I try to do on a regular basis.

Some years ago (without the help of anyone or anything), after having personally discovered and realized through deep thought, reasoning, reflection, and personal experiences—the effects that our *feelings and emotions* can have on a our overall, personal health and well-being—either for good or bad (which is something that I talked extensively about in my previous book *Bipolar Disorder, A Patient's Story*), I decided that perhaps it would be in my best interests, if I learned to regulate and gain control over my feelings and emotions, so that they would help and benefit me, rather than hurt and harm me (mentally, emotionally, physically, and spiritually). And I'm glad that I did. For look at me now. I am completely cured of my mental illness! However, as I had shown earlier in this book, there were other important things — besides controlling feelings and emotions — that were also involved in the healing process as well, as the previous 7 Steps so clearly shows.

True, controlling one's feelings and emotions is not always an easy thing to do. For, unfortunately, there are a lot of things in life that can distress and upset us (some more than others). One example of this is when we happen to run into or be around people that fail to exercise control over their own feelings and emotions—some even displaying bursts of anger or temper tantrums that are directed at us personally. This can present a real challenge to us, because under these circumstances it can be hard to keep calm, cool, and collect, and not retaliate in the same angry spirit, manner, or way. However, for our own health sake it is vital that we remain calm and collected.

Another thing that can be upsetting to us personally, is if we were to learn that we have a serious illness or a potentially life altering or threatening disease. Of course, it would be totally understandable to be upset over this, because it is not an easy thing to face and go through difficult and distressing things of this sort. But for our own personal good and health sake, after we initially learn of the diagnoses, it is vitally important for us to try to stay calm and keep control over our feelings and emotions, so that they don't get the best of us, making matters a whole lot worse. For sometimes our *bad* feelings and emotions can be like pouring gasoline on an open fire!

I didn't realize it during the time it was happening in the past, but I now sincerely believe that my *bad* feelings and emotions contributed to my early depression, and later, to my having bipolar disorder. Of course, it wasn't the primary factor or thing that caused my illness. But, no doubt, it most likely played a significant part in escalating the problem. I know this may seem strange to some—learning that it took so long for me to figure this out, many years down the line. Especially, now, after the damage has already been done. But, how ironic is this! Because, to a certain degree, you could say that this was a sort of self-inflicted anxiety, suffering, and pain (mental and emotional) that I put myself through—something that perhaps could have possibly been totally avoided, had I had proper control over my feelings and emotions. Fortunately, for me, in time, I finally figured this out, and was able to eventually change things to stop this insidious method of self-induced harm—that apparently was being created, triggered, and fed by both the negative environment that I was in at the time, along with the bad personal experiences that I was going through during this difficult and challenging time period of my life.

Unfortunately, if we, personally, are not watchful and careful, there are many things in this world that could cause us to develop and possess a bad spirit, negative thinking, or a destructive attitude that can be damaging to us personally, and also to others—harmful things such as: resentment, hatred, strife, fits of anger, dissensions, divisions, jealousy, and envy, etc.,—things that can erode and destroy the good and beauty in us and also rob us of our personal peace, joy, and happiness. Today, now that I am healthy mentally and emotionally, and I want to continue to stay this way, on a daily basis I try to be ever aware and careful that unhealthy, negative, bad attitudes, and things, that I see reflected and displayed in society and the world around me, no longer influence and infect my healthy mind, thinking, and behavior.

In addition to working to avoid, and keep any *bad* feelings and emotions from surfacing within me, I also strive, each and every day, to have and maintain a calm and joyful mind, heart, and spirit. One way that I do this, is by searching for and opening my mind and heart to beautiful and cheerful things that will bring joy and sunshine into my life and soul. And believe me, I don't have to go too far to find these wonderful things, for they are plentiful, and all around. All it takes is being aware of where they are and where to look.

Another thing — along with looking to have and maintain a cheerful disposition and mood — I also reach out to brighten other people's lives as well (especially family and friends), by regularly sharing with them (on any given day), something good and positive with them that is encouraging—by saying, doing, or giving them something (even if it is something relatively small), that will be uplifting to them individually—something that makes them feel good about themselves and the wonderful things in life!

Unfortunately, for many years, depression and bipolar disorder were really hard on me. They had me in pretty bad shape (mentally and emotionally). Fortunately, in time, I came to discover and realize that I have a lot of power and control over my feelings and emotions—more than I ever imagined! And that, rather than letting them control me in a bad and negative way to my detriment or harm—that I could learn to manage and control them instead—in good, positive, and healthy ways, to my ultimate benefit and good. How did I do this? Well, one way was by changing and safeguarding my thinking. Why is monitoring and controlling one's thinking so important? Because, bad and negative feelings and emotions usually start with our thinking and thoughts, and the more that we think, focus and dwell on them, the stronger these feelings and emotions can grow and become.

In looking back at the amazing success that I've had within a relatively short period of time — in regards to learning to safeguard and control my thinking, feelings, and emotions, — I am so happy that I had worked so hard (on a daily basis) on changing and controlling these things (instead of giving them free reign), by directing my thoughts in upbuilding, good, and positive ways. As a result, I no longer get overly hurt or upset over the negative and discouraging things that others might say or do. Also, instead of tripping, falling, and stumbling so to speak, over disturbing or discouraging issues and things that happen to me (like I did in the past), allowing them to hurt and crush my spirit and tear me down (which can slowdown or impede advancement, progress, and growth), I am now able to stand solid and firm, and run through life unhindered—growing, developing, and flourishing in many healthy and beneficial ways!

Today, instead of being weighed down with *bad* feelings and emotions, how much better it is to have emptied and freed my mind and heart of these hurtful and harmful things, so that, now, there is plenty of room in them for me to not only feed and fill them with amazing, wonderful, and beautiful things of life, but also, so that I can encourage, stimulate, and utilize my thinking and other God-given talents and abilities in good and beneficial ways, to the full!

Yes, learning to control my *feelings and emotions* was a huge discovery and help to me as I traveled along the road to recovery and good health, especially, mental and emotional health. True, it was not always an easy thing to do—to control my feelings and emotions; but through patience and hard work, I was able to successfully battle and eventually take back control over my feelings and emotions and a large portion of my life. However, as good and beneficial as this was, as the next step goes on to show, more was required for me to eventually become completely healed and cured of my bipolar disorder.

Step 9

CHANGING YOUR DIET
AND LIFESTYLE

The *ninth* step or phase that I went through on the amazing road leading to me being healed and cured of my depression and bipolar disorder illness, required that I alter or change my diet and life style.[28] Why was this so important? Well, in many ways, having a good diet and lifestyle is conducive to good health. Often, it can make a big difference in how we feel and function on a daily basis. On the other hand, when we neglect our health by having a poor diet or lifestyle, or both, it can lead to various problems, where we eventually feel and experience the negative effects.

I don't know about you (the reader), if you ever experience this, but in the past, on no particular day, whenever I would eat a load of junk food, the aftermath would often leave me feeling sluggish,

---

[28] Note: I am not insinuating or implying that everyone who suffers from depression or bipolar disorder needs to change their diet or lifestyle. I'm just relating to you what happened to me.

depressed, and downright awful. However, on days when I ate nutritious and healthy things, I would feel so much better!

Truth is, having a poor diet and bad eating habits can lead to poor performance, obesity, diabetes, and other health issues.

True, having and maintaining a good diet and healthy lifestyle is no sure solution or guarantee that we won't ever get sick. However, when we do everything possible within our ability and power to be and stay healthy, we can, to a certain degree, lessen the chance.

In hopes of improving my personal health, one thing that I eliminated from my diet that was unhealthy for me, was refined sugar and products that contained such. Initially, this was a hard thing to do, because sugar is pretty much in everything that's available for purchase at the supermarket. But also, sugar makes things taste good. However, the effect that refined sugar was having on my health was not good. For one, it caused me to put on unwanted pounds. Another thing is that it made me a borderline diabetic. And lastly, it also affected my moods in a negative way.

Interestingly, in the past, prior to eliminating refined sugar from my diet, whenever I consumed it (especially after I had been without it for quite some time), I could immediately feel the reaction or chemical effects that it was having on my brain—particularly in the area of the left hemisphere, within the *sensory area* of my brain. It's sort of hard to explain, but the physical feeling or effects that it produced was not pleasant. To me it felt like a buildup of static electricity, or surges of negative energy of some sort — like there was chemical warfare or a battle was taking place within this area or space within my brain. Interestingly, this feeling stayed with me for a while, that is, until I stopped eating refined sugar and the residual effects of it began to gradually wear off.

Whether or not this strange feeling that sugar produced was something that was good or bad that was taking place within my brain, I don't know. All I know is that I didn't like how it made my head feel. Because of this, and other negative effects of refined sugar, along with reading bad reports about how bad it is for one's health, it led me to believe that perhaps refined sugar is not good for me personally. And so I took the necessary steps to eliminate it from my diet.

Some of the good benefits and results that came from eliminating refined sugar from my diet were: (1) I was able to lose a considerable amount of weight (15 lbs in the first week) and, (2) My health eventually improved so that I was no longer a borderline diabetic, and lastly, (3) My moods improved and stabilized for the better.[29]

Interestingly, over time, because I had become more conscious of my health, especially during the bipolar disorder healing steps or stages that I was going through, I had come to know my body pretty well. But also, I believe that my body, in itself, instinctively knows what is good and bad for it. Because of this, I've learned to listen and pay close attention to it, which has made a big difference in how I treat it now, and also in how I function and feel each day.

As humans, our bodies are a lot like a house, in that it must be kept up and properly serviced and maintained. Because, if we neglect giving it the necessary attention and proper preventive maintenance, and so forth, that it requires on a regular basis, it will eventually get rundown and begin to fall apart. Having this in mind, during Step #9 *"Changing Your Diet and Lifestyle,"* of the bipolar disorder healing process, I started to think of things that I could perhaps do or that I might incorporate in to my personal life that would help to promote good health within me. One thing that I thought about doing is having or incorporating a good and nutritious diet in to my daily lifestyle.

What is a good diet? Well, the good thing is, we don't have to be a nutritional expert to know what is good or bad for our body. Sometimes, it just takes common sense. Also, there is no shortage of professional help in books, and also on the internet about healthy

---

[29] Note: The 15 pounds that I lost was the result of eliminating sugar from my diet and also being on a strenuous exercise program, along with eating a healthy diet of nutritious foods.

diets and good living. Besides this, when it comes to choosing the right foods that are nutritious for us, the guess work is pretty much taken out of basically everything that we may select at the supermarket, because all of the ingredients, and the dietary nutrition and value of the food is conveniently listed on the labels and packages.

According to the World Health Organization (WHO); a healthy, well-balanced, and nutritious diet for an adult consists of eating: fruit, vegetables, legumes, nuts, whole grains, protein, dairy, and also good fats and sugars in proper proportions on a daily basis. If you personally happen to be one who needs help or assistance in this area, you might want to consult your doctor or local nutritionist who will be more than happy to help you.

In essence, all food, no matter what we eat, is essentially made up of chemicals (whether they be natural or manmade), and these chemicals (depending on what they are), when consumed and digested, have certain effects on our body, brain, and health.

Interestingly, it is a common, held notion or belief that one of the possible causes of bipolar disorder is having a chemical imbalance in the brain, namely, *serotonin*, which functions as a neurotransmitter—that helps to relay messages from one area of the brain to another. Subsequently, to help boost low serotonin levels in mental health patients, they are often prescribed antidepressant medications. An interesting thing, is that, theoretically speaking, there is no way of actually knowing for sure what the proper, correct, exact, or normal levels of serotonin are or what they are supposed to be in the human body and brain. There is no way for scientists and those in the medical field to be certain. The reason being is that the human body and brain are just too complex! It is only by means of trials and experimentation that they have noted, that by boosting or increasing the levels of serotonin in bipolar disorder patients, that it seems to somewhat help in treating their depression.

Another reason why it is impossible of knowing what the proper chemical levels are suppose to be in humans, is because everyone is unique and different. In other words, what may be so called *"normal chemical levels"* in one individual; may not necessarily be the proper levels for someone else. Also, it stands to reason that chemical levels would be different in different people, based upon their height, weight, and size, etc. For example, a smaller person (5 feet tall, weighing 100 lbs) would no doubt have a lesser amount or volume of a particular chemical or chemicals in their body, compared to a much larger person (6 ft. 5 in. tall, weighing 200 lbs). Also, it stands to reason that what makes each and every person unique and different from one another, is that, it most likely has to do with, not only their unique, individual, DNA structure, but also, that in all likelihood; it has something to do with the particular chemical makeup of their entire body. No doubt, along with their unique DNA, their unique chemical makeup accounts for the differences in how their unique mind and other things work. The amazing thing is that our body knows how to turn the nutritional foods and things that we eat into the proper chemical groupings or chemical makeup that are unique to our individual body's needs, so as to daily rebuild and replenish us.

Another reason why it is impossible of knowing what the proper chemical levels are suppose to be in humans, is because *all* humans are *imperfect*, with imperfect bodies and brains. So even if there was a way of accurately measuring the exact level or volume of each and every chemical that currently exists in the human body and brain, the measurements that we get, most likely would not be enough to determine what a truly healthy chemical level or balance is suppose to be in humans—compared to what the levels would possibly be if our bodies and brains were in fact perfect. The reason why, is because the chemicals in all *imperfect* humans (which we all are), may be out of whack or out of balance, due to being imperfect. Or perhaps, there may be some unnatural or foreign chemical(s) or substances in the makeup of the body or brain of the imperfect human race now (perhaps even in their DNA and RNA[30]), that were not originally meant to be there when God first made Adam and Eve, the first human pair who were actually created perfect, but then, who later transgressed, lost their perfection, and thereafter passed sin, *imperfection*, and death on to their offspring and the entire human

---

[30] DNA (deoxyribonucleic acid), and RNA (ribonucleic acid).

race. (Genesis 3:1-24; Romans 5:12).

The matter of human perfection and imperfection poses a couple of interesting questions. Could it be that *perfection* or *imperfection* is written in human DNA and RNA? After perfect Adam and Eve (who were originally made to live forever) sinned, did God alter or change the structure or composition of their DNA and RNA from that of perfection to imperfection, so that they would eventually begin to grow old and die?[31] Also, is the DNA and RNA of a person who is perfect (like Adam and Eve were), different from one who is imperfect today? It would stand to reason that this is so. However, there is no way of knowing for sure, because Adam's and Eve's (who lived about 6,000 years ago) DNA and RNA is not available to be found and examined. However, whatever the case may be, it's an interesting thought, to say the least.

Despite the fact that all humans (the descendants of Adam and Eve) are imperfect, when it comes to the matter of our health, it is in our best interest — as far as what we currently know about the body and its functions and things — to try to be and remain as healthy as we possibly can. Interestingly, back in the year 1984, there was thought to be about 30 different types of known chemicals in the human brain. However, today, with more knowledge and research, it's been discovered that there are many more! And like many things in life, often it is important to have and maintain perfect balance, in order to function properly and to be healthy.

Because chemical balance is so vitally important to good health and the proper functions of our body and brain, during Step #9 *"Changing Your Diet and Lifestyle,"* of the bipolar disorder healing process, I began to take a serious look at these things. The reason why is because I felt that if I started eating right, by putting the proper, nutritious foods and things in my body, that perhaps this could help to fix and correct any possible chemical imbalances that might exist—thereby boosting and improving my health, in particular, my mental health. In other words, I felt that the right diet would help my body and brain out by providing them with the

---

[31] Note: The penalty of sin was death.—Genesis 3:1-3.

proper nutrients and building blocks that they require to recover from my illness—to heal, to function properly, and to be healthy. For this reason, I decided to incorporate a healthy and nutritional diet in to my daily life—one that consisted primarily of natural and organic foods—foods containing things that are not artificial or manmade, but instead, are in harmony with the human body's natural makeup and chemistry—things that our minds and bodies seem to naturally thrive and do well on.[32]

The encouraging thing, is that, when we eat the right and proper, nutritional things, it doesn't have to take that long before we start seeing and feeling the good effects and results from them. For example, in God's Word, the Bible, at Daniel 1:1-17, it tells of a true story, about four Israelite youths named, Daniel, Hananiah, Mishael, and Azariah, who refused to pollute themselves with the "delicacies" of Babylonian king, Nebuchadnezzar, although they (the 4 youths), were under the king's orders to regularly eat these things. However, instead of subsisting on a diet of foods that were possibly prohibited by the Mosaic Law to eat—and also wine—the four boys requested vegetables and water for 10 days instead. True, they did this primarily for the purpose of not breaking God's laws and principles. But also, secondarily, it served to prove that these things were healthier and better for them, rather than the so called delicacies of the Babylonians.

To make a long story short, at the end of the 10 days, the four Israelite boys were healthier than all of the other youths in the Babylonian kingdom that were eating the delicacies of the king.[33] I am not highlighting this example for the purpose of saying or demonstrating that being a vegetarian or having a vegan diet is

---

[32] Although I realized that seeking good health through a nutritious diet was going to be beneficial for my overall health, my main purpose in doing this, was to try to restore chemical balance in my brain, so that, perhaps, it could possibly help to heal me of my bipolar disorder illness.

[33] Note: Apparently, the ancient Babylonians ate unclean animals—things that were forbidden to the Israelites under the Mosaic Law. (See Leviticus 11:1-31; 20:24-26; Deuteronomy 14:3-20) Most likely, the King's delicacies included these things. Also, indulgence in a diet of rich foods and strong drink, day after day, would hardly be healthful for people of any age, let alone for young boys.

necessary superior or better, but rather, it just goes to show that what we choose to eat and nourish our bodies with is important, and that our diet can make a big difference in regards to our health. But also, it shows that when we eat the right things, it doesn't necessarily have to take that long before we start seeing and feeling the difference that it makes in how we look and feel. Subsequently, if we eat good and nutritious foods, we will be properly nourishing our body— providing it with the right nutrients and building blocks that it needs to refuel, energize, repair, and restore itself. On the other hand, if we were to eat and subsist primarily on a diet of junk food and unhealthy things, we would be neglecting and starving our body of the healthy nutrients and things that it needs to grow and function properly.

Below is a list of some of the healthy things that I incorporated in to my diet during Step #9 *"Changing Your Diet and Lifestyle,"* of the bipolar disorder healing process. It is a list of natural herbs and vegetables, along with vitamins, proteins, compounds, minerals, and nutrients that they contain. You will also notice that I've listed some of the possible health benefits of each item. Interestingly, some of the things listed are also good for mental and emotional health too.[34]

- Sage: (Vitamin K and B6, iron, calcium, manganese) improves memory, concentration, and brain function, lowers cholesterol and blood sugar levels, lowers inflammation, strengthens the immune system, alleviates skin conditions, such as eczema, psoriasis, acne; strengthens bones, and prevents diabetes.
- Chives: (Vitamins A, C, & K, choline, folate) improves memory functions. May help to prevent the development of dementia and Alzheimer's. Amount: One tablespoon. Larger quantities can cause stomach pain and indigestion.
- Spearmint: High in antioxidants and other beneficial plant

---

[34] Besides regularly eating the healthy things on my list, I also put them, along with various fruits in my green drinks. Note: These are a list of vitamin and mineral supplements, etc., that I take. I'm not recommending that anyone else take them. However, if you wish to take them, I would recommend that you consult with your doctor or other qualified health professionals and nutritionists first, to make sure that they are proper and safe for you personally.

compounds that may help balance hormones, lower blood sugar, and improve digestion. It may even reduce stress and improve memory.

- Rosemary: (Vitamins B6, calcium, iron) Good for improving digestion, decreases risk of leukemia and cancer, enhances memory and concentration, helps prevent brain aging, protects against "macular degeneration" (a disease that affects the retina).
- Kale: (Vitamins A, C, K, B6, calcium, copper, iron, manganese, phosphorus, potassium, high in beta-carotene) Good for healthy moist skin and hair, hair growth, strong bones, healthy eyes,. Lowers cancer risk, and stroke.
- Spinach: (protein, iron, Vitamin A, minerals) Lowers cancer risk and blood pressure, improves bone health. Also good for hair and skin.
- Basil: (Vitamins A, C, K, magnesium, iron, potassium, calcium) Used to reduce inflammation and treat arthritis, also has anti-aging properties.
- Carrots: (Vitamins A, C, E, K, beta-carotene, magnesium, potassium, calcium, folate, manganese, phosphorus, zinc) Good for eyes, reduces risk of cancer and heart disease, delays aging, and improves immune system.
- Celery: (Vitamins A, C, K, potassium) Lowers blood pressure, prevents cancer.
- Cucumbers: (Vitamins A, K, magnesium, potassium, manganese, 3 grams protein, 2 grams of fiber) Helps to keep us hydrated, prevents constipation, helps blood clot, promotes healthy bones, heart, lungs, kidneys, and vision. Helps to prevent osteoporosis, heart disease, and some cancers.
- Radishes: (Vitamin C, K, B-6, calcium, potassium, folate, riboflavin, niacin, magnesium, zinc, phosphorus, copper, manganese, and sodium) Good source of antioxidants to help protect cells from damage. Helps with hydration and skin conditioning. Improves digestion. Helps to regulate blood sugar levels. Blocks the formation of diabetes. Promotes healthy livers. Flushes toxins from kidneys. Helps lower blood pressure. Improves blood flow. Reduces risks of heart disease.
- Chickpeas: (Vitamin K, iron, phosphate, calcium, magnesium,

zinc) All good for building bone structure and strength. Fights inflammation and cancer. Lowers cholesterol. Also good for weight loss, and increasing energy.

- Quinoa: (Vitamin E, B-Vitamins, iron, magnesium, phosphorus, potassium, calcium. Good for weight loss.
- Flaxseed: (Vitamin B1, Omega 3, manganese) Lowers risk of prostate cancer, diabetes, heart disease, and lowers cholesterol.
- Chia seeds: (Omega 3, protein, fiber, calcium, phosphorus, manganese, potassium, copper) Good for healthy complexion, increased energy, decreases weight, and chances of diabetes and heart disease.
- Cilantro: (Vitamins A, C, K, beta-carotene) Decreases risk of obesity, good for hair and skin, increases energy, and helps to decrease weight.
- Mint: (Vitamins A, C, potassium, magnesium, calcium, phosphorus, iron). Good for colds.
- Oregano: (Vitamin E, calcium, iron, omega fatty acids, fiber, and manganese) Protects against cancer, muscle pain, headaches, fatigue, allergies, and menstrual cramps.
- Thyme: (Vitamins A, C, copper, fiber, iron, and manganese) Reduces blood pressure, boosts immune system, and protects against colon cancer.
- Barley: (Vitamin B6, thiamine, riboflavin, niacin, folate, iron, magnesium, phosphorus, potassium, zinc, copper, manganese, and selenium) Lowers blood sugar, improves digestion, aids in weight loss, and lowers cholesterol.
- Marjoram: (Vitamins A, K, magnesium, potassium, and folate) The antioxidants in Marjoram helps to prevent cell damage. Reduces anxiety. Reduces inflammation. Helps to prevent digestive issues. Caution: may interact with certain medications such as blood thinners, and anticoagulants, increasing the risk of bleeding.
- Wheat germ: (Vitamin E, fiber, magnesium, zinc, thiamin, folate, potassium, phosphorus, and natural antioxidants) Aids in boosting immune system to keep heart and cardiovascular system healthy, reduces risk of heart disease, and aids in weight loss.

~

In addition to eating herbs, fruits, and vegetables—along with dairy, nuts, lean meats, and other healthy things, I also implemented some vitamin supplements and things in to my diet as well.

Below are some of the vitamins, amino acids, and herbal supplements that I took, along with some helpful information on the positive things that they can possibly do for the body and brain.

- *L-Tyrosine:* It is an amino acid. It supports brain function, mental alertness, and helps to alleviate stress. According to Webmd.com, MountSinai.org, and others, L-Tyrosine helps the body to produce electro/chemical messengers called, neurotransmitters, that help nerve cells communicate. It is important in the production of epinephrine, norepinephrine, and dopamine. It helps form important brain chemicals that effect mood and sleep. L-Tyrosine can naturally be found in meats, fish, eggs, nuts, beans, oats, wheat, and dairy products.
- *Ginkgo Biloba:* It is an extract from the leaves of the ginkgo tree. It improves brain function and well-being by increasing blood circulation to the brain.[35]
- *Vitamin D3:* Is strengthens bones and immune system. It boost mood. It can improve cognitive function. Some natural sources of Vitamin D3 are: eggs, cheddar cheese, milk 2%, sockeye salmon, rainbow trout, light tuna fish, Atlantic sardines, cod liver oil, chicken breast, beef liver, portabella mushrooms, and white mushrooms. Note: too much of these things can cause high cholesterol.

~

For a full list of vitamins and minerals, and what they are good for, see the *"Vitamins and Minerals Chart"* that I have provided in

---

[35] Caution: According to Webmd.com, it is said that people who are older, or if you have a condition that causes bleeding, or if you have seizures or epilepsy, or if you're pregnant, or if you have diabetes, you should not take Ginkgo Biloba.

the Appendix, on pages 285-298.[36]

Today, now that I have been taking good care of my health, by having and maintaining a good and nutritional diet, I am very careful about what I put into my body, especially when it comes to unnatural, manmade things. Interestingly, whenever I see a new prescription drug or medication that's being advertised on TV or in the media, I begin to wonder how safe it really is for people to take. Because, along with the so called benefits of the drug, also comes a list of negative and potential, bad side effects—some of which can be pretty serious. To me, this is a real eye-opener! Because these bad side effects tells me that some manmade medicines and chemicals can make a person sick; cause diseases; and in some cases even an untimely death! Taking this thought a step further, it also makes me wonder about some of the food products and things that we (the consumer) purchase at the supermarket, that have certain chemicals and manmade additives added to them—foods and things that we are readily eating and putting in our bodies. Could it be that some of these things too, might be causing people to have cancer, depression, or other serious health issues? Unfortunately, it stands to reason that there may be some validity to this question. The important thing, is that, we (the consumer), need to make sure that we, personally, are educated and well informed in knowing what each of the foods and products that we buy actually contains—along with being aware of the effects (both good or bad) that they may have on our body and overall health.

A healthy lifestyle. In addition to having and maintaining a healthy nutritional diet, it is also imperative that we have a healthy lifestyle too. Because, when you think about it, what good is it, if we have a

---

[36] Disclaimer: I do not endorse or recommend that anyone take the listed vitamins, minerals, herbs and amino acid supplements that I took, nor do I endorse or recommend the vitamins, minerals, herbs and amino acid supplements that are listed in the "Vitamins and Minerals chart," on pages 285-298. These things are provided for educational purposes only. Please be sure to contact your own doctor or other healthcare professional or nutritionist to make sure that these things are good and right for you to take. See full disclaimer in the back of this book.

healthy diet, but we are living an unhealthy lifestyle?

What is a healthy lifestyle? Well, that depends on the individual. Because, what may be a healthy lifestyle for one person, may not necessarily be healthy for someone else. The important thing is to choose a lifestyle that is good and healthy for you, personally;—one that promotes good, overall health and well-being—a lifestyle that is free of harmful substances and things that are damaging to the mind and body.

Yes, changing my *diet* and *lifestyle* was a big help to me, as I traveled along the road to recovery and improving my health, in particular, my mental and emotional health. But, as good as this was, more was required for me to be completely healed and cured of my depression and bipolar disorder illness, as the next step goes on to clearly show.

Step 10

FOLLOWING MY DAILY

HEALTH CARE PLAN

The *tenth* step or stage that I went through on the road leading to recovery and being healed and cured of depression and bipolar disorder, required that I put together a *Personal Healthcare Plan* and follow it daily.[37] See the list below.

My Daily Personal Healthcare Plan Schedule:

1. *Pray.* Thank God for the provisions, blessings, comfort, guidance, help, and support that He provides on a daily basis. Also, pray for others too.

---

[37] The daily *Healthcare Plan* was a plan that I personally created and set in place. It was designed solely for me only, for the purpose of improving my overall health and wellbeing, and to also aide in possibly helping to heal and cure myself of depression and bipolar disorder illness. Note: I do not endorse or recommend that anyone follow my Daily Healthcare Plan. Readers are advised to consult their own doctors or other qualified health professionals regarding the treatment of medical conditions, such as depression and bipolar disorder.

2. Read "Day's Text."[38]

3. Do morning body stretches.

4. Do diaphragm deep breathing exercises (5 min).

5. Drink a green drink.

6. Take 1 teaspoon of Royal Jelly & Bee Pollen.

7. Drink plenty of water throughout the course of the day.

8. Take my vitamin supplements.

9. Do a yoga inversion for 1 to 3 minutes.

10. Go for morning walk.

11. Eat breakfast.

12. Sit under SAD lamp (20 minutes).

13. Write down my Positive Affirmations in a notebook.

14. Ride stationary bike for 30 minutes.

15. Do exercises and lift weights at my health club.

16. Drink a protein drink.

17. Take a shower.

18. Eat lunch.

19. Eat dinner

20. During the evening, work on a painting, or on the manuscript for my new book, or do something else that is fun, productive, or creative.

One of the great benefits that came from following my personal, *Daily Healthcare Plan* schedule, was that it insured that the important things on my list, that I felt that I needed to do to recover from my mental illness, and to grow healthy and stronger, was

---

[38] The "Day's Text," is a small booklet that I use that contains scriptures from the Bible. It provides one scripture for each and every day, along with comments on that text.

consistently being done on a daily basis, and that nothing was ever forgotten or left out.

Below are some of the benefits of the things on my list:

Morning stretches: Doing stretches helps to promote flexibility and range of motion in the body's joints, which helps one to be able to move more freely. It is beneficial to include stretches in to your daily activities, especially before beginning exercise or a workout —as a warm up, to help protect you from injury.

Diaphragm Breathing Exercises: These deep breathing exercises are good for lowering the heart rate and calming one's nerves— thereby helping to reduce anxiety and stress. They are also good for strengthening the lungs, cardiovascular muscles, and lowing and improving blood pressure.

Walking: Walking is a good way to get oxygen into the lungs, and the brain, etc. And it is good for stimulating healthy blood flow and circulation throughout the body. Also, it is good for relieving stress, losing weight, strengthening bones and muscles, and improving endurance. Personally, I find that going for an early morning walk is a good way to jumpstart my day—to get my day off to a good start. But also, it gets me outside, where I get to breathe fresh air, and experience and appreciate the beautiful surroundings of nature.

Caution: Before beginning any exercise routine, such as walking, doing stretches, etc., be sure to consult your doctor beforehand to make sure that these are right and safe for you.

Vitamin supplements: These can be good for filling in the gaps of nutrients that we might fail to receive from the foods that we eat.

Caution: Before taking vitamins consult with your doctor or other health professional to make sure that they are good and right for you.

Good old, H^2O: Water is not only refreshing, but it is also good for helping to keep our body properly hydrated. It also, helps the body rid itself of waste through urination, perspiration, and defecation. In addition, water lubricates joints. It also, increases energy levels, and promotes good brain function too. Also, because water has zero calories, it can help you lose and maintain your body weight too.

Caution: Because some people have medical conditions such as heart, or kidney issues, etc., that may limit their water intake needs, be sure to check with your doctor, and then follow his or her recommendations.

SAD lamp: A SAD lamp or "Light Therapy," is a way to treat Seasonal Affective Disorder (SAD), and certain other conditions. SAD happens when people suffer from depression due to experiencing a lack of sunshine during fall and winter seasons, when there are not as many sunny days—due to cloudy, overcast skies. In essence, SAD lamps mimic natural sunlight, which, when exposed to it, helps to trigger the brain to release the neurotransmitter or chemical messenger, *serotonin*—the feel good hormone. It can be an effective way to treat SAD and certain other conditions.

Caution: Before using light therapy (a SAD lamp), be sure to check with your doctor beforehand to make sure that this is good and right for you, personally. Also, he or she may want to monitor the time and frequency of the use of light therapy.

Positive Affirmations: Affirmations are positive statements that a person can either repeat to themselves or write down—that can help them to overcome self-sabotaging and negative thoughts. When they repeat them often enough, and believe them, they can start to make positive changes in their life. Personally, I find positive affirmations to be very encouraging, uplifting, and effective mental exercises that help to build confidence and self esteem, especially when writing them down repeatedly. I talk more about positive affirmations later—on pages 103, 104, 112, and 113.

Inversions, Yoga Headstands, or Alternatives: These are good for the following:

1. Calms the mind and heart.
2. Alleviates stress and depression.

3. Activates the pituitary and pineal glands.
4. Stimulates the lymphatic system.
5. Stimulates and strengthens the upper body, spine, and core.
6. Enhances lung capacity.
7. Stimulates and strengthens abdominal organs.
8. Boosts digestion.
9. Alleviates symptoms of menopause.
10. Prevents headaches.

The following, gentle inversions, are some alternatives for those who are not able to do a yoga headstand. They are:

1. Adho Mukha Svanasana (Downward-Facing Dog Pose)
2. Prasarita Padottanasana (Wide-Legged Forward Bend)
3. Uttana Shishosana (Puppy Pose)
4. Viparita Karani (Legs Up-the Wall Pose)
5. Using an inversion table, such as the "Teeter."

Caution: Before doing inversions, yoga headstands, or alternatives, consult your doctor or other qualified health professionals to make sure that they are good and right for you, personally. Also, *do not* do headstands if you are pregnant, or if you have hypertension, glaucoma, or heart issues.

Green Drinks: Green drinks are good for helping to rid the body of toxins. They arc also a good source of nutrition. What I like about them is that they ensure that I am getting my Recommended Daily Allowances (RDA) of vegetables, fruits, and grains, etc. But not only that, because these things are blended or grounded up in to a liquid form, the body can digest them so much easier.

Caution: Before consuming green drinks consult your doctor or other health professional or qualified nutritionist to make sure that they are good and right for you personally.

Royal Jelly & Bee Pollen: 'Royal jelly' supports healthy brain function, improves memory, and reduces depression. 'Bee pollen' relieves inflammation, works as an antioxidant, boosts liver function and immune system, lowers heart disease, aides in healing, reduces stress, and helps to prevent cancer.

Caution: Bee products may cause an allergic reaction in some sensitive people. As with all dietary supplements, consult your doctor or other healthcare professional before use.

Stationary bike: Stationary bikes increase cardiovascular health, strengthens bones and muscles, aides in weight loss, and reduces stress, anxiety, and depression.

Caution: Before riding a bike or exercising, be sure to consult your doctor or other healthcare professional first to make sure that this is good and right for you.

Weight training: Weight training is good for building strength and strong bones. Also, it burns body fat. And, it is good for cardiovascular health.

Caution: Before weight training consult your doctor or other healthcare professional first to make sure that this is good and right for you.

Protein drinks: Protein drinks are good for reducing appetite—thereby aiding in weight reduction. Also, they aide in increasing muscle mass and strength. And lastly, they boost metabolism and are good for the bones.

Caution: Before consuming protein drinks consult your doctor or other healthcare professional first to make sure that this is good and right for you.

Working on fun projects and personal goals: Personally, I find that working on fun projects and personal goals has many good benefits. One thing that I personally enjoy is writing. It provides good stimulus and exercise for my mind and brain, which no doubt will help to lessen my chance of developing brain diseases such as Alzheimer's or Dementia. Also, writing helps to satisfy my creative itch so to speak, which assists in keeping me feeling happy and good about myself. In addition to this, working on fun projects and healthy goals helps to keep me progressing and moving forward, thereby preventing my life from becoming boring, stagnated, or unfulfilling.

Prayer and Bible reading: Prayer and Bible reading helps to reduce stress. They also help one to build a relationship with God. Also, they give us comfort, encouragement, confidence, peace, faith, endurance, guidance, and hope.

As you can see from the information above, there are a lot of good health benefits that come from following my *Daily Healthcare Plan*. True, it is not always an easy thing to consistently follow through with and do. For it takes a lot of commitment, focus, self discipline, and hard work. However, I realized long ago that I have no other alternative or choice but to motivate myself to do these things, that is, if I wanted to recover from my illness, gain strength, and become healthy again. True, it requires a lot of effort, and it can be a little time consuming at times, but, the overall, good health benefits that it offers are well worth the time and efforts that I spend and put forth.

Another thing that following my *Daily Healthcare Plan* required of me is that I exercise *patience*. The reason why, is because sometimes it takes time before you start to see results. The key however, was to just take and focus on just one day at a time. This way, there would be less chance for me to get upset if progress didn't seem to be coming as fast as I wanted or expected it to occur.

To some people my *Daily Healthcare Plan* might seem a bit extreme. But, sometimes, when you're sick or ill, you have no other alternative or choice but to resort to extreme measures, in order to try to recover from your illness—to become healthy and well again.

It is important to note that when I initially implemented my personalized *Daily Healthcare Plan* into my daily routine, I didn't jump right into doing *all* of the things that are listed on my list at once. But rather, it took time for me to be able to do everything. The key was, slowly adding and incorporating only one thing at a time, until I was able to do everything on the list on a daily basis. In other words, I gradually added all of these things to my daily routine, one at a time, one by one, over an extended period of time, until I was able to complete and do them all. True, there were days when it was hard for me to get motivated. But when I finally got around to completing these things, I felt so much better and happier for having done them!

From personal experience, I've learned that you can get a lot more done when you have and follow a good schedule and routine (such as my *Daily Healthcare Plan*), compared to when you don't have one in place. True, it takes a lot of commitment, time, effort, focus, determination, and self-discipline to follow and stick to it, but the end results show that a good schedule and routine is well worth it!

The wonderful thing, is that, by ritualistically following my *Daily Healthcare Plan*, and routine, each and every day, I was building and sculpting a more beautiful, self confident, powerful, solid, peaceful, and happy person. True, it's not that these things were totally absent or that they were not in me, prior to implementing my personal Healthcare Plan, or that I didn't have or possess them in the past, prior to becoming mentally ill. It's just that, now, I am finally allowing these beautiful and wonderful inner qualities and things in me—that were no doubt hiding or lost in the pain and darkness, to finally emerge and come out—to my great benefit, happiness, and joy!

As we can see from the above information, following my *Daily Healthcare Plan* and routine was a big help and benefit to me as I traveled along the road leading to recovery and improving my health, especially, my mental and emotional health. But as good as this was, more was required to completely heal and cure myself of depression and bipolar disorder, as the next step will clearly show. However, before we consider the next step — Step #11 *"The Push Towards Improving My Health"* — in the bipolar disorder healing process; — for reiteration purposes, I thought that it would be a good idea if I provided you (the reader) with a brief description of bipolar disorder and its prominent two phases. This way it will help you to better understand and appreciate the next step (Step #11). Please note the following description:

Description of Bipolar Disorder: Bipolar disorder involves two separate phases of extreme mood swings that alternate or go from, (1) depressive lows to, (2) manic or euphoric highs. In other words, with bipolar disorder illness you display only two prominent moods—one at a time (either you're very happy, or you're very sad). Because the internal gravitational forces of the illness that takes place from within you, pulls your moods in the direction of either up or down. There is no middle ground.

An interesting fact to note is that the two extreme mood swings associated with bipolar are not like a light switch that quickly turns on, and then off again. These episodes or phases may last for up to weeks, or even months at a time.

Concerning the two separate phases of bipolar, personally, as far as I'm concerned, I would have to say that, by far, the harder of the two to cope and deal with is the *depressive phase*, which I will explain and talk about in more depth in Step #11.

Now that we have gotten all of this helpful information out of the way, I will now go on to explain the next step in the bipolar disorder healing process.

Step 11

THE PUSH TOWARDS
IMPROVING MY HEALTH

The *eleventh* step or next healing stage that I went through on the road leading to recovery and being cured of my depression and bipolar disorder illness, required that I get tough with myself; by forcing and pushing myself to do the healthy things that I devised and set in place to improve my health—namely, by following my personal, Daily Healthcare Plan, routine, and things that I believed could possibly help to eventually heal and cure me of my mental illness. You might ask me: Why did you need to have this kind of drive and mindset? Why was it necessary to *push* yourself?

Unfortunately, when a person suffers from bipolar disorder, a large portion of their life involuntarily gets placed on hold, because the debilitating effects of the illness can be somewhat disabling or crippling, especially when they are going through the *depressive phase* of bipolar—the difficult stage of the disease when they experience dark moods of depression that can be mentally, emotionally, and physically draining—making it hard for them to function in normal daily activities and things. Fact is, this stage of the illness can be so intensely overwhelming and draining that it can completely zap you of your energy and strength, and also, your will and desire to do anything (even things that you may have thoroughly enjoyed in the past), thereby rendering you inactive, feeling totally incapacitated—making it hard for you to even get up and move. Truth is, because you feel so depressed and drained (mentally, emotionally, and physically), often, all you want to do is lie down; bury your head in a pillow and sleep.

Therefore, the *push & drive* forward attitude, spirit, and mindset that I needed to develop and possess during this 11th Step *"The Push Towards Improving My Health,"* was absolutely vital and necessary for me to have, especially because it was not always easy to get motivated, or to find the energy and desire that was needed each and every day to perform my Daily Healthcare Plan, routine, and things.

Because the *depressive phase* of bipolar disorder can be so difficult and debilitating to its victims, I liken this phase of the illness to being stuck in quicksand, where the helpless, trapped victim is slowly sinking downwards, deeper and deeper into the pit of despair and gloom, where they feel that there is little to no hope of ever being rescued. However, in the case of bipolar disorder illness, it is not literal quicksand that has a gripping hold on you and that is pulling you ever downwards into what I call "The pit of misery and despair" (the *depressive phase* of bipolar), but rather, it is the strong, gravitational forces of *depression.*

Personally, for me, the difficult and challenging thing about being in the *depressive phase* (prior to being cured of bipolar disorder), was that, if I wanted to continue to progress and move forward in the battle against my illness—so that I could eventually rise above, overcome, and defeat my unrelenting captors and imprisoners — depression and bipolar disorder,— along with their life-sucking, debilitating (mentally, emotionally, and physically), draining effects, I had to find something or some way to pick me up and motivate me during these often difficult, down times.

Prior to finding a workable solution to this dilemma, I thought:

"What can I do to combat the immobilizing, quicksand-like effect of the 'depressive phase' of bipolar disorder?" And then, it suddenly dawned on me. The answer was: "The *mind* moves the body. So, if I want to get up and get moving—to perform my Daily Healthcare Plan, routine, and things during difficult times, such as during *depressive episodes*, then I needed to jumpstart or motivate my mind *first*, and then the body will naturally follow." But how could I do this? From where would this motivation and push come?

As humans, sometimes it takes a lot of inner-will, strength, and drive to motivate and push ourselves to do things; especially, when we are already feeling weakened, tired, and exhausted from a hard day's work, etc. However, with bipolar disorder illness, the exhaustion and negative effects that you are feeling and experiencing, during the *depressive phase* in particular, is a whole lot worse than this. Because, not only are you feeling tired and drained physically from the effects of your mental illness, but along with this, you are also feeling mentally and emotionally down and depressed from the effects of the illness as well, which can also be extremely draining! True, depressive episodes don't last forever, that is, until the *mania* or *hypomania* phase eventually kicks in— the time when your moods start to improve and you begin to feel better. However, they can prove to be long and disruptive enough.[39]

Because I knew that the often debilitating symptoms associated with *depressive episodes* were; in themselves, not going to go away until after the *depressive phase* had completely run its emotionally painful and disruptive course, I felt that I needed to develop and have a *push through the pain and lethargy* type of attitude, spirit, and drive, especially during this highly disruptive stage or timeframe. This way — without experiencing any interruption or downtime of activity — I could still, on a daily basis, keep progressing and moving forward, performing my important Daily Healthcare Plan, routine, and things that I personally designed and put in place to aid in my recovery—things that I believed would eventually lead to me being healed and cured of my depression and bipolar disorder

---

[39] Note: The depressive phase or episode of bipolar disorder may last for up to weeks, or even months at a time.

illness. However, I soon learned that developing and having a *push & drive* attitude and spirit was easier said than done.

Truth is, it was not an easy thing to motivate and push my mind and body when they did not want to move or be motivated. However, one thing that I soon discovered that helped to motivate and kick my mind, body, and spirit into forward gear during the difficult *depressive episode* phase, was the encouragement and motivation that I got through incorporating *positive affirmations* in to my daily routine.

Affirmations are positive statements that a person can either repeat to themselves or write down, that can help them to overcome self-sabotaging and negative thoughts. Also, they can be used to help motivate and encourage them to perform and achieve positive goals and things too. When they repeat them often enough and believe them, they can start to make positive and productive changes in their life. Personally, I found positive affirmations to be very encouraging, uplifting, and effective mental exercises that helped to motivate me. I also found that they helped me to build confidence and self-esteem too.

When daily working on my positive affirmations, I would audibly say them out loud. But also, in addition to this, at the same time that I was saying them, I would also write them down too, repeatedly, over and over again, in a notebook. The reason why I did this is because I believed that this would have a more powerful effect on me. Because, not only was I hearing them (by saying them out loud), but I was also visually seeing them too, as I was writing them down. In essence, by using this method of both verbalizing and writing my positive affirmations down, I believe that it was making a double impression on my mind and heart, by inculcating and sounding them down deep, where they eventually could take hold of and become a permanent part of me and my personality.

An additional benefit of *writing* affirmations down, is that, because I was actually physically engaged in the process, by writing them down—which takes a lot more effort than just saying them alone—it was good exercise for my mind and brain, helping me to battle and fight to come out of the lethargic, often debilitating state that depressive episodes put me in.

One of the positive affirmations that I personally made up and used to help motivate me during depressive episodes, consisted of just the following four simple words "Get up and move!" Another was, "Push through the pain!" Another affirmation that I came up with and utilized, that was a little longer in length, was: "You are strong and powerful. You can do anything!"

I know that in or by themselves, that these short phrases may not seem like much, but it is truly amazing how effective and helpful that repeatedly saying and writing them down can be!

Another thing that helped to motivate me during the depressive phase of bipolar—that provided me with a good measure of inner strength and drive to get up and keep going when the going got tuff, was that I was able to tap into and draw strength from an attitude and conviction that I displayed in the past, many years ago, in particular, during my youth, when I was growing up and grooming myself as an serious athlete, with aspirations of becoming a professional ball player.

One good and positive thing about being an athlete, is that, it can help you to develop a strong, inner determination and drive, which are highly useful and beneficial qualities that you develop from both personal training and regularly competing in sports — which, back in the day, are things that I personally took very seriously! As a matter of fact, my inner determination and drive was often greater than others. For I use to push myself really hard in both my personal training and practice. For example, when training for a possible future career in professional basketball, some of the things I used to do were:

- **Practice:** I worked on perfecting my basketball skills through daily practice. Often practicing 16 hours in a day.

- **Rigorous training:** To build up and strengthen my *upper body*, I did fingertip pushups, and also lifted weights—

performing a variety of different exercises—bench presses, military presses, arm curls, etc. (often performing a total of 500 reps, utilizing multiple sets per exercise).

And to build up and strengthen my *lower body and legs*, I repeatedly ran up and down long staircases, wearing a 20 pound vest, and also 14 pounds of leg weights on each leg. Also, in addition to this, I did leg extensions, squats, and toe raises using very heavy weights.[40]

- **Conditioning:** I jumped rope for 30 minutes each day, jogged 2 miles on foot, and I also rode my bicycle.

Fortunately, for me, this positive, *push through it and drive forward* attitude and mindset that I possessed in my youth, along with the hard and rigorous training and practice sessions that I put myself through during that time, paid off down the line. For I was able to tap into these built-in memories and past mindset, now, during difficult times when it was hard for me to find motivation—to get me motivated and moving when the going got extremely hard and tuff, in particular, during the time when I was undergoing the most difficult phase of the bipolar disorder illness—*depressive episodes.*

Yes, tapping into this *push through it and drive forward* attitude and spirit helped to encourage and motivate me to move and to keep moving forward, to do the things on my personal, Daily Healthcare Plan, routine, and other healthy things—things that I felt I needed to consistently perform on a daily basis to help me to eventually recover from my mental illness and become healthy again.

Another important and useful thing that I used at times to help to motivate me to get up and keep progressing and moving forward during the bipolar depressive phase or when I would get in a bit of a funky rut, is by just simply getting up and getting started with the

---

[40] Note: Weight training came a little later in my personal training, when I was old enough to lift weights. The reason being is because it was not recommended for youths to lift weights when their body is still growing and in the developmental stage.

goal or task at hand. In other words, sometimes all it took to get moving forward is by just getting up and putting the first foot forward, so to speak. And then, due to the forward momentum, the next step would naturally follow, and the next, etc.

Another thing that can be useful to help with motivation is to team up with a partner. This way you can encourage and support one another. Although, personally, I chose not to take this particular path. One reason why, is because I think that it is important to learn to be a self-motivator — a person who can motivate themselves (which I have always been able to do in my life), rather than depending on someone else to motivate you. Later, I will explain why self-motivation is so important, and how it came in handy during the bipolar disorder healing process. But, whatever the case — whether the motivation comes from you or someone else — the main objective at the time, was for me to have and maintain a *push through it and drive forward* attitude and spirit.

Later, as time progressed, even during times when I felt that I was growing stronger and that my health was getting better with each and every passing day, I felt that I still could not let up on pushing myself forward towards improving my health. In other words, I felt that I had to *"keep the pedal to the metal,"* in doing the positive and healthy things that I believed would eventually lead to me being healed and cured of my mental illness, in particular, by continuing to ritualistically follow my personal, Daily Healthcare Plan, routine, and things. The reason being, was because, out of fear, I felt that if I were to ever let up on doing these important and beneficial things, that I would get discouraged and give up, or that my progress would come to a halt, thereby losing the battle to overcome and eventually defeat my depression and bipolar illness, that was holding my mind and moods captive in a prison-like state. How happy I am now that I never did let up!

Yes, this 11th Step *"The Push Towards Improving My Health,"* in the bipolar disorder healing process, that involved pushing myself ever forward towards my goal of recovery and improving my mental health, was of great aide in helping me—to say the least. However, as good as it was in helping to improve my mental health, more was required for me to be completely healed and cured of depression and bipolar disorder, as the next step clearly shows.

Step 12

INVITE POSITIVE
INTO YOUR LIFE

The *twelfth,* vitally important step or phase that I went through on the curative road of the depression and bipolar disorder healing process, required that I invite *positivity* in to my life, primarily by means of promoting and having a positive mind, attitude or spirit within myself. Why is having a positive attitude so important? One reason why, is because it's been said that: "Attitude determines our altitude." Meaning that having a positive attitude is a key to success.

What does it mean to be *positive?* Positive is the opposite of negative. According to the dictionary, the word positive means: being fully confident, optimistic [*hopeful and confident about the future*], enthusiastic, constructive [*tending to build up*], cheerful, and upbeat.

From the above definition, we can see that being positive is highly beneficial and vitally important for everyone to be. However, this is easier said than done, especially, for one who suffers from depression or bipolar disorder. One reason why, as far as I'm concerned, is because, for a person to truly have a positive attitude, involves more than just working to have a positive *mind* alone. Personally, I believe that it also includes the *heart* (feelings and emotions) too. Because, if your mind is trying to be positive, but your heart is simply not feeling it or with it, or it is suffering or in pain, it is going to be extremely difficult to have and display a positive mind or attitude. The reason why, is because, I believe that our mind and heart are interdependent (closely linked and attached), in that, they act and feed off of one another. In other words, what affects the one (either for good or bad), moves and affects the other. Perhaps that is why so many people are struggling when it comes to trying to have and display a positive mind or attitude—because they are not working on both their *mind* (thinking) and *heart* (feelings and emotions) together.

The interesting thing is that a positive attitude can be feigned or faked by wearing a mask, so to speak, so as to fool and impress others, because it is something that can so easily and conveniently be projected on the surface for others to view and see. In other words, putting forth a false front or facade, in order to project that all is going well, when in truth, it is not. However, to have a *genuine,* positive attitude or spirit goes much deeper than wearing a mask, or just affecting the mind only. It affects the whole or entire soul of the human being—his mind, heart, moods, feelings and emotions. It involves our entire inner disposition and makeup—what we are at heart (figuratively speaking). That is why, I prefer to work on both my *mind* and *heart* together, rather than just working to display a positive mind or attitude alone. I find that this is a much more effective way to approach the problem and for me to be.

Having a positive attitude or spirit is good for anyone and everyone to possess. It can make a big difference in how we feel and function in life. And it can add greatly to our peace and happiness too. Also, it can be an encouragement to other people as well. However, as good as having a positive attitude or spirit is, it is not always an easy thing to possess and keep, especially, when we are going through trying and difficult times, or if we personally happen to be struggling with a serious illness such as clinical depression or bipolar disorder.

Speaking from personal experience, I have to admit that it is not easy to have and maintain a positive attitude or spirit when you are suffering from bipolar disorder. Because your mind, especially, when you are undergoing the dark moods of depression that are associated with *depressive episodes*, has the tendency to cause you to gravitate towards and mentally feed on sad and negative thoughts, feelings, and emotions and things that discourage and pull you downwards.

Fortunately, for me, during this 12th Step *"Invite Positive Into Your Life"* — that I went through, along the road to recovery and being cured of my mental illness — my mind found a way to help me to combat the self-defeating, negative spirit and thinking that the depressive phase of bipolar disorder generated and produced. This required that I change my thoughts and attitude from being *negative* to being *positive* (of course this was easier said than done). But it also required that I work on my heart (feelings and emotions) too. How? Primarily, it was by doing two things: (1) by rejecting and removing negativity from my mind and heart and, (2) by being positive, uplifting, and encouraging within myself, and towards others. In other words, I had to cure both my ailing *mind,* and *heart.* You might ask: How did you do that?

Rejecting and Removing Negativity

Personally, by nature, I have always been a fairly good person, with a big, tender, and caring heart. Unfortunately, however, from the time of my youth on up, I had bad experiences in my life that caused me to battle with a spirit of negativity. Interestingly, during the time it was happening, I wasn't totally conscience or aware of what was taking place—as to what was triggering and feeding the negativity, and especially the harmful effects that this was having on me and my mental health.

Fortunately, in time, in particular, during Step #12 of the bipolar disorder healing process, I was able to finally take a good look at myself, and also my life (both past and present), and observe what it was that was affecting my mind and heart so badly—causing them to be in so much suffering and pain. And then, after discovering and figuring this out, from that time going forward, I was able to take the necessary steps and actions to correct matters. However, because of the severity of the problem — concerning negativity and the detrimental effects that it was having on my mind and heart — I would soon learn that this would not be easy to remedy. Nevertheless, in spite of this, in time, I was able to come up with an effective plan to help me to successfully reverse the damage that had been done in the past, and to develop a positive attitude or spirit going forward. How did I do this?

The first step towards defeating negativity, and also developing and having a positive attitude or spirit, required that I remove all negativity from my mind and heart; in particular, things that I was still holding onto and carrying-over from my past—negative thoughts and bad feelings that I was harboring and having, concerning hurtful and painful things that I had suffered and went through from my youth on up to the present time. Certain, damaging, mental and emotional things that were inflicted on me by certain people that I came in to contact with, and society — things that I both knowingly and unknowingly carried with me for many years.

Yes, if I truly desired to heal and grow healthy mentally and emotionally, and eventually to be completely cured of my depression and bipolar disorder illness, I had no other alternative or choice but to remove and leave behind all of the hurtful and negative things of my past. Interestingly, in order to be fully effective and successful in this, I could not keep or hold on to even one of these negative things. They all had to go! For, just think, how can a person truly be at peace, be happy, and have a genuine positive attitude or spirit, if their mind and heart are always thinking and dwelling on troubling, hurtful, and negative things that happened to them in the past? The answer is, you can't. For its like poking or jabbing at a sore spot, open wound, or injury—making the matter and pain worse by not allowing it to recover and heal. This required that I sincerely forgive people for any and all hurt and pain that they caused me in the past. I had no other choice but to do this, that is, if I wanted to truly heal and be happy and healthy—mentally and emotionally.

Truth is, initially, when I first attempted to remove and leave behind all of the hurtful things of my past, it was not an easy thing for me to do — to completely empty my mind and heart of negativity and to forgive. I had a lot of work to do, for there was a lot of negativity there — both, from my past, and also from distressing and discouraging things that I was presently going through in my life at that time. However, in time, with prayer and a lot of effort, I was able to successfully do this.

The next step that I had to take, if I wanted to have a positive attitude or spirit, is that, I had to reject all negativity *going forward,* by not allowing it to come in to *my peaceful and positive, personal space,* as I call it. In other words, by not allowing negativity to get too close to me, so as to infect and influence my mind and heart.

Although it took time and effort, rejecting any present negativity that I was currently experiencing, as well as also permanently removing any and all negativity and things that might still be lingering in my mind and heart from past, negative experiences that I went through, this was a good and effective thing that helped me to combat a self-defeating, negative spirit, and thinking. However, I soon discovered that something else, in addition to this, was required, if I wanted to truly develop and possess a genuine, positive attitude or spirit. What was it? I had to invite positivity in to my life by doing the next important thing.

Thinking Positive and Being Encouraging

One effective way that I found that I could invite positivity in to my life, is by regularly (on a daily basis) working hard to feed my mind and heart positive thoughts and feelings. How did I do this? Well, I know I talk a lot about this, but one way I did this was by using *positive affirmations*. The reason why I chose to use them is because through application and personal experience, I've found that positive affirmations really work!

A couple of positive affirmations that I custom designed to help me personally to think and be positive, are: (1) "I am positive. I am confident. I am happy. I am successful," and also, (2) "I am strong. I am good. I am beautiful."

Another way that I invited positivity in to my life is by censuring and controlling the subject matter and things that I allowed my mind to think and dwell on each and every day, as well as the subjects and topics that I chose to talk about and discuss with others. In regard to the latter, for the most part, I try to keep things going in an encouraging, positive, and upbeat direction. And, if the conversations that I am having with others start to drift and focus on negative things, I try to quickly change directions by considering and injecting more uplifting things into the discussion instead.

Another way I invited positivity in to my life, is by placing myself in positive environments that feed and stimulate positive, cheerful, uplifting moods, feelings, and thoughts. Also, in regards to the environment within my own home goes, I intentionally built and created a look and feel atmosphere that is peaceful, joyful, warm, inviting, fun, loving, encouraging, and uplifting—a beautiful, cheerful and sunny environment that generates and promotes good thoughts, feelings, and moods, etc. Yes, I truly made sure that my residence is literally "Home Sweet Home!"

Another way that I invite positivity in to my life, is by not allowing my mind and attention to be diverted away from good and beneficial thinking and thoughts. In essence, this means, by not allowing disturbing matters that might randomly pop up in life, to rob me of healthy and productive thinking, as well as my inner peace, and joy—which are qualities and things that are going to benefit me the most, both now and in the future.

An example of the above is: One day, I was driving down the highway, going the speed limit of 60 mph, when all of the sudden a car quickly pulls up behind me—tailgating me. Apparently, to him (the other driver), I was not going fast enough, even though I was driving the maximum speed limit and also driving in the slow lane. So, instead of him (the other driver), changing lanes and driving around me, he decides to tailgate me—so close, that he was practically touching my bumper. Normally, my first response or reaction to a situation like this; would have been to accommodate him, by changing lanes and letting him pass by. However, because I had no other lane to move in to — because I was going to take the exit that was just up ahead, I decided (not out of stubbornness or out of spite to provoke him to anger) to stay in the lane where I was, and let him, if he is in that big of a hurry; drive around me, which he did. However, in the process, he (deliberately), literally tried to run me off the road! And then, afterwards, he sped off, speeding and going straight down the road. This was disturbing—to say the least. However, rather than getting upset and bent out of shape about this, I remained calm and kept my composure. And, I didn't allow him or this incident to upset me at that time or to ruin my day.

The sad thing, is that, if he (the other driver) doesn't change his bad attitude and learn to get control of himself (his thinking, emotions, and actions), he is headed for a crash in some way or another in life, down the road, so to speak. For down the line (if he doesn't change), he will have to pay the penalty and price for his erroneous thinking and bad behavior, which most likely has become a regular pattern of engrained thinking that he has developed.[41]

After the aggressive driver was gone, rather than being annoyed and disturbed by his rude and inappropriate actions (allowing myself to be bent out of shape or continuing to think about it), I remained perfectly calm, and I gave no more thought and consideration to the incident for the remainder of the day. Because, a long time ago, prior to this incident — while traveling along the road to being cured of depression and bipolar disorder — I decided that I would no longer allow anyone or anything to ever rob me of my peace, joy, and

---

[41] Note: Normally, if I am on the highway in the fast lane, and a car drives up behind me, wanting to pass and go faster, I have no problem with this. I will always humbly and happily move over in to the slower lane, so as not to impede their speed or pace. Especially, with the way that drivers are today—with road rage and things taking place. However, in this particular instance, with the stretch of road that we were traveling on, I simply had no other choice but to stay in the slow lane, otherwise, I would have missed my exit.

happiness anymore—no matter what problems or things that I am presented with, or that I happen to face in life. And, believe me, because of this positive thinking, approach to life, and firm resolution; my life is so much more peaceful and happier as a result.

Another way that I invited positivity in to my life, is by staying busy with positive pursuits and things—primarily by keeping myself busy with positive and constructive tasks at hand, whether it was by performing my personal, Daily Healthcare Plan, and routine and things, or doing some other valuable and important tasks. Also, I found that it is best if I didn't get too far ahead of myself. In other words, my thinking or motto is: *"Focus on and take just one day at a time."* This way I would not become overly concerned or worried about what tomorrow or the next day will bring. But instead, I could stay focused on the things that I needed to do now, during the present day, which helped to prevent me from becoming overwhelmed, or getting discouraged, or losing confidence and hope.

An additional thing that built positivity in me, is having and working on personal goals—both short and long term. But, especially, on short-term goals that could easily be achieved. The beautiful thing about goals, when you achieve them, is that they make you feel good about yourself and your accomplishments— thereby building confidence and self-esteem. But also, they help you to keep progressing and moving ever forward.

Another way that I invited positivity in to my life was by reaching out to encourage and help other people too. Because, when I encouraged and helped others, it not only made them feel good, but it also made me feel good too! That's the beauty of reaching out to encourage and help others, because it has a natural, positive, reciprocal effect on us as humans.

Another way that I invited positivity in to my life, is by taking good care of my overall health—by having and maintaining a balanced and nutritious diet, by exercising, and also by getting enough sleep, etc.

Another way that I invite positive in to my life, is by keeping my body clean, my appearance well-groomed, and by dressing nice, etc. I find that doing these things feeds and promotes good feelings and self-confidence. Also, it earns respect from others too. True, it takes a little time and effort to do these things—to be well groomed and, to dress up, etc. But the positive effects that it produces are a huge benefit!

Another way that I invite positive in to my life, is by listening to fun, beautiful, clean, and uplifting music (during appropriate times). Music like, contemporary jazz, or classical music, or selected golden oldies of pop, or R&B, and other delightful genres of music, etc. However, because I prefer to stay upbeat and positive, I found that it is best for me, personally, to avoid certain songs and music that have negative undertones, debasing lyrics, or music that has the tendency of generating sad, melancholy thoughts and moods in me.

Another way that I invite positive in to my life, is by planning and going on fun outings and vacations, even if they are just two or three day getaways. I find that vacations are good, because they help you to relax and unwind, thereby reducing stress. They also recharge and refresh you too!

Another way that I invite positive in to my life, is by finding something that is good, constructive, and beneficial to do and work on—something that I enjoy—that picks me up and makes me feel good, and happy. For me, this is where working on a creative painting, or a fun art project, or on composing a new song, or writing poems and various other forms of literature comes in handy. I love it! For these things and others, bring me a lot of peace, joy, and satisfaction. But also, it's truly gratifying to be able to share these positive and encouraging things with others as well.

Another way I invite positive in to my life, is by not looking back at and dwelling on negative things and experiences that happened to me in the past—something that I used to do. However, now, instead, I prefer to get rid of this ugly, unnecessary baggage, by throwing them all away, and letting them go for good, along with the painful and hurtful thoughts and feelings that they can cause to resurface. To me, these things are not worth revisiting or keeping.

Fact is, the past is the past. There is nothing that I can do to change it. It is forever done and gone. Because of this, there's no sense in looking in the rearview mirror of life so to speak; particularly, at negative things that will only serve to discourage and pull me down. Personally, I'd rather focus on the positive and beautiful things of life now; and also, on the bright and happy future that lies ahead of me, so that my mind and heart can be at peace, and joyful—so that I can enjoy life to the full, and continue to develop and grow in beautiful, productive, and wonderful ways!

Note: An important point to know, is that, when it comes to negative things, is that, *all* negativity is not necessarily bad for us. For example, one thing that is good about certain negative things and experiences that we go through, is that, sometimes we can learn and benefit a lot from them. For example, we learn from the negative effects of *global warming*, that humans have to start taking better care of the earth. This is just one example of something good that can come from something that is negative. Another example — showing that negativity can result in to something good — is that, if we happen to notice that we, personally, are putting on too much body weight, this alerts us that perhaps we need to go on a healthy diet, or that we need to start an exercise program, etc., so that we don't eventually start to develop serious health issues. The same can hold true of other negative things and experiences that we personally go through in life. Although, they can pose a problem and challenge for us during the time that we are going through them — by sometimes making life and things a little rocky and difficult — often, in the end, they can bring out the very best in us.

One day, a friend sent me a text message. He concluded it by saying: "I hope you're doing well?" This got me to thinking that the condition of feeling good about ourselves and life, often has a lot to do with us individually. Because, we as humans have the power and ability to steer and direct ourselves in any direction we may choose to go in life. Essentially, we have the potential to make ourselves and life what we want them to be. But also, we have the power to shape and direct our thinking, mind, and heart in wonderful, uplifting, and positive ways. So, from that beautiful, enlightening day going forward, that is what I am focused on and determined to do!

As the information in Step #12 *"Invite Positive Into Your Life"* shows, inviting *positive* in to my life turned out to be a huge help and benefit to me, as I traveled along the road to recovery and good health, especially, my mental and emotional health. True, it was not an easy thing to do—to change from being negative to having a positive attitude or spirit—especially, when the negative effects of depression and bipolar disorder are pulling you downwards or in the opposite direction. Nevertheless, through focus, concentrated efforts and hard work, I was able to eventually gain mastery over having and maintaining a positive attitude. However, as good and beneficial as this was, as the next step goes on to show, more was required for me to be completely healed and cured of depression and bipolar disorder illness.

Step 13

RELIANCE ON GOD FOR STRENGTH AND SUPPORT

L ife is a most beautiful thing, and yet, as good and wonderful as it is and can be, it is also beset with many obstacles, challenges, and trials too—some big, others small. The good thing is that we can usually handle and overcome most of them individually by ourselves. However, there are times when problems arise that are too weighty or big for us to handle on our own. Fortunately, when this happens, often there are others that we can turn to during these difficult and challenging times for help and support, and they willingly and readily come to our aid. However, sometimes, our problems are just too big for both us and others to handle or solve. In these instances we need help from a much greater and higher source. Here is where turning to God, the Almighty, is of great benefit. For not only does He have the power and ability to help us (no matter how large or serious our problems may be), but also, because of the personal interest and love that He has for us, He also is eager and willing to come to our aid, that is, if we aren't too proud or stubborn to ask for His help.

One problem that we, as humans have, is sometimes, when it comes to asking for assistance or directions when we need help, when we are lost, or with a particular problem or issue that we are having, often we have the tendency to hesitate or refuse to ask for help (perhaps out of pride or stubbornness), preferring to struggle through it alone.

One example of the above, can be illustrated in a true story about my nephew, Stephen, who was about 6 years old at the time.[42] The situation was this: One day, I was helping Stephen assemble a LEGO set that contained a couple of robots (one robot was yellow, the other blue). Now, although, initially, this project seemed fairly simple—it wasn't. Fact is, it was a very detailed and somewhat complicated project with about a zillion pieces! At lease it seemed like that many. Initially, when we first started the project, Stephen, who is an exceptionally smart kid, didn't want to use the provided instructions and directions (containing step-by-step photo diagrams) that came with the building project—instructions on how to assemble the robots. Instead, he just wanted to try to assemble them on his own. However, I insisted that we use and follow the instructions. I told him that we need to follow the instructions because they will help us to succeed in putting the robots together correctly and that it will make it a whole lot easier. Well, making a long story short, we followed the instructions in building the first robot (the yellow one), and we successfully assembled it. However, when it came time to assemble the second robot (the blue one), Stephen, grew impatient and decided that he no longer wanted to follow the provided instructions anymore. I guess he felt that he didn't need help anymore, because he had successfully assembled the first robot. Again, to make a long story short, things didn't go so well with the second robot. Stephen struggled trying to put it together and, in the end, both he and I got frustrated, gave up on it, and walked away.

The next day, when I came to visit Stephen, he was holding the second LEGO robot (the blue one) in his hands. To my surprise, I noticed that it was completely assembled. Impressed, I said to him:

---

[42] The name has been changed.

"Hey, Stephen, you did it! You got the blue robot together! How did you do it?" In response, he said: "I followed the instructions." I flashed a big smile at him, and said: "Great! Good job, Stephen! You see what happens when we look for help and follow instructions." He said: "Yeah!"

What can we learn from the example above? Well, as humans, our lives can get complicated at times, even more difficult and frustrating than trying to assemble a challenging LEGO set. Nevertheless, during these difficult and hard times, things can go a lot better and smoother for us when we humbly ask for and accept help from others, especially, help from God. Why? Because He is the creator of humans and all things. He knows what works best! He has the blueprints for what it takes to build a happy and successful life.

Yes, when it comes to humans, no one knows us better than God, the maker and creator of all things. (Hebrews 3:4) He not only knows what it takes for us to be both happy and successful in life, but also, in His Word, the Bible, He lovingly provides directions and instructions for us too, including real life examples and experiences of others who lived in the past, who had similar weaknesses and problems like ours, and yet, who were successful in coping and dealing with them—encouraging examples that we can draw encouragement, strength, and comfort from. However, it is up to us to read about and use these examples and lessons to our benefit. By doing so, we are not left groping and struggling in the dark to find the way on our own. Instead, by using the examples, instructions, encouragement and help that God provides, our lives will come together, be more stable, and we will be so much better off!

Interestingly, during the 13th step of recovery that I went through on the road leading to being cured of bipolar disorder, it required that I turn to and rely on God for strength and support. Of course, this was not the first time in my life that I did this. Nor was I without God in my life prior to this time. It's just that sometimes we personally go through things in life where we need a little more attention and help than what we normally require.[43] In other words, I had to learn to lean and rely on God more.

Sometime earlier in the bipolar disorder healing process—long before I even got to Step #13 *"Reliance On God For Strength And Support,"*— I had come to realize and discover (on my own), and also believe, that in order for me to be able to be completely cured of my bipolar illness, that I had to address and treat, not just one aspect of the disease, such as the mental health part alone, but instead, *everything* that encompasses me as a person—the *entire* human being. True, this included the mental health part, but it also included the physical, emotional, and *spiritual* aspect of me as well. For I believe that without addressing and treating all of these necessary and important areas and things, that I would not have ever been healed and cured of my depression and bipolar disorder.

The beautiful thing about being conscious of and reaching out to satisfy one's *spiritual* need (which all humans naturally have), is that, God can give true meaning and purpose to our life. But not only this, He can also give our life and character strength and stability. 1 Peter 5:10 says: "He [God] will make you firm, he will make you strong, he will firmly ground you."[44] Also, in addition to these things, He gives us a genuine, deep, fulfilling, and satisfying type of peace, joy, love, happiness, and other things that we simply cannot find anywhere else, or acquire on our own.

By nature, I consider myself to be a pretty proficient and strong

---

[43] Note: I'm not saying that we should only turn to God when we are going through troubling times. We should always look to him and be thankful and appreciative for what He does for us. However, there are times when we need His help and support all the more.

[44] Note: Truth is, being firmly grounded is good for anybody. But, especially, was this important for a person like me who suffered from the debilitating effects that often comes with bipolar disorder, which can make it hard to function on a daily basis. Luckily, during the 13th Step or stage of the bipolar disorder healing process, I came to realize the important role that stability, especially mental and emotional stability plays in having and maintaining good mental and emotional health—and I reached out to acquire it with the help and support that God supplies.

person in many ways—a person that can accomplish and achieve just about anything that I set my mind and heart to do—sometimes a little too independent. However, just like anyone else, when it comes to certain things in life, there are some things that can be hard to cope and deal with or to overcome and conquer on our own. With these things, I needed the wisdom and power that comes from above. This is where trust and reliance on God, the Almighty, comes in handy. Because, according to His Word, the Bible, He says He can provide us with: "Power beyond what is normal." (2 Corinthians 4:7-9). Fact is, with help from Him, nothing is impossible. (Job 42:2). For He can give us power to move mountains — be it mountain-like obstacles; or if it is God's will, even literal mountains. (Matthew 21:21).

The Bible informs us that Almighty God is the most powerful person in the entire universe. Concerning Him, Isaiah 40:26 says: "Lift up your eyes to heaven and see. Who has created these things? It is the One who brings out their army [stars] by number; He calls them all by name. Because of his *vast dynamic energy* and his *awe-inspiring power,* Not one of them is missing." Interestingly, we, personally, can tap into God's power by means of prayer, which can give us strength to do things that we cannot accomplish on our own. Philippians 4:13 says: "For all things I have the strength through the one [God] who gives me power.

In addition to giving us power and strength, God also loves us and is sensitive to our individual needs. He is even concerned about the lowly and afflicted. Psalms 72:12 says: "For he will rescue the poor who cry for help, Also the lowly one and whoever has no helper." Also, Psalms 34: 18, 19 says: "Jehovah is close to the brokenhearted; He saves those who are crushed in spirit... Many are the hardships of the righteous one, But Jehovah rescues him from them all." Also, Psalm 55:22 says: "Throw your burden upon Jehovah himself, and he himself will sustain you."[45] Interestingly, the psalmist, David, wrote those words when he was greatly distressed. (Psalms 55:4)

---

[45] Note: Jehovah is God's name. Psalms 83:18. King James Version.

I would have to say that, while I was traveling along the road to recovery and being cured of my depression and bipolar disorder—that out of all of the things that I personally have come to discover, realize, and understand that I needed to acquire, in order to be and stay healthy—that beyond a shadow of a doubt, the *spiritual* aspect is one of the most, if not the most important part. Why? Because, as humans, we were not meant to live without or be without God in our lives. Just like the air we breathe, and the blood that flows through our veins, we need Him. But also, because of overwhelming issues, problems, and obstacles that we sometimes go through in life, we need courage and strength that is beyond normal—courage and strength that only God, the Almighty can supply. Fortunately, for us, He is a loving, all powerful, generous, and caring God, who is willing, capable, and readily available for help and support, even during our most difficult and trying times.[46] (Isaiah 40:26; 2 Corinthians 4:7, 8; Psalm 116:1-19)

Personally, I have found through experience that God brings out the very best in us and makes our lives so much better! Some of the things that He has done for me are: He helped me to develop and possess, to a much greater degree, the qualities of peace, patience, joy, love, and other beautiful qualities that have added real enjoyment and happiness to my life. He also helped me to forgive others for the wrongs that they committed against me (real or imagined), which would have been virtually impossible for me to do on my own. This forgiveness was essential for me to be able to recover from the hurt and pain that others had caused me, and also for my future health and happiness. Because having a forgiving spirit works good as a curer. For it helps one to overcome things such as hurt feelings, resentment, and hate. In turn, it produces

---

[46] Note: I am not insinuating or saying that everyone who suffers from depression or bipolar disorder does not rely on God for comfort, help, strength, and support. Neither am I saying that this is something that I was not accustom to doing myself. I'm just relating to you (the reader), what I happened to realize and make further application of during this particular time period or stage of my life. Also, bipolar disorder is not a spiritual disease. But rather, it is a medical illness. However, leaning on and relying on God, the Almighty, for comfort, help, strength, and support, can be highly beneficial when we are undergoing stressful, painful, and difficult things in our personal lives.

peace, joy, contentment, and happiness. Interestingly, through personal experiences, I've come to discover and see firsthand that peace, joy, and love have powerful healing properties. And as far as these things are concerned, no one can give us both the *quality* and *quantity* of these things that only God can provide.

True, it's not that God will necessary heal us of our illnesses or medical problems (by means of performing a miraculous cure), but He can give us the courage, strength, and ability to face up to them and cope. But more than this, He can also bring us true peace, joy, and refreshment.

Today, thanks to God, I can now see and appreciate the real beauty and things that surround me in life, and the world—things that I could not see and appreciate when I was loaded down with the anxieties and depression that are associated with bipolar disorder illness.

Yes, today, I have true peace and joy that is beyond compare! Without sounding corny or too over the top, I'd like to say that, ever since I've learned to look to and lean on God more, I can see beauty in just about everything now, even in the so called simple things of life. For example, I can see beauty in a peaceful walk through a newly cut path in the woods. I can see beauty in frisky animals at play, in the flight of an eagle, a patch of wild flowers, Minnesota lakes and bubbling brooks and streams. I can see beauty in the calm and peacefulness of night, and bright sunny days that flood the earth with warmth and radiant light. I can see beauty in encouraging my family, neighbors, and friends with a positive word or cheerful note. I can see beauty in people who do or say something to make me giggle, laugh, and smile. I can see beauty in myself—that each and every day, I can see and learn something new and grow. Yes, I see peace, joy, and beauty, wherever I am, and go!

For anyone to be able to observe, experience, and appreciate the things above, along with so many other delightful and wonderful things in life—can be good for anyone's overall health, especially, their mental and emotional health. How fortunate I was to be able to take full advantage of these things as I traveled along the road to recovery from my illness. However, in addition to relying on God for help, strength, and support, there is another important thing that goes hand in hand with this that I needed to do, along the road leading to being cured of my depression and bipolar disorder, as the next step shows.

Step 14

LOOKING FORWARD
TO A BRIGHT FUTURE

The *fourteenth* step or stage that I went through on the road leading to being healed and cured of depression and bipolar disorder illness, required that I have and maintain a positive hope for a bright future, in regards to what I believe future world conditions and also my own personal health will bring.

As humans, we naturally have a keen interest and curiosity in what the coming future holds—and for good reason. Because without the hope of a bright future, it can be a little distressing or unnerving—to say the least. But, not only that, if the future is looking a bit grim or uncertain, it can rob us of a measure of peace, joy, and happiness, which, in turn, can affect our overall outlook in life, and even our mental and emotional health to a certain degree. For many people, anticipating a bleak future can cause worry, fear, frustration, anxiety, and even depression.[47]

---

[47] Note: I am not insinuating or implying that everyone who suffers from depression or bipolar disorder lacks hope. I'm just relating to you what happened

As imperfect humans, no matter how genuine our desire and efforts may be to bring about a just and better world, we often lack the power and ability needed to accomplish this or to solve or rectify certain troubling problems that the human race may be facing. Nevertheless, there is no need to get discouraged or downhearted over these things, because there still remains genuine hope. For according to God's word, the Bible, it informs us that Almighty God can produce and bring about real and permanent changes for the betterment of the earth and humankind, which is something that He promises to do in the not too distant future, under the Kingdom rule of his son, Jesus Christ. This is the Kingdom government that Christians often pray for to come in the "Our Father" or "Lord's Prayer." (Mathew 6: 9, 10)

Below is a list of some of the amazing things that the Bible says God's kingdom will bring about and accomplish in the near future:

1. Under the management of God's Kingdom, the earth will gradually become a global paradise. (Luke 23:43)

2. A perfect ecological balance will return. There will even be harmony between man and beast. (Isaiah 11:6-9)

3. Wars will disappear. (Psalm 46:8, 9; 72:7, 8.)

4. No more hunger and food shortages. (Isaiah 25:6; Psalm 67:6; 72:16.)

5. No more crime and violence. (Psalm 37:9, 10; Proverbs 2:22.)

6. No more housing problems and shortages. (Isaiah 65:21-23)

7. No more pollution. (Revelation 11:18)

8. No more sickness. (Isaiah 33:24; Isaiah 35:5, 6; Revelation 21:3, 4.) This means that, gone will be all physical and

---

to me.

mental illnesses, including depression and bipolar disorder.

9. Pain and death will be no more. (Revelation 21:3, 4; Isaiah 25:8; 26:19; John 5:28, 29; 1 Corinthians 15:26.

10. All earth's inhabitants will find, "Exquisite delight in the abundance of peace."—Psalm 37:11.

~

The above things are just some of the wonderful things that God promises to do and bring about in the near future. There are many more!

Yes, having these encouraging things to look forward to gives us a bright and solid hope for the future. It's not that I didn't possess hope for a bright future in the past, prior to falling ill, or that I lacked hope during the time when I was sick with bipolar disorder illness, it's just that during the 14th Step *"Looking Forward To A Bright Future,"* of the depression and bipolar disorder healing process, my focus and confidence in these promises became even stronger. Why? Because I found it to be immensely calming and encouraging looking forward to the wonderful, prosperous, bright future that God's Word, the Bible, promises to come. It brought me a tremendous amount of peace, joy, satisfaction, comfort, and contentment.

Yes, keeping an eye on the wonderful promises of the amazing future that are outlined in the 10 things that are listed above, as well as other encouraging things that the Bible foretells, is good and beneficial for anybody's mental and emotional health. Even in the midst of a worldwide pandemic of Covid-19, or other troubling problems or situations that we personally may be going through in life. Because it shows, that, despite these distressing things, the future is extremely bright!

Also, in conjunction with providing a bright hope for the future, God can also give us peace, joy, and happiness in our lives now! Personally, I am ever so grateful and thankful for the wonderful gifts of peace and joy that He provides, because they have greatly enriched and enhanced my life. Today, at this particular stage or time period in my life, I would have to say that I am happier and more at peace than I have ever been in my entire life! As a result, my heart and mind feel extremely good!

Yes, looking forward to a bright future was extremely helpful and useful to me, as I traveled along the road to recovery and being healed of my mental illness. However, in spite of this, I found that there was still something else, in addition to this — something that is similar to, but yet, somewhat different to having a bright hope for the future — that was required for me to be completely cured of my depression and bipolar disorder, as the next and final step goes on to show.

Step 15

HAVING A POSITIVE VIEW AND OUTLOOK ON MY PRESENT LIFE

The *fifteenth* and final step or phase that I went through on the road leading to me being healed and cured of my depression and bipolar disorder illness, required that I have and maintain a positive view and outlook about my life, *now*, during the current and present time, each and every day.

True, as we learned in the previous step (Step #14), having a bright outlook in regards to the coming *future* is good and beneficial. But in order for me to be truly happy and healthy, mentally and emotionally, I came to realize and appreciate during the 15th Step *"Having A Positive View And Outlook On My Present Life,"* that I also needed to have a positive outlook, *now*, in regards to my present life too—each and every day. For having and maintaining this type of mind frame and outlook, *now,* would not only aid in helping me to recover from my mental illness, but it would also help me to lead and live a more positive, productive, joyful, and meaningful life.

According to the dictionary, the word *outlook* means: "a

person's point of view; mental attitude; a person's way of understanding and thinking about something; or general attitude of life. Example: *"He has a positive outlook on life."*

What are some things that might help one to have a positive view and outlook on life, *now*? Well, one important thing is the matter of how we personally view ourselves. In essence, we should feel good, confident, and comfortable about whom we are as a person. Why is this so important? Because, if we don't appreciate, value, respect, and love ourselves for who we are, it can have an unhealthy and negative effect on how we view life and things, which can begin to rob us of our peace, joy, and happiness.

Another thing that can help us to have a positive view and outlook on life, *now*, is by not looking back at and dwelling on distressing things of the past, in particular, on the bad, negative, hurtful, and painful things that might have happened to us in life. This will only serve to drag us down and becloud our judgment, view, and outlook on life now, during the present time. But it can also cause us anxiety and depression too. When you think about it, it makes sense to leave a painful past behind. Because, in reality, if one is suffering from depression or bipolar disorder, how can they ever expect to get well mentally and emotionally, if they are continuously dwelling on sad and hurtful things?

Personally, as far as my situation goes, I've learned to view and treat these things (past issues and problems) like an old, worn, tattered, and stained garment, that has absolutely no use but to be disposed of. In other words, like a raggedy, old garment, I've found that it was best for me to strip off the painful things of my past and throw them completely away. Then, after trashing them in the garbage where they belong—to leave them there and totally forget about them. And then, thereafter, to move on—to start afresh and new, by obtaining and clothing myself with a new garment, so to speak—a way of living, thinking, and being that will be a much better and healthier fit for me—a life that will make me feel more positive, confident, and happy about myself and life.

Truth is, sometimes life and things can beat you down so badly that it makes you feel completely worthless and defeated—thereby, sucking the joy and life out of you. This can happen to anybody, even to the rich and famous. The beautiful thing, is that it is never too late to recover from these things and change (even if things haven't gone well for us in the past), as the following poem, entitled *"Rewriting Life's Script,"* clearly shows.[48]

Rewriting Life's Script

Whatever person you have become,

To wherever in life your path has run

It's never too late to change your course,

To recover from a life that has brought remorse

For you have the power and ability in your mind,

To step backwards in the stream of time

To use the knowledge and wisdom gained,

To redirect the goals that you wish to obtain.

~

Another thing that can help us to have a positive view and outlook on life, *now,* is by feeding our minds and hearts good and healthy things that will build strong character in us and increase our value and beauty as a person. True, each and every one of us is already important, valuable, and beautiful from the moment of birth onwards. Nevertheless, there is always room for development, growth, and improvements. This is one of the amazing things about life, which makes it so delightfully challenging, progressive, ever-changing, and beautiful!

An additional thing that can help us to have and maintain a

---

[48] The poem "Rewriting Life's Script," is a poem that I personally wrote. It can be found, along with a compilation of other inspiring poems, in my book, entitled *"Poems That Touch Home,"* on Amazon.com.

positive view and outlook on life, *now,* is by having healthy goals in place (both short-term and long-term) that we are working on. This can give us a sense of real accomplishment and make us feel good about ourselves and life—especially when we meet and achieve our goals.

Another thing that can help us to have and maintain a bright and positive view and outlook, *now,* is by associating with positive and encouraging people who have a bright and positive outlook on life and things. But also, they should be people that truly value, respect, appreciate, and love us for who we are—people that have our best interest at heart.

Another important thing that can assist us in having a positive view and outlook, *now,* is by reaching out to encourage and help other people too, especially those in need. Because, when we help and build others up, we, in turn, also help and lift ourselves up too. Because, giving of ourselves, time, and energy to others naturally has a reciprocal influence and positive effect on us. Interestingly, God's Word, the Bible, says: "There is more happiness in giving than there is in receiving."—Acts 20:35.

Another thing that helped me to have a positive view and outlook on life, *now,* especially when I was suffering from depression and bipolar disorder, was by having and maintaining total confidence and faith in myself—that, someday, I will, not only get better, but also, that I will eventually defeat depression and bipolar disorder—being healed and cured of these menacing illnesses once and for all time.

From personal application and experiences, I've come to discover that, not only is having a positive view and outlook of our life, *now,* important for our personal happiness and success, but also, it is good for our overall health and well-being too, including our mental and emotional health. For without having a positive view and outlook, we simply don't fare as well.[49] However, on the other hand,

---

[49] Note: I am not insinuating or implying that everyone who suffers from depression or bipolar disorder lacks a positive view and outlook. I'm just relating

with it (a positive view and outlook), our mind, heart, and soul can thrive and flourish. Yes, it is absolutely essential to have a positive view and outlook. We need it! And we must reach out and strive to obtain it. It is similar to plants reaching out to the rays of the radiant sun, because they know that it is their source of nourishment, health, and life!

Unfortunately, today, there are a lot of problems in the world. And as time advances, it seems like even more issues and problems are continuously being added to the list from day to day. Because of this, if we are not careful, these things could begin to negatively influence and affect our view and outlook on life and things, causing us to lose hope and become downhearted. That is why, for the most part, I personally try not to become too overly concerned with the problems and cares of the world. It's not that I don't care, because I do. It's just that I'd much rather focus on positive, joyful, peaceful, and more uplifting and encouraging things instead—things that won't get and pull me down—thereby affecting my mental and emotional health in a negative way.

Sad to say, most of the problems inflicting the world today are things of mankind's own making. In other words, they are *manmade* problems, which can be alarming, stressful, and discouraging to many, because he (man) has a long history or track record of not only causing world issues, but also, of being incapable of fixing or resolving them. Nevertheless, despite the negative and challenging things that currently exist, or discouraging things that may be looming on the horizon, I for the most part am able to remain optimistic and cheerful. The reason being, is because, I've learned to have and maintain a positive view and outlook on life and things, *now*.

It's not that I don't live in the real world, because I do. I can't help but to live here, because, I'm in it, and part of it—it's all around me. However, because of the negative direction that the world seems to be headed and the distressing things that often take place within it, I've learned to go in the opposite direction by developing a bright,

---

to you what happened to me.

sunny, and beautiful view and outlook on life. One way that I do this is by filling my life full of things that are good, healthy, and uplifting to me, and to those with and around me. And, believe me, because of the large variety of beautiful, fun, and exciting things that I regularly have to choose from (when making selections of things to do and be involved with), there is never a shortage or dull moment! But not only this, I find that my new, bright, sunny, optimistic disposition, attitude, view and outlook on life is so much better for my overall health and well-being, especially, my mental and emotional health.

I realize that there will most likely be naysayers, skeptics, and critics who will criticize my optimistic viewpoint, outlook, and approach to life, and the beautiful environment and world that I have created for myself—thinking that I just want to escape from reality or not face the truth. But that's okay. As far as I'm concerned, they can criticize and condemn me all they want, because, in contrast to them, I am truly peaceful, joyful, content, and happy with myself and my life. Besides, I've already lived a life of depression and bipolar disorder. And as far as I'm concern, I don't ever intend on going back there!

When it comes to life and things, having a bright viewpoint and outlook on life is vitally important and conducive to having good health, especially good emotional and mental health. This makes sense, because if we are always worried, angry, or upset about everything and everyone, this can rob us of our inner peace, joy, and happiness—causing discouragement, pain, and misery to our mind, heart, and soul, which can cause us undue stress, making us more susceptible to developing major health issues, and so forth. How much better off we are when we have and develop a love and appreciation for beautiful things, along with the people that surround us in the world. When we do this, life takes on a whole new meaning, and our attitude, viewpoint, and outlook becomes bright and cheerful, which is good and healthy for our overall happiness and health.

There is an old adage or proverb that says: "We are what we eat." Personally, I feel that this applies, not only to our diet of physical food, in regards to what we feed our body, but also, to our mind and heart too—as to what type of diet of things that we take in and feed them also. I believe that, like a well balanced diet of nutritious physical food that nourishes the body—thereby promoting good physical health and well-being—that also, if we regularly feed our mind and heart good, positive, uplifting, and healthy things, that this will also be good and beneficial to our mental and emotional health. Fact is, the entire universe, as well as the earth, and many people on it, are amazingly beautiful. Often, it is life's troubles; problems; the depressing and discouraging daily news; and our own negative thinking that gets in the way, thereby disrupting or distorting our positive view and healthy outlook of things, so that we don't observe, see, and appreciate the true beauty of the wonderful things that surround us in life.

Well, there you have it. This final step — Step #15 *"Having A Positive View And Outlook On My Present Life,"* completes the 15 amazing steps that I took, which led to me being 100%, completely healed and cured of my depression and bipolar disorder illness. The question is: "Now that I have been totally cured, is there any chance that I will someday relapse and come down sick again?" The final chapter, entitled *"Turning Over A New Leaf,"* will go on to answer this and other important questions.

TURNING OVER A NEW LEAF

Today, I am absolutely thrilled to finally be cured and free of the distressing, menacing effects of my mental illness. What a huge difference it has made, to now be able to truly enjoy each and every day of my life to the full!

Never, ever, do I want to go back to the painfully dark and gloomy days that I suffered through mentally and emotionally in the past, when I suffered from depression and bipolar disorder. And, as long as it is up to me, I will do everything humanly possible to prevent it from ever happening again, which, in itself, could pose somewhat of a challenge, due to all of the problems, distresses, and stressors that currently exist in the world.

Unfortunately, because of the way that the world is going today, with all the mounting issues and problems that we see taking place, along with the anxieties, pressures, and stressors that often come along with them, it is my prediction that, if things don't improve and get better, that there will be an increase in the number of people with depression and mental health issues in the not too distant future. As a matter of fact, because of the way that things are going, it makes it all the more important that each and every one of us, do everything possible, now, to protect and take care of our personal health, in particular, our mental and emotional health. By doing so, perhaps we can ward off any possible problems or harm to our personal health that could possibly arise down the line (in the future), hadn't it been for us taking the necessary precautions and steps, now, to safeguard ourselves mentally and emotionally. Because, once a person becomes mentally ill with clinical depression, bipolar disorder, etc., it can be hard to break free, recover, and grow healthy again. For the strong grip and hold that mental illness exercises and exerts on its victims can be overwhelming and debilitating—rendering them feeling completely helpless and without hope. Personally, in my case, when I was suffering from and undergoing deep depression in the past (prior to being cured of depression and bipolar disorder), at times, I felt like a prisoner being held captive in a dark prison, with little to no hope that I would ever be released or set free.

During the time that it was taking place (when I was suffering from depression and bipolar), I wondered what it would take to break free from the overwhelming gravitational forces that were holding my mind and moods bound and captive? The answer that I discovered from personal examination and experiences was that it would take an even *greater force*—something that is stronger than depression and bipolar to set me free. What was that force, and from where does it come?

Through personal experiences, I've discovered that the primary force that I needed to break free from the engulfing black hole of the strong gravitational forces of depression and bipolar disorder — that was unrelentingly holding my moods captive — was strong *self-determination* and *motivation*, with an enormous amount of power and energy behind it! From where would this powerful force come? It was a force that had to come from or be generated from within myself—internally—from within my *mind*.

Yes, in order for me to effectively and successfully battle and defeat the enemies—depression and bipolar disorder — first, and foremost, my mind had to believe, that, not only was this possible, but also, that it was stronger than depression and bipolar disorder—

that it could overpower and defeat them. Of course, not instantly or overnight, for this would be unreasonable and unrealistic to expect. But instead, to gradually and progressively (over a period of time), battle and defeat them. The important thing, was for me to not get discouraged and let up on the ongoing struggles, battles, and fight that were taking place from within me.

An interesting point, is that, in the past (prior to being cured of bipolar), I used to think that a person had absolutely no control over this illness, especially, the dark moods that are associated with the depressive phase of bipolar disorder. I even wrote about this in my previous book *"Bipolar Disorder, A Patient's Story."* At that time, I believed that the bipolar victim simply had no choice during these depressive episodes, but instead, that they had to just sit back and let them run their ugly, disruptive, and debilitating course. That is, until I personally got tired of being this way, and I decided to get tough with myself and fight back! And, believe me, it was not an easy thing to do—to battle and fight to free myself from the tenacious, unrelenting clutches of my bullies and enemies—depression and bipolar disorder, that were holding my mind and moods captive. It was an all out battle and war!

Personally, I feel that depression is comparable to or a lot like having a really bad *habit*—one that has become deeply ingrain in a person. And that, if they want to break free and completely rid themselves of it, they have no other recourse but to put up a hard struggle and fight against it, in order to eventually overcome, break free, defeat, and remove it permanently from themselves and their life.

One of the things that I discovered, in regards to working and fighting to get rid of depression and bipolar disorder, was that I had to (without letup), on a daily basis, condition my mind to think and behave differently—to train it to go against the grain, in the opposite direction that my mental illness was pushing my mind and moods to go. In other words, I had to fight the strong tendency of giving into the sad and negative feelings that depression and bipolar disorder were producing in me, rather than allowing them to control me. I had to take hold of and control of the reins, so to speak, and steer and direct my mind and moods in healthy and positive directions, where I preferred and wanted them to go.

Truth is, it was not an easy thing to do—to fight to overcome and defeat depression and bipolar disorder. I had to be a determined and relentless warrior and fighter—often battling and scrapping with every ounce of strength and energy that I could muster up, to force my mind and moods to be positive and upbeat, rather than allowing them to be sad and downcast. Because the enemies — depression and bipolar disorder — were intent on pulling me downwards and inflicting pain and suffering on me. The important thing was that I had to be a *self-motivator.*[50] No one could do it for me. I had to fight my own internal battles and demons. This is the reason why I highlighted earlier in my discussion, in Step #11, the importance of being a self-motivator, rather than depending on others to motivate us. Because, I realized that without being a self-motivator, that I would not have been able to defeat depression and bipolar disorder.

Another important thing that helped in my battle and fight, was for me to get to know the enemy. To become thoroughly familiar with depression and bipolar disorder, and how they function, operate, and work, etc. This way, I could devise and put together a good strategy or effective war plan, to wage a successful battle against them, with the intent to eventually overcome and defeat them!

Another valuable and important thing for me to know was: Why were these enemies — depression and bipolar disorder — attacking me? Was it something that I ignited or initiated? For example, what was causing my depression? Also, was it just one thing alone that brought in on, or was it caused by several things? Well, after extensive thought, consideration, and examination, etc., I came to discover and believe, that in my individual case, that it was primarily one thing in particular that caused my bipolar disorder, which was the all encompassing makeup and structure of the overly critical and

---

[50] "Self motivator," meaning: a person who is motivated by himself—one who does not require or need assistance from anyone else to help him get motivated to perform a task, etc.

negative, bad *environment* that I was in. Although, in addition to this, other things were involved too. Fortunately, in time, my mind was able to figure all of these things out (consciously and unconsciously), and, thereafter, to devise and put together an effective 15 step plan (taking one step at a time) to supply myself with the necessary tools and things that were needed, along the road to recovery, to eventually rid myself completely of the debilitating effects of depression and bipolar disorder illness.

You might ask: How important were each of the 15 steps in the healing process? Well, when I look back, I can see that each and every one of these individual steps that I took on the road to recovery (although, within or by themselves, they may have seemed to have been somewhat insignificant during the time that I was going through them), in the end, they played an important, vital, and necessary role in helping to cure me of my depression and bipolar disorder. Personally, I feel that I could not have done it, hadn't I gone through *each* and *every one* of these important steps. Sure, I might have gotten somewhat better if I would have done only half of these things. But I don't think I would have been completely healed of my mental illness. In other words, each and every one of these steps was necessary for me to go through—for if just one of them was missing, a complete and total cure would not have been possible.

In reviewing the depression and bipolar disorder healing process, in the following information, note what each of the 15 individual steps did for me.

Step #1 — *Finding Yourself.* What did finding myself do for me? It brought me a lot of comfort, peace, and joy. It gave me self-confidence. It helped me to appreciate and love myself for who and what I am. It helped me to find my place in the world.

The main lesson here, is that, I had to come to know and love who I am as a person. Because, when one doesn't find, get to know, and learn to love their self, it can cause a certain degree of mental and emotional anguish, distress, and pain, which can lead to feelings of emptiness, un-fulfillment, or being lost, which can trigger feelings of frustration, anxiety, sadness, and even deep depression. But also, when you truly get to know who you are—as being a distinct and individual person, it contributes greatly to obtaining peace, joy, happiness, and contentment in your life.

Step #2 — *Open Your Heart to Peace, Joy, and Love.* What did opening my heart to peace, joy, and love do for me? It helped to remove the hurt and pain that I was feeling and going through in life. It removed anxiety, and stress. It helped me to let go of resentment and hate, and to forgive others. It opened my mind and heart to see and appreciate the wonderful and beautiful things that surround me in life and the world—things that I didn't notice or fully appreciate in the past. It beautified, enriched, and enhanced my life and soul. It improved my overall health and well-being. And it helped to cure me of my depression and bipolar disorder illness.

The main lesson here, is that, I needed to open myself up to receive, have, and maintain, inner *peace*, *joy*, and *love*. Because, these highly valuable and beneficial qualities can help me to feel good about myself, and also, about life and people in general. But also, they are good and beneficial for my mind, heart, spirit, and soul too, because they helped me to heal, grow, and thereafter, to stay healthy—mentally, emotionally, physically, and spiritually.

Today, now that I have found and possess a great amount of peace, joy, and love, and I have experienced and observed the amazing benefits and things that they have brought to my health (mental and emotional), and life; from now on, going forward, I simply refuse to let anyone or anything ever rob me of these beautiful and healthy qualities again!

Step #3 — *Respect Yourself.* What did learning to respect myself do for me? It gave me confidence and self-esteem. It helped me to be more positive. It gave me peace of mind and heart. It brought me joy and happiness. It fortified and strengthened my character in many ways—making me solid, strong, and complete in ways that I hadn't been in the past. No longer did I have to depend on or look to others for their approval (erroneously thinking that this was going to help me to gain self-worth). It helped me to truly love, appreciate, and value myself for who and what I am.

The main lesson here, is that, I had to learn to respect and love myself for who I am. Because, without having a good and proper measure of self-respect and self-love, it can make life a lot more difficult.

Note: Many of us spend our lives looking for love, acceptance, and happiness in all of the wrong places, believing that if and when we eventually find them, that our emptiness will somehow be magically filled, and from that time going forward, we will be truly happy and complete. Not realizing and knowing that a large portion of these things already exist, if we just take a good look within ourselves. True, as humans, we also need to be loved and appreciated by others too. However, much of our joy and happiness depends on us and how we view and treat ourselves.

Step #4 — *Make Joy Your Close Friend.* What did making joy my close friend do for me? Personally, I found *joy* to be a powerful medicine, healer, and curer! For it helped to relieve me of the suffering, misery, pain, and despair that my depression was causing me. It picked me up, lifted up my spirits, making me feel calm, confident, and happy. It made me feel good about myself, and life. It helped to eventually heal and cure me of my depression and bipolar disorder illness.

The main lesson here, is that, I needed *joy* in my life, because, not only is it the opposite of sadness, but joy picks me up and makes me feel good mentally and emotionally. But, not only that, joy is also good for my physical health too. I'm not talking about a transitory joy, or joy that is shallow or only on the surface, but instead, a type of true joy that creates a sense of happiness deep down within our heart and soul. Because of this, I tap into this type of joy as often as I can, and I carry it wherever I go.

The quality of *joy* has become so valuable and important to me, that I view it as being like *sunshine* that brightens my day. Along with this, during this stage — Step #4 *"Make Joy Your Close Friend"* — of the depression and bipolar disorder healing process, I decided to view and use my mind and heart as *joy-catchers* that reach out to catch and hold onto beautiful and delightful things that will bring joy and sunshine into my life. True, *joy* may not come natural to some of us, and sometimes it can be a little hard to find, that is, if we are looking in all the wrong places or for riches and material things alone to bring us joy. That is why I have learned to also have internal joy—a joy that resides within me—that is generated and flows deep from within my soul. Fortunately, I've discovered through personal experiences that finding and having this type of genuine and lasting joy requires a change of one's thinking, attitude, viewpoints, outlook, and beliefs. And now that I have obtained and possess it (joy), I refuse to let anyone or anything ever rob me of my joy again.

Step #5 — *Finding the Root Cause of My Illness.* What did finding the root cause of my bipolar disorder illness do for me? It brought me a sense of real comfort and relief. It showed me that my having bipolar disorder illness was not heredity or due to genetics (something that was passed on to me through an ancestor or parent), but instead, that it was primarily the result of my *environment* that caused it.[51] It helped me to understand why I personally contracted the illness. It stopped the bleeding, so to speak, by relieving a lot of the mental and emotional pain and suffering that I was feeling and going through. It helped me to learn how to better cope and deal with my illness. It brought me peace of mind and heart. It gave me hope. And, it added to the *15 Step* process and tools that I created (consciously and unconsciously), and put in to place; that I both needed and used to work towards healing and curing my depression and bipolar disorder illness.

The main lesson here, is that, I had to find the root cause of my mental illness, so that I could stop the bleeding (the pain and suffering that I was going through from not knowing the source of

---

[51] "Environment," meaning: All of the external factors that have a formative influence on a person's physical, mental, emotional, and moral development. The environments that I'm referring to are *long-term environments*—those that we spend a considerable amount of time in, such as at school, at work, or in our neighborhood, etc.

my illness, etc). Finding and knowing the root cause of my illness also helped me to realize and see that I could possibly work to remedy and remove the things that had and were continuing to make me sick (mentally and emotionally), the things that were triggering, feeding, fueling, and causing negative thoughts, thinking, moods, and emotions in me—that were producing frustration, anxiety, anger, sadness, depression, self sabotaging thoughts, etc—thinking and actions that made me feel even worse. In addition to this, it also showed me that I had to take whatever steps necessary to try to *reverse the damage* that had been done in the past. And lastly, it helped me to put in to place good, positive, and healthy things that would stimulate and promote *healing* (mental, emotional, physical, and spiritual)—things that would eventually lead to me being healed and cured of depression and bipolar disorder illness.

In the end, as things turned out, finding the root cause of my illness wound up being a very powerful tool that produced many good and positive results!

Step #6 — *Finding the Right Environment.* What did finding and placing myself in the *right environment* do for me? By removing myself from my *old*, overly critical and negative environment, and placing myself in a *new*, positive, uplifting, and encouraging one instead, it took away the triggers—the things that existed in my old environment that were causing and feeding frustration, anxiety, depression, and pain in me. It brought me peace, joy, contentment, encouragement, and a positive spirit. It also, improved my overall health and well-being, especially, my mental and emotional health, which aided in helping me to eventually be healed and cured of my depression and bipolar disorder illness. Yes, my new environment made me feel good about myself, and life. It brought out the very best in me!

The main lesson here, is that, I needed to find and place myself in a good and healthy environment to recover, mend, and heal from my mental illness. I needed a highly positive and curative environment that would stimulate and promote healing, growth, and good health in me, especially, good mental and emotional health. True, no environment is ideally perfect. But, if I wanted to be healed of depression and bipolar disorder illness, and to remain healthy thereafter, I needed to place myself in a warm, loving, caring, positive, and healthy environment that encouraged, stimulated, and generated good and positive thinking, thoughts, feelings, moods, and emotions in me—an environment where my mind, heart, and soul could be properly nourished and encouraged to grow in healthy and beneficial ways—a place where I could find true inner peace, joy, and happiness. The wonderful thing, is that, this worked, for my *new environment* helped to eventually heal and cure me of my depression and bipolar disorder illness!

Yes, just like a healthy, luxuriant plant or tree, I finally began to grow and flourish—all because I found and planted myself in a good and healthy, *new environment.* The reason why, is because I was being properly fed and nourished (mentally, emotionally, physically, and spiritually) with all of the good, healthy, and right things!

Some people might criticize me for removing myself from my old environment, perhaps even going so far as to wrongly accuse or label me as being nonconforming or antisocial. But this would be farthest from the truth! Because, I don't have a problem with conformity (if it is just and right), nor do I have a problem with people in general. In regard to the latter, personally, I have a lot of beautiful friends, family, and people in my life. Truth is, I am the kind of person that can communicate and socialize with just about anybody. However, for health purposes, I decided not to stay in an overly critical and negative environment that was harmful and detrimental to my health. For if I were to stay there, it would only keep triggering and feeding mental and emotional hurt and pain, which would only make matters worse. Because, that unhealthy, bad environment that I was in, in the past, was making and keeping me sick.

My situation can be compared to a person that was a heavy smoker in the past, who, for health reasons, decided to completely quit after many years of nicotine addiction. In so doing, he also realized and decided that it would be best for him, to stay away from cigarettes, and to remove himself from any compromising situations or tempting environments, such as being in a room full of smokers that are blowing cigarette smoke in the air and in his face—places where it would make it hard for him to stay true to his promise and resolve to quit smoking permanently. Because, not only would being in a smoke filled environment be highly tempting, but also, the matter of taking in secondhand smoke would be harmful and detrimental to his health too. Well, the same is true, in regard to my past, bad environment. Truth is, it was making and keeping me ill. Therefore, if I wanted to heal and get better, I had no other recourse, but to totally remove myself from it. And then, in turn, to find and place myself in a good, beneficial, and healthy, *new environment* that stimulates and promotes peace, joy, happiness, and good health (mental, emotional, physical, and spiritual). The wonderful thing, is that, this decision and move that I made worked, because it eventually helped lead me to being healed and cured of my depression and bipolar disorder illness.

Step #7 — *Putting on a New Personality.* What did putting on a new personality do for me? It gave my character strength and stability. It made me solid. It gave me positive thinking, and self-confidence. It helped me to adjust and function better in various environments, especially, in my previous, bad environment, whenever I had to temporarily reenter it—that overly critical and negative environment that had previously posed serious problems for me. It helped me to look at and deal with people in a reasonable and balanced way. It helped to improve my mental and emotional health, which eventually led to me being healed and cured of my depression and bipolar disorder illness.

Note: In regard to social environments—it is important to have people in our lives. This is both good and healthy for us. However, to be of true help and benefit to us, it is best if they are people that encourage, respect, love, and support us. For example, if we are not watchful and careful we can let society, and peoples erroneous and negative viewpoints, thinking, teachings, hatreds, etc., distort and change the healthy image and viewpoint that we have of ourselves, and life. They can even start to erode and destroy the beautiful person that we are inside, which can rob us of our peace, self-esteem, joy, happiness, and even our health (mental and emotional), or even worse. Personally, that is why, for the most part, I now make it a point to surround myself with good and positive people who love, value, respect, and encourage me.

The main lesson here, is that, if I wanted to fair well in any environment, especially, in my old, overly critical and negative one (during times when, due to no choice of my own, I had to occasionally reenter it), I had no choice but to adjust and balance out certain aspects of my personality, so as not to allow the harmful effects of the bad environment (that was in conflict with certain good aspects or qualities of my personality), cause me any more mental and emotional harm. For example, my quality or trait of being *overly nice* had to be properly balanced out so that people would no longer take advantage of me, and so forth. Also, my trait of being a *deep thinker* (which can be a good thing if used in a balanced and right way) had to be self-monitored, properly channeled and balanced out, so that I was no longer focusing and dwelling on negative subjects and things that would discourage and tear me down. In other words, I made the necessary adjustments and changes to my personality that would benefit me, rather than hurt or harm me. For example, instead of over thinking harmful matters that triggered and fed frustration, anxiety, hard feelings, and depression in me, I focused and dwelled on positive and uplifting things instead—things that encouraged, built me up, and made me feel good about myself, and life—things that brought me peace, joy, and happiness! The amazing thing, is that this worked, for it helped me to heal and eventually be cured of my depression and bipolar disorder illness.

Step #8 — *Controlling Your Feelings and Emotions.* While *good* feelings and emotions are good and healthy for us, on the flipside of things, *bad* feelings and emotions can be harmful and damaging—to where they can cause serious issues, even to the point of making us sick, that is, if we allow them to overwhelm, control, and get the best of us. What did learning to control my feelings and emotions do for me? It gave me power and strength. It gave me self-control, in that, I no longer allowed people or things to affect and influence my feelings and emotions in a bad or negative way. It improved my outlook on people and life. It also improved my overall health, especially, my mental and emotional health. And lastly, and most importantly, it helped to eventually heal and cure me of my depression and bipolar disorder illness.

The main lesson here, is that, because feelings and emotions (both good and bad) play a significant role in how we feel and function in life, and also in our overall health and well-being, I had to learn to monitor and control them, in particular, *bad* feelings and emotions, so that they did not wind up robbing me of my peace, joy, and happiness. But also, so that they would not be harmful and detrimental to my health, in particular, my mental and emotional health.

The secret or key to controlling my feelings and emotions was for me to not allow room for bad feelings and emotions to begin to enter my mind and heart in the first place. However, if or whenever negative or bad thoughts did begin to surface, I had to take action to get rid of them immediately, by pushing them out of my mind, so that they would not take root and start to grow, thereby causing me potential issues and problems down the line. In return, I had to replace the bad feelings and emotions with good, positive, and healthy ones.

Another thing that helped to create good feelings and emotions in me, was by adding or incorporating good and positive things in to my daily life, and home environment, etc.,—things that generated, stimulated, and promoted good feelings, moods, and emotions in me—things that were uplifting, encouraging, peaceful, joyful, and healthy for me personally. In other words, I created and promoted a positive and healthy atmosphere and environment that brought out the very best in me, whether I am at home or wherever I am and happen to go.

Note: In the past (prior to being healed of depression and bipolar disorder illness), I possessed somewhat of a negative spirit (not all of the time of course, but all too often), which fostered bad feelings and emotions in me. Unfortunately, my bad attitude and emotions were often triggered and fed by the overly critical and negative environment that I was in at the time. This was not good, because it was harmful and damaging to my mental and emotional health.

However, after I discovered through personal experiences the harmful and detrimental effects that *bad* feelings and emotions can have on a person's health and well-being; I worked hard to rid myself of these things, including a negative spirit. And then, after removing these bad and negative things; in return, I worked to replace them with a positive attitude and good emotions, such as peace, joy, love, kindness, goodness, etc. Fortunately, for me, these positive things created a new spirit and good feelings and emotions in me, that, not only helped to protect my mind and heart from harmful and damaging feelings and emotions, but also, it eventually helped to heal and cure me of my depression and bipolar disorder illness as well.

Today, I am so grateful and happy that I finally defeated bipolar disorder, especially, that I no longer have to suffer from the painful depression and dark moods that it produces. Now, unlike the past, rather than wallowing in misery, pain, and sorrow; my mind, heart, and spirit feels all so good, and free, and they are soaring high!

Step #9 — *Changing Your Diet and Lifestyle.* What did changing my diet and lifestyle do for me? It improved my overall health. It gave me more energy. It helped me to remove unwanted pounds. It made me feel healthy and physically strong. It helped me to shape and mold a more confident and positive person and spirit. It made me feel good about myself, and life—thereby improving my overall outlook, and my self-esteem. It supplied both my mind and body with the necessary tools, and things — vitamins, minerals, etc., — that were needed to replenish, regenerate, recover, and repair themselves, and to function properly. And lastly, and most importantly, it aided in helping me to eventually be healed and cured of my depression and bipolar disorder illness.

The main lesson here, is that, I needed to make some positive and healthy changes in my diet and lifestyle, in order to improve my overall health, especially, my mental and emotional health. This required that I start and keep a healthy, nutritional diet in place, which I did.

In addition to changing my diet, I also changed my lifestyle too, by *removing* any and all things that I felt might be undermining my health (mental, emotional, physical, and spiritual)—things that might be harmful and damaging to my personal development, growth, and well-being. Also, I *added* or incorporated good, positive, healthy, and constructive things in to my life too—things that encouraged and promoted strong character, a positive spirit and outlook, and good health.

Step #10 — *Following My Daily Healthcare Plan.* What did following my personal, *Daily Healthcare Plan* do for me? It gave me good and healthy goals and things to work on, that kept me active and moving forward in the right and positive direction. It made my life more productive. It gave me self-confidence and positive energy. It helped to build and strengthened my character. It helped to shape and remold my mind, thinking, and actions from being negative, self-sabotaging, and destructive, to becoming positive, optimistic, and constructive. It helped to rewire or reprogram my brain, thinking, habits, and actions in healthy and beneficial ways. It helped me to defeat and break free of the debilitating, strong, gravitational forces of dark moods of depression that are associated with bipolar disorder—which was holding my mind and moods captive in a prison-like state. It gave my life organization, order, and stability. It gave me energy, strength, and motivation. It helped to boost my moods. It improved my outlook on life and things. It gave me an upbeat and positive mind and spirit. It improved my overall health (mental, emotional, physical, and spiritual). And lastly, and most importantly, it helped me to eventually be healed and cured of my depression and bipolar disorder illness.

The main lesson here, is that, I needed to promote good, overall, personal health and well-being in myself, including mental and emotional health. This required that I have and keep my *Daily Healthcare Plan*, routine, and things in place—that would encourage and promote it.

Note: Prior to being cured of bipolar disorder (during the time when I was attempting to try to heal myself of my mental illness), I discovered from personal experiences and experimentation on myself, that when it comes to treating bipolar disorder, that it's best and a lot more effective to treat, not just one aspect of the person alone, such as their mental health, but rather, the *entire* human being. This includes the *mental* aspect of course, but also, the *emotional*, *physical*, and *spiritual* part of the individual as well. Personally, I wanted to be complete, whole, and healthy in all respects. That is why I came up with or devised, developed, and put in to place my extensive *Daily Healthcare Plan*, routine, and things, which helped me to recover from my mental illness, gain strength, and heal in all of the important areas of my life.

Step #11 — *The Push Towards Improving My Health.* During this step in the depression and bipolar disorder healing process, it was vitally important for me to develop, incorporate, possess, and maintain a *push and drive* forward attitude, spirit, and mindset. What did this do for me? It helped me to continue to *keep moving* ever forward in my quest to recover and be healed of my illness, especially, during difficult times when I was undergoing depressive episodes, when it was hard for me to get started or motivated to perform my Daily Healthcare Plan, routine, and things (the things that I had created and put in place to help me to heal and get better). It helped me to *fight back*—to successfully battle against and defeat the dark moods and depressive episodes of bipolar disorder that were holding my mind and moods captive. It helped me to be productive and enjoy life, rather than just sitting around and letting my life become stagnated, inactive, and wasted—allowing my mental illness to drain and control me. It helped me to fight to take back my life. It helped to eventually heal and cure me of my depression and bipolar disorder illness.

The main lesson here, was for me to not let my mental illness control and defeat me, but instead, I had to battle and fight hard to take back control over my thinking, emotions, and life—the things that depression and bipolar disorder had taken from me to a large degree.

Yes, through personal experience, I've learned that I had to be a fighter that *pushes and drives* forward to achieve my goals and aspirations—including medical health goals. That I simply cannot just idly sit by and let my depression, bipolar disorder, or whatever illness I have, dominate and control me. Instead, I must fight back! by forcing my thinking, mind, feelings, emotions, and moods to be positive, upbeat, and joyful, instead of feeling sad and depressed. In other words, I had to break the *bad habit* of feeling down and depressed, by developing *good habits* that would possibly become a permanent part and fixture of my internal makeup and being. Interestingly, I found that this eventually worked, because the more that I pushed and applied myself to being joyful, happy, and upbeat, the easier it became to have and reflect a genuine, positive, and joyful spirit. Also, in addition to this, my mental health kept improving more and more, each and every day!

Note: In the past, I used to believe that there was simply nothing that a bipolar disorder patient could do, in particular, during *depressive episodes* to pull themselves out of the dark moods of depression that it produces. I even stated this in my previously released book *"Bipolar Disorder, A Patient's Story."* One of the reasons why I believed that this was true, is because, at that time (that is, up until the time that I cured myself of bipolar disorder), in the mental health medical community and elsewhere, this was the generally accepted, popular, held belief at the time. But not only this, my own personal case of the illness (bipolar disorder), and the overwhelming effects that the disease, in particular, the depression was exerting and having on me — which often left me feeling mentally, emotionally, and physically drained and disabled; seemed to confirm this teaching or belief to be true. However, during Step #11 *"The Push Towards Improving My Health"* phase in the bipolar disorder healing process, I decided to do something else, instead of just sitting back and letting my mental illness control and defeat me. What did I do? I decided to take an unconventional approach in dealing with the problem, which was something that no one else had tried nor was able to successfully do prior to that time. What was that? I decided to battle and fight back! Why?

The reason why I decided to fight the effects of my bipolar illness, in particular, the *depressive phase*, was because I had grown tired of letting it pull me down and control me—leaving me feeling drained, depressed, crippled, debilitated, and defeated. So, rather than continuing to throw my life away, letting it go to waste, by just sitting there feeling paralyzed, helpless, frustrated, completely awash in an overly depressed, mentally and emotionally painful state, I decided to do something about it, by getting aggressively tough with myself. How? By forcing my mind, thinking, moods, feelings, and emotions to go in the opposite direction that my mental illness was forcing them to go. This required that I not only stop my mind and heart from gravitating towards depression, but also, that I had to force my mind and heart to be positive, upbeat, and joyful instead. True, it was a very difficult thing to do, to fight and defeat the powerful enemies—depression and bipolar disorder. It took a lot of time, energy, willpower, strength, focus, consistent efforts, and personal drive. But I was determined to scrap and fight hard, with every ounce of energy and strength that I could muster up, to get back control over my life, which eventually I did.

Today, now that I look back, I would have to say that out of all of the tools and things that were useful to me in winning the battle against my illness, that having a *push and drive* forward attitude (a fighting spirit); is one of, if not the most powerful weapons that I could have come to develop and possess. For I believe that I would not have been able to successfully battle and defeat the ugly, powerful, and relentless enemies, depression and bipolar disorder, without it!

Step #12 — *Invite Positive Into Your Life.* What did inviting positive into my life do for me? Inviting positivity in to my life, did a lot of good things for me: (1) It boosted my moods, (2) It helped me to oppose and reject negativity, (3) It gave me the power to overcome discouragement and things that can get and pull me down, (4) It gave me control over my thinking so that it doesn't dominate and control me in negative ways to my harm, (5) It gave me hope, (6) It helped me to cope with my illness and trials, (7) It helped me to keep my head up, and to keep moving forward, advancing, developing, and growing in good and beneficial ways, (8) It brightened my viewpoint and outlook on life and things, (9) It brought me peace, joy, and happiness, (10) It improved and strengthened my character, (11) It made me feel good about myself, and life, (12) It helped me to encourage others, (13) It improved my overall health and well-being. And lastly, and most importantly, (14)

It helped to eventually heal and cure me of my depression and bipolar disorder illness.

The main lesson here, is that, I had to develop and maintain a positive attitude or spirit to overcome discouragement, and to defeat the negative thoughts, moods, feelings, and emotions of bipolar disorder that were pulling me downwards, especially, during the depressive phase or episodes of bipolar. Also, by having a positive attitude it promoted peace, joy, and happiness in me, thereby improving my viewpoint and outlook on things and life. And also, equally important, inviting positivity in my life encouraged others, promoted good friendships, and improved my relationships with others.

Note: Prior to becoming upbeat and positive, which thankfully I am today, I was in a highly toxic, overly critical and negative environment that often brought out the worse in me. It was so bad that, not only did it trigger, feed, and breed negative thoughts, thinking, and feelings in me (not all of the time of course, but enough), but it also, had a detrimental effect on my self-esteem, and my potential to develop and grow in certain areas too. And even worse, it produced anxiety, stress, and depression in me, thereby robbing me of my peace, joy, happiness, and health (mental and emotional). Fortunately, I eventually wised up, broke away from, and left that ugly and destructive environment. Fact is, I believe that if it wasn't for that unhealthy environment, that I would not have ever come down sick with depression and bipolar disorder in the first place.

Now, instead of living in toxic negativity each and every day, I search for and find positive, uplifting, delightful, fun, and highly constructive things to focus on, work on, and do—things that bring a tremendous amount of joy and sunshine into my life, which helps out tremendously! For I now have a lot of delightfully colorful, enjoyable, exciting, good, and positive things going on in my life. All because I opened up and invited *positivity* in to my life!

Today, I am extremely happy and pleased with the huge turnaround that my life has made for the better. What an amazing improvement! However, this was no accident. Most of it was due to conscience efforts and a lot of hard work! The encouraging thing is that, others (no matter who they are or where they come from) can change and improve their life too, if they really want to. Like I highlighted earlier in this book (in Step #15 *"Having A Positive View And Outlook On My Present Life"*), I honestly feel and believe that, no matter how ugly or disappointing one's life may have turned out to become — due to painful or horrible things that they may have suffered and went through in their past — that, if they truly desire and want to, they have the power and ability within themselves to completely dump it, get rid of it, and leave it all forever behind. And then, thereafter, from that time going forward, they can go on to remake and reshape themselves and their life in to whatever they prefer and want it to be. True, it may take some adjustments and a certain amount of time and effort to do, but it can be done, as my life's encouraging example so vividly shows and proves!

Yes, being positive promotes a lot of good things, including good health and well-being, especially, good mental and emotional health. That is why I will continue to pursue and invite it, each and every day, in to my life. For, by personal choice, being positive has become my preferred way of being!

Step #13 — *Reliance on God for Strength and Support.* What did relying on God for strength and support do for me? He gave me power and strength beyond what is normal. He gave me the strength to endure and cope with problems and to overcome obstacles and things that I could not have possibly accomplished in my own strength or on my own. He provided me with encouragement, hope, and comfort. He gave me the courage and strength to cope and deal with my depression and bipolar disorder illness. He built up, improved, stabilized, and strengthened my overall character. He gave me a heart to forgive others. He made me stand on solid ground. He gave my life true meaning and purpose. He filled my heart with an abundance of true peace, joy, love, and happiness — a genuine, deep, and lasting type of peace, joy, love, and happiness that is much greater and more valuable than I could have ever found anywhere else in life or in this world. And lastly, He improved my thinking, viewpoints, outlook, and overall health and well-being for the better.

The main lesson here, is that, I needed to turn to and rely on God for strength, help, and support, if I wanted to enhance and improve my life for the better.

Note: Although I don't believe that God necessarily heals us of our sicknesses and diseases (by means of performing a miracle), I do believe that He can give us the courage, comfort, strength, hope, and ability to be able to effectively cope, endure, and deal with them.

Interestingly, in regards to my personal case, when it came to coping and dealing with my depression and bipolar disorder illness, fortunately, I was able to tap into my innate, God-given abilities and talents, by utilizing my mind, thinking, and reasoning skills in positive and productive ways to devise and put together an effective, 15 Step Plan, that led to me eventually being healed and cured of my depression and bipolar disorder illness, which I am so grateful to God for. Because, if it hadn't been for Him originally equipping and supplying me with the wonderful tools and things (the innate gifts of my brain, mental facilities, reasoning abilities, and problem solving skills, etc.), I would not have been able to accomplish this amazing feat!

Step #14 — *Looking Forward to a Bright Future.* What did looking forward to a bright future do for me? It took away anxiety, worries, and stress. It gave me a bright outlook, and positive thinking. It gave me confidence, encouragement, and hope. It made me feel good about myself, life in general, and also in the bright days that the future will bring. It brought me peace, joy, and happiness. It improved my health, especially, my mental and emotional health. It aided in helping me to eventually be healed and cured of my depression and bipolar disorder illness.

The main lesson here, is that, I had to have and maintain a positive hope for a *bright future* — for the earth, mankind, and especially, in regard to my personal, future health, well-being, and happiness. Having this type of faith, hope, and strong conviction gave me a positive attitude and spirit. It also, helped to fortify and strengthen my belief and hope that I would eventually be healed and cured of my depression and bipolar disorder illness someday, which, in the end, eventually came true!

Step #15 — *Having A Positive View And Outlook On My Present Life.* What did having a positive view and outlook on my present life, *now,* do for me? It made me feel good about myself, my life, and others. It gave me a positive spirit and thinking. It helped me feel confident, good, and comfortable about who I am as a person. It brought me peace, joy, and happiness. It helped me to lead and live a more productive, positive, and meaningful life, *now.* It boosted my moods. It gave me positive energy. It improved my overall health and well-being, especially, my mental and emotional health. It aided in helping me to eventually be healed and cured of my depression and bipolar disorder illness.

The main lesson here, is that, I had to have and keep a positive outlook, in regards to my present life, *now,* that is, if I wanted to be happy and make the most of my life. And, most importantly, if I wanted to rebound, recover, and heal from depression and bipolar disorder illness.

~

Note: Along with the effective 15 steps above, there were other helpful things that I also personally devised, set up, and did to heal and cure myself of depression and bipolar disorder (as I traveled along the road to being cured of my illness). For a comprehensive and detailed discussion of these things, see the informative and encouraging information *"Coping with Bipolar and Depression,"* in the Appendix, on pages 198-237. Also see "A Recipe for a Healthy Mind," on pages 238-239, and "Things that Can Help Fight Added Depression," on Pages 240-243.

~

Yes, as you can see from the effective 15 steps above, they did some truly awesome and magnificent things for me and my health, especially, my mental and emotional health! Today, thanks to them, I no longer have or experience any of the symptoms of my former illness, bipolar disorder, along with the dark moods of depression that it often produces. For I am 100%, completely healed and cured of depression and bipolar disorder, which makes me extremely happy![52]

One person asked me (after I was cured of my mental illness): "When did you realize or recognize that you no longer had bipolar disorder? Did the awareness of it happen gradually or was it overnight?" My response was: "From what I remember, the complete awareness of it happened within the timeframe of about six months—between one of my scheduled doctor visits with my psychiatrist. Although, there were certain signs or indicators before this that I was feeling and getting a lot better; the last phase of the healing process (that was leading to me being completely cured of depression and bipolar disorder illness), seemed to take a giant leap forward! During that time, it was as though it filled in the last or remaining piece of the puzzle, so to speak—the piece that was needed to complete the entire picture or scene, thereby providing and confirming without a doubt (both to me and others), the full recovery of my mental and emotional health!

As you (the reader) noticed in examining the 15 steps; it took, not just one thing alone, but rather, *all* 15 steps to heal and cure me of my bipolar disorder. As a matter of fact, I believe that if just one of these important steps was left out or missing, I would not have been completely cured.

Now that I look back, I would have to say that the thing that fascinates me the most—in observing the incredible step-by-step healing process that I went through—is how each of the individual steps, one by one, were gradually leading me, one step at a time, closer to being healed. And, what was even more amazing, is in, personally, being there, seeing and experiencing *firsthand,* how the human mind and body have the power and ability to heal

---

[52] Disclaimer: I do not endorse or recommend that anyone follow the 15 step course that I took, along with other things that I did to cure myself of depression and bipolar disorder. Readers are advised to consult their own doctors or other qualified health professionals regarding the treatment of medical conditions such as depression and bipolar disorder and their prescribed medications.

themselves. Although, sometimes, we have to provide them with the necessary tools and things that they need to recover and fix themselves, which is something that I did.

The big question is: "Going forward, do I have to continue to follow these 15 steps today and in the future, even though I am now totally cured of my depression and bipolar disorder illness?" The answer is, *no*. At least, not to the degree or extent that I did in the past, prior to being completely healed. In essence, all of the hard work and necessary repairs that had to happen for me to heal and be cured of my illness have already taken place. Nevertheless, for preventive maintenance purposes, and to continue to lead a healthy life, I will continue to apply and do some of the things in the 15 steps, but to a lesser degree. The main thing, is for me to continue to live a life that is good, healthy, and beneficial for me, so that I will remain in good, overall health, especially, good mental and emotional health; now, and in future days, months, and years to come. And believe me, I will! Because I don't intend, nor do I ever want to come down sick again—like I did in the past—no, never again!

In further examination of the 15 Step healing process that I went through, and how the amazing cure for my mental illness took place, I can clearly see that, in order for me to be completely healed and cured of depression and bipolar disorder, that, my *mind, body, environment,* and *lifestyle* had to undergo a significant metamorphosis or change. In other words, there were specific aspects and things about me, my life, surroundings, and things (some major, some minor) that needed to change—things that were *physical, chemical, mental, emotional,* and *spiritual* in nature. Interestingly, the required changes that occurred, did not happen immediately or overnight. But rather, they took some time for them to happen and take place. The good thing, is that, prior to making these and other important changes, I had prepared myself mentally for a long haul, so to speak, just in case changes and improvements took longer than I had anticipated or expected. This way, I would not get discourage or disappointed if progress was slow. The important thing however — as it turned out in the end — was not how fast I could possibly be cured, but that, initially, I had created and put in to place my necessary *Daily Healthcare Plan*, routine, and other effective tools and things that were needed for me to heal myself of depression and bipolar disorder illness — which I believe helped to speed up the recovery and healing process.

Looking even closer into how the healing and cure took place, I noticed that it was my *brain* or *mind* that took the initiative and lead in finding and orchestrating a cure for my depression and bipolar disorder illness. I believe the reason why it did this, is because it was the primary organ or thing that was being negatively affected and attacked by the disease. Interestingly, in addition to finding a way to heal itself, my mind also had to find a way to cure my ailing *heart* too. Why? Because the heart (the seat of human emotion), which is closely connected and linked to the brain, was also, being negatively affected by my illness too. This leads me to believe that bipolar disorder is not just a mental illness alone, but rather, that it is both a *mental* and *emotional* disease combined. Whatever the case, I find it to be an absolutely fascinating subject!

When you think about it, in order for positive changes to occur or take place within my body, in regard to potentially healing and curing my depression and bipolar disorder illness, my *mind*, had to be organized first. Why? One of the reasons why, is because our brain or mind controls and drives our body and everything that we do.

How the human mind works is truly amazing! Personally, I believe that when it came to finding a remedy and cure for my depression and bipolar disorder illness, that, initially, from the very beginning (before all of the healing began), that my mind knew exactly what it would take to heal and restore itself. But not only this, it also led me, step by step, through the progressive healing process. What is even more amazing, is that, even though my mind possibly knew in advance, every individual step that I had to take or go through to eventually become healthy and well again (mentally and emotionally), it didn't reveal it to me all at once, but instead, it revealed it on a need to know basis, one step at a time, as I was going through them. Perhaps, so that I wouldn't become too overwhelmed with too much information, or so that I could focus on just one step or thing at a time. What tremendous organization! This leads me to echo the same sentiments of King David, who, in the Bible, said of God, concerning the way that He designed and made the human body: "I praise you [God] because in an awe-inspiring way I am wonderfully made. Your works are wonderful, I know this very well." (Psalms 139:14). Isn't this the truth! For the more that we learn about the human body, the more we find ourselves awed by the unmatchable wisdom that is shown in God's creation!

Nevertheless, in spite of the fact that the human body is amazing—that it has both the power and ability to strengthen, heal, and repair itself; sometimes, there are things that we personally have to do to encourage and help it along in the process. For example, by supplying it with the necessary nutrients, tools, therapy, exercise, rest, and other important things that it needs to make needed repairs, to recover, to grow stronger, etc. But also, we have to work along with it, instead of against it. This way recovery and repairs can perhaps take place sooner, so that we can possibly have a speedy recovery. In response, you might say: "This is all good, fine, and dandy but, sometimes, I simply don't know what to do to help my body, because I don't know what it needs or why I am sick." This is true. However, this is where physicians and hospitals can be of aid, for they often possess the knowledge, medicines, and tools that can perhaps help treat whatever is ailing us.

Unfortunately though, as much as physicians, doctors, and the scientific community, etc., have come to discover, learn, and know about the human body over the years, reality tells us that there still remain diseases such as cancers and things that they are still working hard on to understand, so that they can more effectively treat, or even possibly cure them. The same is true regarding mental illnesses too, such as clinical depression, bipolar disorder, and so forth. Although a lot has been discovered, there is yet a lot to be learned, for the pathway to finding a cure for these things has simply puzzled and eluded them. That is why, in treating my depression and bipolar disorder, I eventually, personally, decided to step in and take a different path, by helping and treating myself, rather than looking to or depending on someone else, such as doctors, and psychiatrists, etc., for help. Fortunately, for me, in the end, it worked out to my great benefit, for I am now completely healed and cured of my depression and bipolar disorder illness, something that I believe would not have happened, hadn't I done what I did.[53]

Yes, I cured myself of depression and bipolar disorder. It's not necessarily that I am smarter than doctors, psychiatrists, or scientists, etc. Perhaps, it's just because I was in a much better position than they were, in that, I had the advantage of personally seeing and working with the disease *firsthand*. In other words, because I had bipolar disorder and I lived with it daily, I had a greater perspective or advantage point, in that, I got to see and experience firsthand how the disease works and affects its victims, and also discover what works to help. And because, by nature, I have a highly inquiring, analytic, and exploratory mind, it therefore put me in a good position to find a workable remedy and cure.

Yes, by nature, apparently, I was born or equipped with a problem-solving mind. To give you an example of this: In the past, I used to work for one of the largest and top pacemaker and defibrillator companies in the world. I worked on the Material Review Board. Unfortunately, at that time, the company was faced with a serious problem or dilemma that they needed to immediately resolve and fix. The problem was that eight cardiac patients or customers who had our company's Implantable Cardioverter Defibrillator (ICD) implanted in them, died, due to product failures. As a result, the Food and Drug Administration (FDA) shut us down, and our company was not allowed to build and sell any more of that particular defibrillator product line until the problem was completely resolved and fixed. In addition to this, in the event that if and when the problem did get fixed, our company was then also required at that time to prove to both the FDA and the Medicines and Healthcare products Regulatory Agency (MHRA) that our product is now perfectly safe and that it no longer poses any

---

[53] Disclaimer: I am not suggesting or encouraging others to do what I did in working to cure myself of depression and bipolar disorder. Readers are advised to consult their own doctors, psychiatrists, or other qualified mental health professionals regarding the treatment of medical conditions such as depression and bipolar disorder.

dangerous health risks. Yes, it was an extremely huge deal, to say the least!

To make a long story short, I was given the job to solve and fix this serious problem. Interestingly, before I was given this important responsibility, many others, including top-level engineers and managers had tried to remedy or resolve the situation, but without success. Because of the sheer difficulty of the project and the work involved, not one of them could resolve and complete it. Fact is, for about 4 years (prior to me receiving the project), this project was passed on from one person to another. However, no one was able to solve and correct the problem, that is, until I was given the project.

At the time that I took over this huge FDA driven project, my department manager, who was also an electronic engineer by profession, and highly knowledgeable and experienced, had been working on the difficult assignment himself; and he was having an extremely difficult time getting it done. While working on the project, he had even personally applied for and was granted thirteen, separate, time extensions, by upper management. But, now, they had finally grown impatient with him for his lack of progress and his failure to get the project resolved and completed, and they were not going to allow him anymore extensions.

To my surprise, shortly after I received the FDA driven project, I recognized that others who had the project prior to me, had been going in the wrong direction with it! Once I personally figured this important part out and discovered how to proceed with the project, etc., I was able to both complete it and get it approved by the FDA and MHRA, all within the matter of the short time span of about one to two months. In response, my department manager, his boss, and upper management were absolutely ecstatic and thrilled! They were so happy that this huge and difficult project was finally completed! Because now our company was out of the woods with the FDA. But also, they could finally start building their defibrillator product line once again, without harm or threat to future customers!

Upon completion of the job, my manager, personally and privately thanked and praised me for taking on and completing the important FDA driven project, which apparently ended up saving his job. Confiding in me, he told me that upper management had given him a final deadline, and that they had even seriously threatened to fire him if the project wasn't completed on time. Because, even though I was personally working on the project, he as my manager was still the one that was responsible for it. What's interesting and good is that I completed the project about a month before his deadline had passed.

One of the electronic engineers in my department and work group, who was highly impressed by what I had did and accomplished, in regard to the complexity and difficulty of the work assignment and the timely completion of this extremely important FDA driven project, said to me: "Wow, Chuck, what you did was amazing! I wish I was you when it comes to work performance review time! You're going to get a big promotion and pay raise!"

After this, my department managers placed me in the position to head all future projects in the manufacturing process—to make sure that everything goes smoothly and that they, not only get done, but also that they are completed in a timely manner.

The above is just one example of problem-solving that I have tackled and solved in life. There are many more that I could go on to relate.

Today, although, I still have a problem-solving mind and I would like to take full credit for the cure for my depression and bipolar disorder, I simply cannot, because, in essence, I believe that it was essentially my God-given brain that cured me of my mental illness. How? It was by means of its leadings and directing—it walking me through, and up and out of the clutches of depression and bipolar disorder. In other words, my brain instinctively knew the pathway to a cure for my illness. I just had to acquiescence, by intuitively listening to and following its lead.

Yes, thanks to God, I was able to tap into my innate abilities, and also the natural healing properties and powers of the human mind and body, which were required to cure myself of depression and bipolar disorder illness.

Interestingly, without realizing it (during the time it was happening), it appears that when I was going through the 15 step healing process, that I (unconsciously) gave my mind and body a complete overhaul or renovation. I think the reason why, is because my mind, in particular, wanted to ensure that I won't ever become mentally ill again. And also, perhaps to ensure or make certain that things within me, both now and in the future, function and work more effectively than they did in the past—thereby making me more robust and stronger in many ways. I guess you could say that my depression and bipolar disorder, and the subsequent healing stages that I went through, ended up bringing out the very best in me!

I know that there will most likely be critics and those who scoff at the ideal of self-diagnoses and treatment, but I simply had no other choice, because I had grown tired of suffering and allowing the overwhelming and overpowering, painful disease of bipolar disorder and depression destroy and control me and my life.

Yes, depression and bipolar disorder were pretty mean, cruel, and detrimental to me in many ways—and for many years. But that's okay. Because, in the end, even though they were like relentless, overpowering, strong bullies, I ended up having the last laugh, so to speak. Because I was able to figure them out and overcome and defeat them! How? It was primarily by outthinking them—by thinking and working my way out of my mental illness. I guess you could say that my bad habit of over-thinking things finally came in handy—at least, in regard to this vitally important matter! This goes to show that some of the so called negative or bad traits that we personally possess — that often pose and create problems for us — can also be utilized for good too, that is, when we use and direct them in positive and constructive ways.

Another thing that I believe helped me in finding a cure for my depression and bipolar disorder illness, is something concerning myself, that I was born with—which is, an *innate gift or ability* that I wasn't aware that I possessed—that is, until the discovery of it in the year 2001. What was it? It turns out that I have a high level of

"Spatial intelligence."[54] They said that it is: *"Off the charts!"* They also said that my intelligence level is found in just one percent of the population, and that I am the kind of person that makes changes and a difference in the world for the good and the betterment of mankind. Apparently, these are things that were discovered and revealed by means of extensive testing that I was being put through at a professional IQ testing facility at that particular time in my life—when I was seeking an employment career change.

At the time of the diagnosis and revealing, I was not as impressed as others were with the finding that I have an extremely high level of spatial intelligence. For one, at that time, I did not know exactly what spatial intelligence was. Another thing, is that, I felt that it was most likely just a useless, innate ability and gift to have. The reason why, is because, at that time (at least, as far as I was concerned) it didn't seem to me that spatial intelligence would have any practical value or use in the real world. However, today, now that I look back and see how this innate ability was highly instrumental in helping me to find a pathway and cure for my depression and bipolar disorder illness, I have a whole new understanding and appreciation for it!

Nevertheless, in spite of possessing a high level of spatial intelligence, and as good as it may be to have certain knowledge, abilities, talents, and so forth, or even the personal *Daily Healthcare Plan*, routine, and things that I eventually put in to place (that I believed could possibly help heal me of my mental illness), I discovered that there was something that was perhaps even greater and more powerful than these, that I also needed to possess, to overcome and defeat depression and bipolar disorder. What was it, you might ask? It was the internal desire, willpower, and strength to *fight back*. Yes, fight back! Why? Because the enemies — depression and bipolar disorder — that were holding my mind and moods captive, were not going to voluntarily relinquish their hold on me or be easily defeated.

---

[54] Spatial intelligence is a combination of multiple intelligences that deals with spatial judgment and the ability to see or visualize with the mind's eye.

But, not only this, in addition to the *internal* struggles of depression and bipolar that I was dealing with from within myself, to make matters even harder and worse for me, I also had *external* things that I had to put up with and contend with too, such as coping and dealing with a non-supportive, difficult environment (which was the bad, past environment that I was in), along with other troubling and trying things. However, despite whatever negative and challenging things that I was going through at the time, and no matter how hard and difficult they were or had become, I was determined that I was not going to let these things or anything else for that matter, distract, discourage, or stop me from taking care of myself, and doing the necessary things that I needed to do to become mentally healthy again. Yes, this is where having strong determination and the *spirit of a fighter* came in handy!

I am so happy that I've discovered within myself, how much power and control that I actually have over my own mind and body, especially over my mental and emotional health. That I have the power and ability to control and improve, not only my thinking, feelings, and emotions, etc., but also, to heal myself of depression and bipolar disorder illness. True, although I wish that I would have discovered this much sooner in my life, I am absolutely excited and thrilled that I finally figured and worked all of these things out. But also, in addition to this, I'm extremely grateful that I also know what I need to do from now on and going forward, to maintain good, overall health, and that I have the positive mind frame, desire, determination, and personal drive to carry it out and apply it in my life.

Yes, having strong willpower, personal drive, and the *spirit of a fighter* cannot be overemphasized. Because, without it, I believe that I would not have been able to successfully conquer and defeat the enemies—depression and bipolar disorder illness. Interestingly, prior to being cured of my mental illness, I had come to discover or realize that if I wanted to recover, heal, and grow healthy mentally and emotionally, that, although others could encourage and help in certain ways, that, for the most part, it was all on or up to me personally to do it. No one else could do it for me. Because battling depression and bipolar disorder is a personal, *inner* struggle and battle that takes place from *within* the individual—a battle that takes place within the mind, heart, and spirit.

Yes, it takes a lot of personal strength and willpower to fight the overpowering and overwhelming strong forces of depression and bipolar disorder—to battle and resist them, instead of allowing them to control and pull you mentally and emotionally downwards— especially, when you are undergoing depressive episodes associated with bipolar. However, despite this, and the enormity of the gravity and difficulty of the tasks at hand, I decided to battle and fight it— to force myself to go in the opposite direction that the illness was pulling and forcing my thinking, feelings, emotions, and moods to go. How? By forcing my mind and moods to be positive, upbeat, joyful, happy, and at peace, instead of being down and depressed.

Interestingly, in the past, prior to being cured of depression and bipolar disorder illness, I believed that a person had no control over the strong forces of bipolar disorder illness, in particular, the dark moods that are associated with depressive episodes. I felt that the victim or patient simply had no choice but to let them run their disruptive and painful course. I even stated this in my previously released book *"Bipolar Disorder, A Patient's Story."* However, now, through further trial and personal experiences, I've come to discover within myself (while traveling on the pathway towards being healed and cured of depression and bipolar disorder) that this thinking and belief is wrong. That it is better to resist and fight back—to battle the effects of the disease, rather than allow them to control you, especially, the depressive phases that were causing my mind and moods to gravitate towards and sink into deep depression—or what I call "The pit of misery and despair."

But, that's not all. Along with battling and fighting the strong gravitational pull and tendency to be drawn into depression and dark moods, I also had to literally direct and force my mind, thoughts, feelings, and actions to go against the grain, so to speak, by pushing them in the opposite direction to where the disease was pulling me. This required that I daily feed my mind and heart heavy doses of positive, uplifting, and encouraging things, etc.,—things that generated good thoughts, feelings, and moods in me. True, this internal struggle and tug of war was an extremely challenging and difficult thing to personally go through. However, the good thing is, it eventually became easier the more that I applied myself, and with the passage of time.

Yes, this is where having strong willpower, inner drive, and self-motivation comes in handy! In regard to this, at this time, I would like to say that, personally, I believe that no one can actually cure another person of their depression or bipolar disorder illness—not their spouse, not family, nor friends, not doctors or psychiatrists, not even prescribed medications, etc. It is only we, the patient or victim of the disorder that can do it. True, others can provide encouragement and support but, we, the patient or victim of the illness is the one that has to take the initiative. And then, thereafter, to follow through to do whatever we can and have to, in order to mentally and emotionally pull ourselves up and out of our depression and bipolar disorder. No one can do it for us. The encouraging and wonderful thing, is that, we, as individuals, can and have both the ability and power to do it, as my personal experience, and inspiring, true story clearly proves![55]

One thing that was very helpful to me during the extraordinary, metamorphic changes that I was going through, in regard to reversing my depression and bipolar disorder illness, and in improving my health and well-being, was understanding that change does not happen quickly or occur overnight. But rather, it takes time. The key was for me to not get discouraged or give up, but to keep consistently pressing ever forward in doing the necessary things — such as following my personal, *Healthcare Plan*, routine, and things that I had put in to place—that I felt were needed to improve my mental health. For by regularly doing these things, I sincerely believed that, in time, I would eventually start to reap and see the good results from my persistence and hard work.

---

[55] Disclaimer: Although I was able to heal and cure myself of depression and bipolar disorder on my own. I do not recommend that anyone else try to do this. But rather, you should consult with your Doctor, Psychiatrist, or other medical health professionals as to what is right and best for you.

When I think about it, it is truly remarkable how my mind figured out how to completely heal itself and also my heart of depression and bipolar disorder illness. However, that was the easy part. The hardest thing was the application—applying the knowledge that my mind was providing me with—by consistently doing the positive and healthy things that my healing mind was telling (not literally of course), and leading me to do, which can be very difficult to do when you're feeling completely down and drained from depression. Fortunately, in time, I was able to muster up the inner strength, determination, and drive, to not only comply, but also, to carry it through to its completion. One thing that helped me during difficult times was focusing on the potential future outcome that it could possibly lead to—that of being cured of depression and bipolar disorder illness, rather than thinking about and dwelling on how hard things were at the time, or the misery and pain that I was going through on a particular day. The important thing was for me not to get discouraged and give up in doing what was good and healthy for me when I didn't see immediate results, which I'm glad that I did not do.

Today, even though I have been completely healed and cured of my depression and bipolar disorder illness, going forward, I am determined to continue to work to improve and protect my overall health, especially, my mental and emotional health.

Life in the Real World

Sometime later, after I was completely healed and cured of depression and bipolar disorder illness, there was an occasional day, here and there, when I was not feeling as up emotionally, as I normally am. At first, I was a little concerned by it, but then, I had to tell myself *"This is perfectly okay. That I'm going to have a bad day every now and then. Everybody does! This is simply nothing more or other than being human. It doesn't mean that you are losing ground or reverting back to your old self. So, keep your head up and keep moving forward."* As it turned out, I was right, because the next day, and many days afterwards, I was perfectly fine!

Truth is, in this life, none of us (no matter who we are or where we come from), will ever be completely trouble and problem free. Nor can we navigate through life untouched, avoiding any and everything that might cause negative side effects, or potential problems down the line. Unfortunately, the structure or anatomy of imperfect, human life in general, is one that presents random challenges and obstacles that we have to go through (some more difficult than others), including those that cause hardship and pain—things that we often have to individually face. However, the encouraging thing is that we can cope and get through them, as other people have, who have successfully gone through similar things.

An interesting thing, is that, personally, I often learn and benefit more from my mistakes, weaknesses, failures, and the negative things that happen to me, than I do from anything else. For example, in regard to my having depression and bipolar disorder illness—in the end, they turned out to be an asset and good thing, rather than something completely negative or bad. For, not only, did I personally benefit from them, by learning a lot about myself, life in general, and other important things, but also, I was able to use the valuable lessons and experience that I've gained from going through them to encourage and help others too, especially those who are undergoing the same health issues or problems that I was. It's not that I personally prefer to have bad or negative things happen to me, because I don't. However, when they do happen to occur, often, in the end, I wind up using these negative things in positive ways to help to improve myself and my life for the better, in some form or way. This is a good example to show that, not everything negative that we go through or that happens to us in life is necessarily an ugly or bad thing. On the contrary, they can turn out to be a valuable, good, and beneficial thing!

There is an old adage or saying that goes: "You can't change the past." However, I beg to differ, because I did! How? By reversing the damage that the past did to me and my health (mentally and emotionally). And now that I am totally cured of my mental illness and healthy, going forward, I intend on protecting and taking care of myself, from now on, and far into the future.

Taking Care of Your Future Health

Yes, now that I have been totally healed and cured of my depression and bipolar disorder illness, I want to make sure that I stay that way, by continuing to take good care of my health, especially, my mental and emotional health. However, there have been some disturbing developments that have surfaced in recent years in the world that could pose some possible challenges going forward, not for me only, but for people in general. The thing that I'm referring to is troubling world problems and conditions, including the social climate and attitudes of people that were affected by the Covid-19 (Coronavirus disease) pandemic, and other world shaking events that have risen since then, such as the tragedy that happened to Mr. George Floyd, and also the Russia / Ukraine war, and so forth.

Unfortunately, in noting just the results of the Covid-19 pandemic alone, and some of the negative side effects and lingering aftermath that the menacing virus, along with the succeeding variants of the disease, imposed on the general public's mental and emotional health; it is something of interest that is worth mentioning or taking note of.

As things turned out, because of the distresses, and imposed hardships, and so forth, that the Covid-19 pandemic brought upon the human race—with its subsequent restrictions, lockdowns, food shortages, etc—it now seems to appear that these things had a traumatic effect on people's mental and emotional health—to say the least. Today, since the emergence of Covid-19, I've noticed that there are more people than ever that suffer from anxiety, worries, and depression, than in the past. There is no denying it. Not only is it etched on their faces, but also, you can see it in their actions and in their dealings with others. Fact is, so many people have become distressed, downhearted, and depressed, that it is almost as though depression has become a pandemic in itself!

As it turned out, many people had an extremely difficult time trying to cope with and get through it all—trying to find or reassemble some type of happiness or normality in their life.

Being forced to stay at home during Covid-19 lockdowns and trying to find some type of relief, comfort, and joy in their lives, many turned to alcohol, which no doubt will give rise to future cases of alcoholism. Others succumbed to overeating (some perhaps even gorging themselves on food), and thereby, gaining a lot of weight as a result. Whatever the case, it's interesting in observing what humans might resort to that temporarily makes them feel better; or that they feel will help them to cope, get through, and survive difficult, challenging, and stressful times. Unfortunately, in regards to the latter situation mentioned above, personally, I have never in my life seen so many obese Americans, which, most likely, is going to have negative repercussions on their future health, giving rise to possible cases of diabetes and other serious health issues, if they don't try to do something immediately to reverse it.[56]

Upon further examination of some of the negative effects that Covid-19 had on people's mental and emotional health in the United States, I've noticed, in particular, in the surrounding area where I live, that Covid has resulted in creating a somewhat callas, rude, high-strung, impatient, short-tempered, angry, and selfish type of people in general—people that have become extremely rude and overly aggressive with one another. This is readily apparent in people's attitudes and actions, in their everyday dealings with one another—at grocery stores, shops, and various businesses, etc., but, especially, on the roads and highways, where drivers are racing down the road, far exceeding speed limits, aggressively tailgating vehicles in front of them, practically pushing other drivers off the road, in order to get to where they are going. I've never seen anything like this before! In some instances, it seems like the world has gone mad! And who knows what all of this may escalate or lead to in the days, months, and years to come.

---

[56] Note: I'm not judging or condemning people for their chosen life styles. For people have the right to choose for themselves what they want to do, and how they want to live. I'm just reporting on how the distresses of the Covid-19 pandemic affected people in general.

Unfortunately, all of this is showing that the ever challenging, trying circumstances, situations, and stressors of the Covid-19 years have and are continuing to take their mental and emotional toll on many, which no doubt will give rise to related mental health issues in the near future. However, along with this, it no doubt is going to present a challenge to the public in general, going forward, in having to face and deal with the negative and overly aggressive social climate and attitudes that Covid-19 produced. And this is just some of the effects of Covid-19. Not to mention additional stressors and other problems that the world is currently facing.

In light of the foregoing examples, and what is to possibly come in the days, months, and years to come, in regards to future problems, issues, and stressors that we (the human race) may be presented with; it is all the more important for us to take good care of our personal, mental and emotional health, *now,* so that we can possibly ward off any possible issues or problems that might have perhaps resulted to us personally down the line (in the future), hadn't we taken the necessary steps, *now*, towards safeguarding and taking care of our overall health and well-being, especially, our mental and emotional health. Personally, this is something that I intend on continuing to do. Because, what we do with our lives now (during the present time), in regards to protecting and working to improve our health and well-being, can possibly make a big difference in how things turn out for us in the future.

Fortunately, for me, with the positive changes, improvements, strengthening, and fortifications that I have made to myself, my life, and health — which had taken place along the road to recovery and being healed and cured of my depression and bipolar disorder — it has better equipped me to be able to function, progress, and succeed in coping with the many difficult and challenging situations and circumstances of life now. What an amazing turnaround I have made! No doubt this incredible transformation that I have made will go on to continue to help me in future years to come!

Although it was not a pleasurable thing to have to cope and deal with depression and bipolar disorder illness, in looking back, I would have to say that walking myself through and out of depression and bipolar disorder was the most amazing, unforgettable journey and experience that I have ever had! But also, in addition to this, I am very thrilled and appreciative that I could do something to contribute to the advancements of health and science, by finding a cure for my mental illness. Interestingly, when you think about it, we, as humans, never truly know what tomorrow will bring—in regards to ourselves, the world, and others. Personally, up until the time that it actually happened, I never would have thought or even imagined in my entire life that I would be the one to go on to find a cure for a major illness—bipolar disorder. But I guess this is one of the things that makes life so incredibly wonderful and beautiful— when a person like me, an everyday, ordinary citizen, winds up doing something that is totally unexpected, truly remarkable, and useful—something that is extremely beneficial, not only to myself, but that could also go on to inspire and encourage so many other people too! What an amazing turnaround I have made!

Some people say that sometimes it is hard to tell, from an outward appearance alone, as to whether an individual suffers from mental illness or depression. Because, unlike other illnesses that often have specific signs or symptoms that show up on the outside of a person when they are sick (outward signs indicating that they are ill)—mental illness or depression on the other hand, is not always visibly apparent or recognizable in a person, in that, it does not necessary show up on the outside of the individual. However, I believe otherwise. Personally, I can often see mental illness reflected in a person, in particular, in their eyes. For example, in regard to myself, when I look at the before and after photos of myself, that show what I looked like when I had depression and bipolar disorder in the past; compared to current photos of myself today (now that I have been cured), I notice that in my past photos, that my eyes look dull, lifeless, and sad. Whereas, in my more recent photos, my eyes shine, are full of energy, life, and joy. What a huge turnaround and difference being cured of my illness has made!

In view of the foregoing, now that I am totally cured of bipolar disorder, I would like to change or revise something that I stated in my previously released book *"Bipolar Disorder, A Patient's Story."* In Chapter #1, on page 8, I made the false statement that bipolar disorder is *not* curable. Although this was something that I sincerely believed back then—during the time I was writing my book. One reason why I believed this was true, was, because, at that time (that is, up until the time that I cured myself of bipolar disorder), in the medical community and elsewhere, according to psychiatrists, doctors, psychologists, mental health organizations, professionals, experts, specialists, etc., (throughout the entire world), there was no known cure for bipolar disorder. For according to them, bipolar disorder is a chronic, incurable, lifelong condition. However, look at me now! I proved all of them to be wrong. For I am now 100%, completely healed of my mental illness! What an amazing turnaround I have made in my mental health! For this reason, today, I completely change my previous thought and held belief that bipolar disorder is *not* curable, especially, in light of my being totally healed and cured of my mental illness. Now, today, I am happy to say that this erroneous, false belief and statement that bipolar disorder is *not* curable, can now be updated and changed to read: "Bipolar Disorder *is* curable!" This is both exciting and wonderful news—to say the least!

Another thing in my book *Bipolar Disorder, A Patient's Story* that I would like to change, is my theory about what it was that caused my bipolar disorder. In my previous book, I stated that I believe that it was *environment alone,* that caused my bipolar disorder.[57] However, now, after further, personal examination of my life and experiences, and other things associated with my mental illness — at considerable length and depth — I now believe that, although *environment* was the *primary* cause of my illness, I have come to personally discover and believe that there were also other factors and things that were involved as well. For a complete explanation of this *new theory* of mine, please see the information "Cause of Bipolar Disorder," in the Appendix, on pages 270-284.

---

[57] "Environment," meaning: All of the external factors that have a formative influence on a person's physical, mental, emotional, and moral development. The environments that I'm referring to are *long-term environments*—those that we spend a considerable amount of time in, such as at school, at work, or in our neighborhood, etc.

In closing, I would like to reemphasize that, just because a person suffers from anxiety, depression, or bipolar disorder, or any other mental illness, it does not make them a bad person. These things can happen to anyone—no matter who they are or where they happen to come from. However, I would also like to add—that if we (victims of mental illness) can personally find ways to encourage and bring comfort and relief to ourselves and others (even if it is in just small ways), it's a good thing. Fortunately, I just happened to find a cure for my mental illness. And hopefully my personal story can be an encouragement and inspiration to others, to keep hope alive, that perhaps someday, they too may be cured of their mental illness too!

Today and going forward, I have a personal, simple approach to good health and life. My motto is: "Be easygoing. Be nonjudgmental. Stay focused on good, positive, uplifting, peaceful, and beautiful things. And lastly, don't let anyone or anything hinder your personal, positive development and growth." Yes, even if society, the world, or things around me are completely falling apart, I, for my part, am determined to personally keep it together, and remain individually solid in all respects—physically, mentally, emotionally, and spiritually.

Because I suffered from depression and bipolar disorder for so many years (prior to being cured), some might reason or say that in the process I lost a lot of time in my life. However, to me, personally, it's all about perspectives or how you look at things. True, some fellow sufferers of mental illness might feel this way about the years they have personally lost due to their illness. However, my belief or thought is: "Better is the outcome of a matter, than its beginning." How true this is in my case, for, although, it was difficult going through past, stormy days and times of darkness, today, now that I have been completely healed and cured of depression and bipolar disorder illness, I am enjoying every moment and having the time of my life!

True, the pain and suffering that I went through during the years that I suffered from depression and bipolar disorder was extremely difficult and tuff on me—to say the least. However, in the end, having gone through all of the things that I did, I would have to say that they wound up bringing out the very best in me. For my illness triggered and put in to place my 15 step process of recovery and healing that gradually made me more solid and complete in so many ways—things that I believe would not have happened, hadn't I gone through what I did. Thanks to all of this, I am living and experiencing a full, peaceful, happy, and highly productive life—at a level and degree that perhaps I would never have ever experienced, hadn't I gone through the things that I did.

Yes, today, unlike the past (when I was suffering from the negative effects of depression and bipolar disorder), my mind, heart, and soul now feel great! So much so, that I even composed a happy little song about it, containing both music and lyrics that I fully wrote/composed, performed, and produced on my own. Although simplistic in nature, it's a beautiful little song that expresses the enormous amount of peace, joy, and happiness that I now feel in my heart, mind, and soul. The song is all original. The title of my song is: *"I'm Walkin In Paradise."* Maybe someday, I'll release it to the public, so that others can hear and enjoy it too. But, for now, my dear friends—peace be with you. And may God bless!

Appendix

BIPOLAR DISORDER

U nfortunately, in the year 2010-11, I was diagnosed with bipolar disorder. I was 54 years old at the time. What is bipolar disorder? Bipolar disorder, formerly known as "Manic Depression," is clinical depression, a mental illness. This type of depression is much different and more severe than the ordinary, common or garden variety depression, the regular, normal ups and downs of life.

One prominent characteristic or feature of bipolar disorder is that it involves two distinct and separate phases of extreme mood swings that alternate between lengthy episodes of an overwhelming sad state of depressive lows, to manic highs. In other words, a person with bipolar experiences severe mood swings that go from depressive lows, to euphoric highs.

An interesting fact to note is that the mood swings associated with Bipolar are not like a light switch that quickly turns on, and then off again. These phases or episodes may last for up to weeks, or even months at a time.

As respects bipolar disorder, there are two main types. They are: "Bipolar I," and "Bipolar II." Both are mental illnesses. However, it is important to note that, although patients with Bipolar I, and

Bipolar II experience mood swings, there is somewhat of a slight difference between the two groups or categories as noted below:

Bipolar I: The symptoms of Bipolar I, consists of a sequential cycling that alternates between two severe mood swings, both low and high. They are: (1) the "Depressive Episode," and (2) the "Mania Episode," with at least one episode of full-blown mania in a person's lifetime. Mania meaning: Euphoric or great excitement, marked by hyperactivity.

Bipolar II: This is similar to Bipolar I. And yet, it is somewhat different. Its symptoms include a vacillating or alternating between two separate and different mood swings, which are: (1) the "Depressive Phase," and (2) the "Hypomanic Phase," that never erupts into or reaches full-blown mania, which is more severe.

Bipolar Depressive Phase

Speaking from experience, I can honestly say that bipolar disorder is one of the worst, if not the most difficult and painful things to live with in life. Often, in my case (prior to being cured), the bipolar *depressive phase* produced an extremely sad and hopeless feeling, type of condition or state—a sort of deep and gnawing, emotionally painful sadness, that consumed, overwhelmed, and ate at my soul. At times, it was so extremely anguishing, distressing, miserable, and intense, that it made me groan, and even weep and cry. During this time, I felt like my heart was shattered or broken, or like I was mourning the death of a loved one, but only ten times worse! Also, in addition to being mentally and emotionally painful, the depressive phase can also be physically and mentally draining too, so much so, that you don't even have the energy, desire, or strength to go anywhere or to do anything. Often, all you want to do is lie down and sleep.

Along with producing agonizing and tormenting internal pain, and mental and physical fatigue, bipolar disorder can also kill your emotions, and also your will or desire to do things, even things that you may have thoroughly enjoyed in the past. It can leave you feeling empty and lifeless inside, making your heart insensitive, unresponsive, or non-expressive to natural feelings such as love and joy that normal, healthy people regularly have and show. At times, it can be so overwhelming that it's virtually impossible to even muster up a smile.

Due to the unrelentingly sad and overwhelming degree of mental and emotional pain that is often associated with bipolar disorder, it can cause feelings of hopelessness, that perhaps your heart will never ever feel true joy and happiness again. You look for comfort and seek relief, but these things seem to have vanished from off the face of the earth. At times, things can get so bad! that you loathe your life, and you wish that you had never been born. You feel like the man of ancient times in the Bible, named, Job, who, because of the severity of his unceasing misery, pain, and sufferings, cursed the day he was born.—Job 3:1-26.

Speaking from experience, at times, it feels like the only way for the sufferer to gain possible relief from the misery and pain would be to just lie down and die, which is something that I often prayed and hoped for. It's not that I would have actually killed myself (although at times the thought did enter and then quickly leave my mind); it's just that I didn't want to live like that anymore, with all of the internal suffering and pain. Fortunately, my will to live for both me, and my family, and also my love, hope, and faith in God was stronger than taking the so-called easy way out.

What about medications? Can they help? Yes, prescribed medications can be helpful in treating bipolar disorder. But, truth is, they cannot heal you, nor can they bring back the past (when you were perhaps healthy)—making you healthy and "normal" again. For the most part, they often mask the pain, leaving you feeling numb. I know that this might seem bad; however, this can be better than not receiving any help at all.

Because bipolar disorder can be so painful and difficult to personally cope and deal with, there are times when you need people to show you that they care—those who are willing to sympathize with you and comfort you during your time of need. But, sad to say, many times you don't get the understanding and support that you desire but, instead, people often avoid you, or treat you unsympathetically. What's surprising is that, I can honestly say that I was not angry or upset with them for acting or behaving this way, because, unless they themselves have experienced what it's like to be bipolar, how are they to really know and understand what you are actually going through. Also, due to bad publicity and the stigma that's often attached to bipolar disorder, many are simply misinformed. Thankfully, in my case, I had a very loving and supportive family, which helped tremendously!

Bipolar Mania Phase

In addition to the bipolar *depressive* phase, there is also the *manic* phase, which is the flipside of things, at the opposite end of the bipolar spectrum. Although, with 'Bipolar II' the hypomanic stage never reaches full-blown mania, as it does with 'Bipolar I', where the manic phase can cause a euphoric, excited and energetic state that can foster excessive physical activity, and even make one feel superhuman.

During the manic phase, a person seldom needs rest and sleep, because their mind and energy level is on maximum overload, being pumped up and on the constant go! Often, when other "normal" people are sleeping, a person in manic phase might be up all night working on a project, or be on their hands and knees cleaning every inch of the house with a toothbrush, so to speak. Interestingly, this euphoric phase can go on for days, and even weeks at a time.

One time, when I was undergoing a manic episode, I painted and redecorated — pretty much non-stop — the entire interior of our huge, three story, rental home, which at the time my wife and I were sharing with our daughter and her children. The house had six bedrooms, three full size bathrooms, a large kitchen with seating area, a formal dining room, and a big family or entertainment room, and more.

As it turned out, in the end, this gigantic painting project wound up costing me a pretty penny (a small fortune). Because, even though we didn't own the property, I decided to personally pay for all of the paint myself. The reason why, is because, knowing the home owners or landlords thinking or mentality, I knew that if we were to request that the interior of the house be painted, that they would squawk in complaint, and refuse to pay for the paint and labor costs of having to contract a professional painter to do it. But even though this was the case, I still desired to have it done. Sure, the cost and work that I did was a lot; however, in the long run it paid off. For putting a nice, fresh coat of paint on the walls, along with adding a little colorful and decorative décor, enhanced our home's dull appearance, thereby providing a more uplifting environment for me and my family to live in. But most importantly, it gave me something to burn all of my dynamic, manic energy on.

The thing that was most interesting about this large painting and redecorating project, is that I worked hard at it for several days; nonstop, with very little to no rest at all, until it was completely finished. And then, after this was done, I went on to work on another big project.

The crazy thing, is that, when it comes to both the *manic* and *depressive* stages of bipolar, if I could have chosen which one I would've preferred, I would have chosen to be in the manic phase all of the time, because it makes you feel great, rather than having to cope and deal with the painful depressive phase. However, as good as this might seem, in reality, this too — the manic, up and energetic phase of bipolar — is unnatural and abnormal behavior for a person.

Racing Thoughts

Another notable feature or symptom that comes with manic depression, is that, one's mind often races out of control. While normal, healthy thinking usually consists of moderately paced, deliberate, and structured channeled thoughts that follow a certain or particular directed path. With bipolar patients it is often different. For example, in my case, I often found that my mind rapidly changed from one idea or thought to the next. This made it very hard to focus and concentrate on things, and also to listen to other people when they were speaking, etc. And then, there were times when my mind was racing so nonstop and fast that I couldn't shut it down, not even to get needed rest during bedtime. Luckily, if it wasn't for sleep inducing medications that are used to combat this, there were nights when I think I wouldn't have gotten any sleep at all.

Hypersensitivity to Sound and Light

Another symptom of bipolar disorder, is that, one's ears can be overly sensitive to noise. Often, the tiniest, little sounds can be amplified many times over—some sounding like gunshot blasts! This can be pretty startling, especially if they occur randomly or are totally unexpected. Personally, when I was at home, I often had to wear ear protection (the heavy duty kind of ear muffs that are normally used at a gun range) to muffle out harmful and annoying noises and sounds. Other times, when I happened to be out and about in public, and was in need of relief, I preferred to wear ear plug inserts, which are not as noticeable.

In addition to the ears being highly sensitive to noise, another annoying thing, is that, bipolar disorder patient's eyes can be extremely sensitive to lights.[58]

Having to deal with hypersensitive ears and eyes can make being in social gatherings and crowds very challenging. For the most part, I tried to avoid them as much as possible, because it was so easy to become aggravated and annoyed. I don't know what causes the human body to react this way, but when you think about it, usually, when a person is ill or sick, their senses (vision, hearing, taste, smell, and touch) often have a heightened sense of feelings and sensitivity—becoming overly sensitive. Whatever the case may be,

---

[58] Although there are additional symptoms, the things listed above were just some of the symptoms of my mental illness. Also, as respects other bipolar patients, they may experience similar symptoms, or they may have some symptoms that are different than mine. The same is true respecting the degrees of intensity. Some patient's symptoms may be more or less intense than others.

some of the symptoms that I mentioned above, which often and unavoidably come with bipolar disorder, seems to confirm that it is in fact an illness.

Bipolar Facts

How many people suffer from bipolar disorder? According to the National Institute of Mental Health (NIMH) report, "An estimated 2.8% of U.S. adults had bipolar disorder in the past year." That's roughly about 9.2 million people within the current United States population alone. Interestingly, in some people, bipolar disorder has been diagnosed early, when they are in their teens.

Providing us with another perspective — as far as the scope and prevalence of bipolar disorder illness is worldwide — the World Health Organization (WHO) reported: "In 2019, 40 million people experienced bipolar disorder."

Who are susceptible to getting bipolar disorder? As it is, bipolar disorder shows no distinction. It does not target any one type of person or group in particular. Both males and females are equally affected, no matter what age, race, ethnic group, or social class they may belong to.

What causes bipolar disorder? Although, there are some thoughts as to what might cause it, as it currently stands, it is unknown.

Is bipolar disorder a genetic disease? Even though some indicators seem to suggest genetics may be involved, it still remains uncertain if this is an actual cause.

Do emotional traumas, or environmental conditions cause bipolar disorder? In some cases, emotional traumas have been known to trigger bipolar disorder. And as far as environmental factor or influence is concerned, it is uncertain as to whether this causes it. However, for some people, I personally believe that environment can and does play a significantly large role in one's developing bipolar disorder, which is a theory I will attempt to prove later in my discussion. But, of course, I will leave it up to you the reader to decide, once you have considered all of the presented evidence and facts.

Is bipolar disorder treatable? Yes. Some of the things that are often used to treat bipolar disorder are: Medications, Psychotherapy, and Electroconvulsive Therapy (ECT), things which I will now briefly discuss.

Prescribed Medications

There are a variety of medicines that have been developed over time to help treat bipolar disorder. There are mood stabilizers, antidepressants, and anti-anxiety medications.

As it stands, bipolar medications, like any other healthcare medications, are prescribed by a doctor. In this case, it is a mental health professional or clinical psychiatrist who prescribes them—based upon the patient's needs and the effectiveness of the drug. It is his or her duty to properly evaluate their patient's medical condition and prescribe medications or treatments based upon individual need, medication effectiveness and success rate, and so forth—things that are not always easy to quickly diagnose and determine. The reason being, is because, it takes time to analyze and properly evaluate a person's symptoms and arrive at proper conclusions, which involves closely monitoring and evaluating their moods, behavior, etc., over an extended period of time. Also, what works for one patient, may not necessarily work for another.

Some of the medications that are used to treat bipolar disorder are: Prozac, Lithium, Seroquel, Zyprexa, Risperdal, and the list goes on.

Are there medication side effects for these drugs? Unfortunately, the answer is yes. What are they? Well, although side effects may vary per medication and individual, some common side effects of these medicines include: nausea, headaches, tiredness, dizziness, drowsiness, and weight gain.

One medication that I was initially given during the early stage of my bipolar illness, made me feel like a zombie. After a couple of weeks I had to stop taking it, and I asked my doctor to prescribe me something different, which he did.

Another medication, named Ambien, which I was taking for sleep, actually caused some very strange effects. Interestingly, this I would not have known, if it weren't for my son, Joseph,[59] and other telltale, visible signs.

My strange experience with Ambien was this: Late one night, about 2:00 am or so, Joseph (who was in his twenties at the time), and I were up watching TV together. Also, in addition to this, I was cooking some food on the stove. Okay, so what's so strange about these things, you might ask? Well, the strange thing was, during the entire time, I was sleepwalking!

The scary thing is, initially, at the time, both Joseph and I didn't know that I was actually sleepwalking. But as time elapsed, he began to notice that something just didn't seem right with me. So, he awoke and alerted his mother (who had gone to bed earlier that night), about the strange situation. He said: "Mom, I think that Dad is sleepwalking!" In the meantime, I had gone back to bed, but in our guess bedroom.

The next day, when I woke up in the morning, I was quickly informed about what had happened to me the night before. However, not before I had discovered something else first. As is so happens, to my utter surprise — when I had awakened that morning — I was surrounded in bed by fudgsicles and ice-cream sandwich rappers! One ice-cream sandwich, which, apparently, I was holding onto for quite some time during my sleep, was even melted in my hand, which made a sticky and gooey mess.

The curious thing, is that, I don't know how many nights prior

---

[59] The name has been changed.

to this that I might have sleepwalked. All I know is that I had been taking Ambien for some time, and because I had recently and unexplainably been putting on a lot of weight, the evidence seemed to suggest that I was possibly sleepwalking and eating at night on a regular basis, over an extended period of days and time!

Later, I informed both my psychiatrist and mental health therapist about my bizarre, sleepwalking episode, and they told me to cease taking Ambien immediately! This was a good decision, seeing that I could have hurt myself or others, or possibly that I might have even burned down the house!

Help for Anxiety

Along with clinical depression, often comes the feeling of anxiousness. But there are also medications that can help with this too.

Some of the medications that are used to treat and reduce symptoms of anxiety associated with depression are: Ativan, Lexapro, Zoloft, Celexa, KlonoPIN, etc. Interestingly, new medications are becoming available all of the time. By the time this book is published and released to the public there will probably be others on the market.

Are there any medication side effects for the drugs listed above that are used to treat anxiety? Unfortunately, the answer is yes. Although, side effects may vary per medication and individual, some common side effects of these medicines include: insomnia, drowsiness, dizziness, and upset stomach.

Concerning prescribed medications associated with bipolar disorder, sometimes you feel a little bit like a guinea pig or lab rat that is being experimented on, because doctors often have to change your medication or try several different kinds. Nevertheless, this is something that may be required at times, in order for them to be able to find the right medication that is best for you, because not all medication works the same for everyone. What works for one person may not work for another. Also, sometimes the medications that you may have been taking for quite some time, might eventually lose their effectiveness. And so, you may be prescribed or given something else to take its place.

As with many things in life, with prescription drugs there are usually certain known side effects. And these may not always be easy to have to cope with or endure. But often, the positive benefits that the medications offer can far outweigh the negative experiences. The important thing for bipolar disorder patients, is that, once you begin taking your medications, it is important to stay consistent with them, for if you stop taking them, you can possibly suffer a mental relapse.

Chemical Imbalance

It is a commonly held belief that people who suffer from clinical depression have a chemical imbalance in the brain. Interestingly, back in the year 1984, there was thought to be about thirty different types of known chemicals in the human brain. However, today, with more knowledge and research, it has been discovered that there are many more! And like many things in life, often, it is important to have a perfect balance, in order for things to function properly or to be healthy.

Of the many chemicals in the human brain, one that seems to be notably off balance or low in volume in those who suffer from bipolar disorder is *serotonin*. Serotonin functions as a neurotransmitter, which helps to relay messages from one area of the brain to another. Subsequently, to help boost low serotonin levels in mental health patients, they are often prescribed antidepressant medications. An interesting thing, is that, theoretically speaking, there is no way of truly knowing for sure what the proper, correct, exact, or normal levels of serotonin are or what they are supposed to be in the human body and brain—there is no way for scientists and those in the medical field to be certain. The reason being, is that, the human body and brain is just too complex! It is only by means of trials and experimentation that they have noted that by boosting or increasing the levels of serotonin in bipolar patients, that it seems to somewhat help in treating their depression.

Psychotherapy

Psychotherapy is another alternative treatment that can be used to treat bipolar patients. Psychotherapy, is talk therapy, which usually takes place between the bipolar disorder patient, and a mental health therapist. However, this is often offered in both individual and group settings, depending on what method is preferred by the patient.

The goal of the mental health therapist is to listen attentively and patiently to their patients, allowing them to express their true feelings and concerns, and then to offer any suggestions that might aid in helping them to cope with their disorder. Also, the patient's are taught how to recognize when a mood shift is about to occur, so that they can be better equipped to handle it when it does arise. In addition, patients are also taught effective stress reducing methods and techniques.

Both individual and group settings for psychotherapy can be very helpful. However, usually, when it comes down to it, it all depends on what a person's preference is. Personally, I've had both (group and individual psychotherapy). Interestingly, as far as group sessions are concerned, while personally attending them, I found other bipolar patients to be very encouraging and supportive, both to me and to one another. Also, it was very comforting to learn that some of them were actually going through some of the same problems or things that I was experiencing.

Electroconvulsive Therapy

Electroconvulsive Therapy (ECT) or "shock treatment" as it is sometimes referred to, is another form of treatment that can be used to treat bipolar patients.

ECT is a procedure that is administered under general

anesthesia, which involves intentionally feeding small currents of electricity into the brain, for the purpose of inducing a brief seizure. Although, it is not fully understood how it works, it has been known to offer relief to some bipolar patients who suffer from debilitating depression.

"Electroshock therapy," as ECT was formally called in the past, was given a lot of bad publicity in 1975, with the release of the highly popular and acclaimed theatrical blockbuster movie entitled *"One Flew Over the Cuckoo's Nest"* — starring in the main character roles: actor, Jack Nicolson, as the mischievous and rebellious patient "Randle Patrick McMurphy," and actress, Louise Fletcher, as the mean and ironfisted nurse named, "Ratched." However, ECT can be an effective form of therapy that can be helpful in administering needed relief to mental health patients suffering from debilitating depression.

Interesting to note, is that, ECT therapy is a sort of last resort type of therapy that is usually warranted and recommended only when nothing else, such as medications, psychotherapy, and other things... don't seem to be working. Nevertheless, it is totally a personal decision to pursue.

At one time in the past, ECT treatment was actually recommended and prescribed for me personally, which I was even hospitalized to have done. However, later, during the preparation process, and with further consideration (based upon receiving more information about the procedure, and its possible side effects), my family, and I, for personal reasons, decided that it was best for me to forgo the treatment at that time. Nevertheless, there are many people yearly that have ECT therapy treatments administered, and it has worked well for them.[60]

---

[60] Disclaimer: I do not recommend or endorse any medications or treatments. This book is not intended to provide medical advice or to take the place of medical advice and treatment from your personal physician. Readers are advised to consult their own doctors or other qualified health professionals regarding the treatment of medical conditions.

Bipolar Myths

The following bulleted items below are some incorrect myths about bipolar disorder. They are:

- *People with bipolar disorder have mood swings that shift back and forth quickly, like the flip of a light switch.* (False) The depressive phase, as well as the mania (or hypomania) phase, can last for weeks or even months at a time.

- *Bipolar disorder people are insane or crazy.* (False) Interestingly, in talking to and listening to many people, I've noticed that the word *bipolar* is often synonymously used with the word *crazy,* when people are discussing, evaluating, or explaining a bipolar person's mental state; as if these two things are both alike in significance and meaning. However, linking these two things together, as though they mean the same thing, is totally incorrect. Because the actual medical definition of bipolar disorder does not mean that a person with this condition is crazy. It simply means that they suffer from manic depression. So, to suggest or say that bipolar people in general are crazy, is completely wrong. Bipolar people in general are not nuts or mentally deranged, but rather, they simply suffer from cycles of depression, and mania (or hypomania).

- *Bipolar disorder patients are violent people.* (False) Although, some people by nature may be overly aggressive or physical, this does not mean that all bipolar people are violent. In general, they are not monsters, or ticking time bombs lying dormant, just waiting to explode. Take for example, United States of America President, Abraham Lincoln, who was bipolar. He was known to be a pretty mellow individual by nature. I couldn't even imagine him going ballistic on someone. He didn't even attempt to fight back when his half crazed wife, Mary Ann Todd Lincoln, frequently would punch, hit, and beat on him.

- *Bipolar disorder people are non-spiritual people that do not have God's spirit, approval, blessing, and support.* (False) A person's spirituality or relationship with God has nothing to do with bipolar disorder. Bipolar is not a spiritual illness but, rather, it is a medical illness or disease.

If you happen to be a bipolar patient, or if you know someone who is, it is nothing to be ashamed of. For many people bipolar is a way of life, something that they learn to live with. As a matter of fact, some of the most gifted, talented, creative, inspiring, intelligent, highly successful, influential, and productive people in the world—both past and present—were/are bipolar. In view of this, if you are bipolar, you can consider yourself as being in pretty good company, and also as being a very beautiful and special person—someone that you can be very proud of. Below is list of famous bipolar people, both past and present.

Famous Bipolar People:

- Vincent van Gogh – artist and painter.
- Edgar Allan Poe – poet and writer.
- Ernest Hemingway – writer and journalist.
- Charles Dickens – writer.
- Abraham Lincoln – American president.
- Florence Nightingale – founder of modern nursing.
- Mark Twain – writer and humorist.
- Vivien Leigh – actress.
- Kim Novak – actress.
- Marilyn Monroe – actress.
- Jimmy Piersall – Boston red sox hall of famer.
- Delonte West – professional basketball player.
- Mel Gibson – actor and director.
- Richard Dreyfuss – actor.
- Robert Downy Jr. – actor, and film producer.
- Judy Garland – actress, and singer.
- Patty Duke – actress.
- Rosemary Clooney – singer, actress.
- Rene Russo – actress, and model.
- Jim Carrey – actor, and comedian.
- Maria Bamford – comedian.
- Linda Hamilton – actress.
- Carrie Fisher – actress, writer, comedian, activist.

- Catherine Zeta-Jones – actress.
- Jean-Claude Van Damme – martial artist, and actor.
- Connie Francis – singer.
- Nina Simone – singer, songwriter, pianist, and journalist.
- Dusty Springfield – singer.
- Frank Sinatra – singer, and actor.
- Charlie Sheen – actor.
- Jimi Hendrix – guitarist, singer, and songwriter.
- Jaco Pastorius – musician, composer, and producer.
- Charley Pride – country singer, and musician.
- Kurt Cobain – singer, songwriter, and musician.
- Britney Spears – singer, dancer, and actress.
- Selena Gomez – singer, actress, songwriter, and producer.
- Sinéad O'Connor – singer, songwriter, and musician.
- Chris Brown – singer, dancer, and actor.
- Demi Lovato – singer, songwriter, actress, and model.
- Mariah Carey – Singer, songwriter, record producer, actress.
- Dick Cavett – television personality and former talk show host.
- Jane Pauley – television anchor, and journalist.
- Ted Turner – Entrepreneur, television producer, media proprietor, and philanthropist.
- Jesse Jackson, Jr. – American civil rights activist, and politician.
- Jonathan Winters – actor, and comedian.
- Ben Stiller – actor, comedian, and filmmaker.
- Burgess Meredith – actor, producer, director, and writer.
- Francis Ford Coppola – film director, producer, and screenwriter.
- Winston Churchill – prime minister, and journalist.
- Theodore Roosevelt – American president.
- Ludwig van Beethoven – composer, and pianist.
- Wolfgang Amadeus Mozart – composer, and pianist.
- Virginia Woolf – Novelist.
- Rembrandt Van Rijn – painter, and printmaker.
- Pablo Picasso – painter, sculptor, printmaker, poet, and playwright.
- Sir Isaac Newton – physicist, and mathematician.

*Sources[61]

---

[61] For sources, see *"Sources,"* on pp. 300-305.

COPING WITH BIPOLAR
AND DEPRESSION

L ike many other illnesses, bipolar disorder or manic depression is a disease, and those afflicted by it have no other recourse but to fight it; otherwise, it can eat them alive. With this factor in mind, after a person is diagnosed with bipolar disorder, which initially can be a hard thing for them to personally accept; the first step in the battle, recovery, and coping process, is that they need to reach the point when they finally acknowledge and accept the fact that they actually have the illness and that it is something that they most likely will have to cope and deal with the rest of their life.

Although being diagnosed with bipolar disorder can be a difficult thing for one to accept, this is not something to be ashamed of, for it can happen to anybody. However, with the right encouragement, support, and help, one can learn to successfully cope with the often debilitating disorder.

Fortunately, when it comes to dealing with bipolar and the depression that comes with it, there are many things that can help one to successfully cope—things that can comfort, encourage, refresh, and cheer a depressed soul—things such as: being in a positive and uplifting social and home environment; having positive thinking and a healthy outlook; a good diet, and exercise; and receiving encouragement and support from family and friends. Also, in addition to these basic needs, there are many other things that one can choose to incorporate in to, or eliminate from their lives that can help, which I will touch on in this section of my book.[62]

Interestingly, when it comes to searching for, finding, and using things that can help one to cope and deal with bipolar disorder, there is no one thing alone that will do the trick—like swallowing a magic pill or something. Personally, I have discovered that it takes the utilizing of a combination of a number of things. Let's consider some of the things that I used, one at a time.

A Positive Social Environment

When it comes to a person's mental and emotional health, a positive and uplifting social environment is vital for everyone. Not only is it an important factor in one's development and growth as an individual, but it is also good for their overall health and well-being too.

Positive environments are absolutely essential. The reason why, is because they provide encouragement and support—the basic elements and ingredients that all humans desire and need to feel secure, happy, appreciated, and loved. On the other hand, negative environments can be harmful and detrimental to one's overall health and well-being; especially, if they are overly critical and negative. Because they are often devoid of or fall short of the love, encouragement, and support that human's need to be well-rounded and happy individuals.

All people need positive social environments, but especially, is this absolutely necessary and essential for bipolar disorder patients who suffer from debilitating depression. The reason why, is because it makes them feel better when they are around people that value and

---

[62] Although prescribed medications can help people to cope with bipolar depression, I won't be touching on this particular method of treatment at this time.

treat them with love, understanding, dignity, kindness, and respect. On the other hand, overly critical and negative environments can create insecurities, sadness, and even depression in people, which will only further add to and feed the depression that bipolar disorder people are already experiencing—making matters a whole lot worse!

Unfortunately, when it comes to environments, most of us don't have much of a choice or say as to what kind we live or grow up in. Often, we are left to make the most of a good or bad situation (depending on what it's like). However, in regard to some aspects concerning environments and our individual involvement in them, there are certain things that we personally have the ability or power to improve or change, even if it's just to a minimum degree—things that can have a significant and positive impact upon both ours and other people's overall health and well-being.

An interesting thing, is that, social environments are a lot like people or personalities, in that each has its own distinct features or characteristics that make them unique and different from one another. Some are warm and inviting, others are cold and aloof, some are encouraging and supportive, while others are overly picky and critical, and so forth. And then, there are those that have a mixture of these things, and more. The social environments that I'm referring to are *long-term environments*—those that we spend a considerable amount of time in, such as at school, work, or in our neighborhood, etc.

When it comes to the overall makeup or structure of environments, it is often virtually impossible to significantly alter or change them; because their characteristics or personalities, generally, are already solidly fixed or set in stone. And because of this, the only three choices that people usually have are: (1) they can choose to stay within their present environment, and adapt and become like it. Thereby contributing to its growth and success, and sharing in its failures, and so forth or, (2) they can decide to remove themselves from it to avoid its effects and influences or, (3) they can hate it and complain about it, and yet, decide to stay within it, and be unhappy and miserable.[63]

Interestingly, there are some environments that we fit into better than others. Also, what works for one person, may not be a good fit for another. Truth is, no environment is perfect, and if it becomes necessary to choose one, it often comes down to selecting the one that suits us the best—an environment that we can at least tolerate and function within to a reasonable degree.

But, what if the environment that we find ourselves in is just too overly critical and negative, so much so, that it is to the point of being harmful or damaging to us? What do we do then?

Avoiding overly critical and negative environments. Environments can be an important factor in regard to our personal peace, happiness, health, development, and growth. Often, they can make or break us, depending on whether they are supportive and encouraging, or unsupportive and discouraging.

Interestingly, it is not uncommon for people who suffer from bipolar disorder to have feelings of worthlessness or low self-esteem. And when they are in the company of people who view and treat them like they are insignificant or useless, it only serves to intensify those negative feelings. Personally, in the past, there were times when I found that it was best for me to avoid *overly critical and negative* people—environments or places that made me feel this way, because I found them to be counterproductive, discouraging, emotionally draining, and damaging. It's not that I avoided them because I thought that I was better than others, because I'm not. It's just that I realized that there were certain things in the environment that were feeding my depression—making it worse. And that it was

---

[63] Sometimes there may be an overly challenging, negative environment that we find ourselves in, because we have no other choice but to stay and try to function within it, because due to one reason or another we cannot leave or remove ourselves from it or we simply have no other place to go. For help on how to develop, grow, and be productive in an overly challenging and negative environment, see the information *"Growing in a Negative Environment,"* in Appendix A, on page 269.

best for me to steer clear of these for my own emotional health and well-being. The fact is, at the time, I was already mentally down and beat-up as it was. I didn't need to add to this, by allowing others to cause me further suffering and pain.[64] To see the bad and negative effects that criticism can have on a person, see the information *"Constructive Criticism?"* in the Appendix, on pages 267-268.

To me, having major depression was like continuously battling or wrestling with a relentless enemy—one who is bent on trying to tear you down and defeat you. Therefore, it was important for me to never let down my guard. Instead, I had to be ever vigilant to avoid situations, areas, things, and even certain people at times, that might feed my depression and cause me further mental and emotional pain.

In regards to people, most of us know what it's like to be around difficult individuals, such as a bully, or an overly rude person, or a person who is a killjoy—one who spoils, crushes, or kills any and everything that we say or do (even if we have positive and valuable things to say or share). These types of people are like damaging *weeds* that sprout up in a garden and eventually overtake and choke the growth, vitality, beauty, and life from the healthy plants. Unfortunately, throughout history, these damaging weeds or individuals have taken their tow on many people, crushing and destroying their potential good, goals, and dreams.

Due to the discouragement, and excessive severity of some negative influences, and the bad and harmful effects that they may have on us personally, sometimes, in the past (when I was suffering

---

[64] Notice that I said that I tried to avoid *overly* critical and negative people and environments, and not just critical or negative people and environments in general. The reason why is because negativity can be found everywhere. This is just a normal part of everyday life. And it is something that we must get used to dealing with. However, it is the extreme, *overly* critical and negative ones that put it over the top, which sometimes makes it very hard to cope and deal with. These are the ones that, because of my depression, and the environment's harmful effects on me, that I personally tried to avoid. Note: I'm not recommending this way of handling these kinds of situations or environments to others. It's just something that I found that I personally needed to do at that particular time in my time.

from depression and bipolar), I found that it was necessary for me to avoid overly critical and negative environments and people that were having a harmful effect on me. And then, in return, I needed to replace these negative ones with positive ones that were healthy for me (emotionally and mentally)—good environments and people that were helpful and supportive to me, that encouraged me, and uplifted my spirits; especially, in times of need.

But, what if it is not feasible for us to bodily remove ourselves from an overly negative and critical environment, because for one reason or another, we happen to be stuck there, with no other place to go? What might we do so that its harmful influence doesn't impact us too greatly? Well, one thing that can help is by having a realistic view of life and people in general.

Having a realistic view of life and people. Life is a beautiful thing, and there are a lot of wonderful, fun, and exciting things around us—things that make life pleasant and enjoyable (things that we often take for granted). However, on the flipside of things, there are also negative things that we often have to contend and deal with too—trying and challenging things that can sometimes make life tough and hard to deal with.

One thing that can make life difficult or challenging, is that, we have to daily navigate our way through a vast sea of people that possess a variety of likes, dislikes, attitudes, personalities, ambitions, lifestyles, and goals, etc., that are often completely different from our own. And because of this, we must learn to accept variety or diversity. But we also have the challenge of staying true to ourselves, by not allowing the often highly opinionated, pushy, and domineering world around us squeeze us into its mold, which can cause us to lose sight of our own distinct individuality—the special features, unique characteristics, and things that make us who we are.

In addition, the attitude or spirit of the world around us can be highly competitive. Many people are daily fighting for dominance in one thing or another—whether it be for attention, power, prominence, jobs, money, or material wealth, etc. These things are so important to some people that they will do just about anything to succeed or obtain them, even if it means stepping on the heads and toes of as many people (no matter who they are) as they can, as they scratch and claw their way to the top. Unfortunately, sometimes we unforeseeably get in the way or path of these overly aggressive and ambitious one's and, as a result, we become a victim of misfortune. Often, in the end, we are left there, lying in bewilderment or pain alongside of the road, shaking and scratching our heads in utter disbelief, as we try to figure out or piece together what had just happened, or what the person's problem is.

Another challenging thing that can be hard to cope and deal with at times is human imperfections. Fact is, none of us are perfect. And because of this, both we and others are going to say and do things at times that may hurt and offend one another. Knowing and understanding this in advance can be very helpful, because if someone happens to hurt or offend us in the future, which they inevitably will; we won't be too quick to get upset or take offence, allowing it to ruffle our feathers, so-to-speak.

Another thing that can help, is when we don't expect too much from others, but instead, we are willing to accept and put up with them—appreciating and accepting them for whom and what they are. I'm not saying that we should necessarily compromise our standards or beliefs. What I am saying, is that it helps when we are not too overly demanding and critical of people. For if we have the habit of setting the bar too high in what we expect from others; we are sure to be disappointed. But on the other hand, if we allow for errors, imperfections, and differences in others, then we won't be too devastated or bent out of shape when they disappoint us.

Another thing that can help us to cope and fair well within an overly critical and negative environment, is when we are willing to *forgive* others for the hurt or harm that they cause us, whether it is done intentionally or unintentionally.

Practice forgiving. An old, yet wise, and familiar proverb says: "To err is human; to forgive is divine." Meaning that it is human nature to sin and make mistakes. And yet, God freely forgives us. And when we forgive others we are being like him.

Unfortunately, many of us are still harboring hurtful things today, that happened to us in our youth or distant past—highly disturbing and troubling things that someone either said or did to us, that left emotional scars—things that keep resurfacing and that don't seem to ever be going away. And yet, at the same time, not realizing that the reason why these things are continuing to linger on and bother and torment us, is because we refuse to release and let go of them.

What can help us to change, so that we no longer have to suffer from these things, and go on to lead a happier and more productive life? The answer is to *forgive*, and then move on.

What does it mean to be *forgiving*? It means to *completely pardon* or let go of a wrong that a person committed against us. To cease from feeling resentment and anger towards them, and not wanting, desiring, or seeking retaliation or revenge.

Personally, in the past, where I went wrong in my life, was that I allowed the highly discriminatory, overly critical and negative environment around me, along with the hurtful experiences that I was suffering at the hands of others, influence my thinking, in particular, in regards to their judging and dictating my self-worth, which led to me suffering from a lot of crippling emotional pain and depression. Unfortunately, these hurtful experiences and things changed my viewpoint, focus, and thinking, from that of being wholesome and healthy, to being negative and critical of pretty much everyone and everything, including myself. But it also led to me not wanting to be around certain people; out of fear that I would become a victim of further cruel judgments, pranks, and remarks. As a result, I became somewhat of a loner in life (partly, not completely), which sometimes can serve as a protection, because it can shield us from additional pain. However, it can also be crippling to us too, because we can develop tolerance and valuable coping skills from being around other people, even difficult and challenging ones.

Unfortunately, by letting the bad experiences that I had with people stumble me, it wound up stunting my emotional development and growth to a certain extent. Consequently, it kept me from gaining a certain level of maturity and stability in certain aspects of my life. And it also robbed me of a considerable measure of inner peace, joy, self-appreciation and love. But not only this, as a result, I didn't set a good example for others. Now, when I think back on these things, I realize that I would have been much better off, if I had been forgiving, and didn't take things so personal, allowing frustration and anger to take root and grow. Fortunately, in time, I eventually wised up, learned from my past mistakes, and made the necessary changes and adjustments in my life and personality to improve, grow, and become highly successful.

Why is *forgiving* so important? Well, one reason why, is because we are all imperfect humans who are in need of forgiveness. It is also important because there are good benefits that come to us when we both willingly and freely forgive others. For one, it helps us in our relationships and friendships with others. But it is also good for our overall health and well-being too. Because when we forgive and forget we don't have to carry around the heavy weight and burdens of feeling resentment, hurt, anger, or even hatred—all of which are strong deterrents and barriers to our own inner peace, joy, and happiness. But also, being unforgiving can be harmful to our personal health. For living with bad feelings and emotions can make us ill.

The role feelings and emotions play. As humans, we were created with the amazing ability to be able to express a wide range and variety of feelings and emotions. We can express: love, warmth, affection, goodness, kindness, generosity, thankfulness, joy, peace, mildness, patience, empathy, humility, compassion, and the list goes on.

While *good* feelings and emotions can add color and spice to our lives, making it more enjoyable; on the flipside of things, if we are not watchful and careful, certain *bad* feelings and emotions can do the exact opposite. They can bring us sorrow and pain. But even worse than this, they can be damaging to our health, because our deep feelings and emotions support our overall health and well-being—physically, mentally, and spiritually. Interestingly, human emotions can run so deep that people have been known to literally die from a broken heart. Also, fits of uncontrolled rage and anger can be damaging to one's health. They can cause high blood pressure, respiratory issues, digestive troubles, skin diseases, hives, ulcers, and a host of other health issues.

Personally, in regard to myself, I think that my bad feelings and emotions were one of the factors or causes of my clinical depression—negative feelings and emotions that were agitated and brought on from growing up and living within an overly critical and negative environment, that viewed and treated me unjustly and unloving.

As we can see from the above, *bad* feelings and emotions can be harmful and detrimental to our health and overall well-being. However, on the other hand, *good* feelings and emotions can be the exact opposite—they can be good for our health. Interestingly, in the Bible at Proverbs 16:24 it tells us: "Pleasant sayings are a *healing* to the bones." Meaning that positive and uplifting words of encouragement that we receive from others can have an uplifting affect on our moods and health, in that, they can cheer us up and make us feel better.

Because *bad* feelings and emotions can run deep, sometimes it can be a real challenge to gain control over them; especially, if we are undergoing or experiencing extremely difficult and trying situations. But, in spite of this, for one's own health and well-being's sake, it is best for us to try to have and maintain a positive attitude and spirit. One way that I found, that eventually helped me to have a positive spirit, was by having support and help from others who are interested in my well-being. However, not all associates are helpful in this regards, as a matter of fact, some may be the exact opposite. Instead of encouraging a positive attitude, they may promote a negative spirit and attitude in us. With this being the case, what might we do that can help us in this area?

Watch your associations. It's been said: "Show me who your friends are, and I'll tell you who you are." There is a lot of truth to this statement, because those with whom we choose to associate, we often become like. The reason why, is because, people have the tendency to rub off on us. And before you realize it we begin talking and acting like them.

In addition to having a powerful influence on us, people that we associate or hang out with can either build us up or tear us down. Because of this, depending on whether we wish to fair well or bad, it is important to choose our friends and associates wisely. This includes not only physical friendships, but also, associates that we invite in to our lives through the media, television programs, and the internet, etc. These too are our associates. And they can either have a positive or negative influence on us. To give you an example of this, personally, in the past, I used to watch (pretty much on a daily and ritual basis), the daily news reports on TV. However, sometime later, because of the discouraging and negative effects that they were having on me, I had to stop watching them, because they made me feel sad and depressed. Because of all of the bad reports and news that they reported on.

Interestingly, after I had quit watching the daily news, within a relatively short period of time, I noticed that my thinking and outlook changed for the better. Because I was no longer allowing the bad, sad, shocking, and discouraging things that were often being reported on to influence my moods in a negative way. Sure, occasionally, I'll catch something on the news here and there (concerning the weather or sports or something), but, for the most part, I try to avoid the news altogether. I guess it's sort of ironic when you think about it, but, sometimes the less that we know or the less informed that we are about certain things, the better off we are. I know this to be true in this case — in regard to the daily news — because by not watching it, I am no longer allowing the sad and discouraging news reports to trigger and feed depression and pull me downwards (both mentally and emotionally).

Yes, from life's experiences (in particular, when I was suffering from depression and bipolar disorder), I've come to discover that there were certain situations, areas, subject matter—like the TV

News reports, and even specific people at times that would feed and breed depression in me, and that for my own mental and emotional health, well-being, and protection, I needed to be ever aware of what or who these might be. And, based upon the degree or severity of a particular situation or thing, and the bad effects that it was having on me (if it happened to be within my power and ability to control or change matters), then I needed to take the appropriate actions or necessary steps to either minimize the negative effects and influences that these things were having on me, or to remove myself from them entirely. However, when it came necessary to avoid associations with certain people, there is a certain caution that I needed to be aware of, which was the trap of falling into isolation.

Avoiding total isolation. Although I felt that avoiding certain negative environments and people were necessary for me to do from time to time (in particular, when I was suffering from the effects of depression), there was need for caution in this area. Fact is, this can only be done to a limited degree, for total isolation from people can be damaging to us personally. The reason being, is because, by nature, humans are meant and made to be social creatures. For the most part we need other people in our lives to communicate and socialize with, for this can be good, beneficial, and healthy for us. True, sometimes we need a little solitude; some private and quiet time alone, for this can have its benefits too. However, too much time alone is not good. With this in mind, if you happen to be suffering from depression, fight the urge or tendency to want to lock yourself alone in your room, although, initially, this may feel somewhat good, in the long run it can be crippling and damaging to us personally.

Another thing that I've discovered, is that, when it comes to life; although a bit of self-sufficiency and self-reliance has its place in the world, that, it is best not to try to go through life alone, but instead, to have and solicit support and help from family, friends, and others, who can encourage us and uplift our spirits along the way. Interestingly, it doesn't have to be a large group. It could be just one or two people, who together with ourselves, make up a strong and supportive team. This is vitally important, because life can be hard, and there will be trying times when we need a little encouragement, direction, support, and help from others. In the Bible it says: "Two are better than one... for if they fall, the one will lift up his fellow: but woe to him that is alone when he falleth; for he hath not another to lift him up."—Ecclesiastes 4:9-10.[65]

A Positive Attitude and Healthy Outlook

Cultivating a positive attitude and healthy outlook. Traveling on the ever-changing and challenging road of life is much better when we have and cultivate a positive attitude. This can help the road to be a little smoother and easier to travel on. But it can also make the difference between either leading a peaceful, contented, and happy life, or living a miserable one.

I say to *cultivate* a positive attitude, because having a positive attitude is something that many of us have to regularly work hard at manifesting or displaying in our lives. The reason being, is that, it doesn't necessarily come easy. As a matter of fact, having and maintaining a positive attitude or healthy outlook can be one of the most difficult things that we can do in life. Why? Because we already have the deck stacked against us, so to speak, in that, we are all imperfect creatures, and sometimes our own shortcomings, or those of others, can discourage and get us down. Also, there may be certain difficult situations or circumstances that we may be facing that can be downright challenging and trying to us.

Another thing that can make having a positive attitude challenging, is having bad health, for it can negatively affect one's thinking and outlook, because when we are suffering or in pain, it can be hard to focus on the positive aspects of life and things—to see and appreciate the good and beautiful things around us. To give you an example of this, let me tell you a true story about what happened to me. The problem was this: In the past, because my family and I live in the northern state of Minnesota, where the cold and snowy winters can be a little tuff, we often liked to vacation in sunny Clearwater, Florida (an annual three week vacation or trip in

---

[65] King James Version of the Bible.

which we use to drive). Well, one year during our drive there, I suddenly developed a toothache. Initially, the pain was controllable through the use of a little aspirin. But, the further we drove, the greater the pain got. Finally, when we arrived at our destination, the pain was so intense that I had to seek emergency dental help from a local dentist, who started root canal work immediately on the bad tooth—a process, which at the time took three separate appointments. Well, after the first part of the dental procedure was done, the dentist set up the next appointment, and then sent me on my way. Interestingly, initially, the first portion of the work that was done on my tooth seemed to help somewhat, that is, until the Novocain wore off. Then, I was in excruciating pain all over again!

Now sunny Clearwater; mind you, is very beautiful. The scenery is absolutely breathtaking! With its decorative palm trees, its delightful array of various blooming flowers, white sandy beaches, and crystal blue waters. However, because the tooth pain that I was experiencing was so excruciating and unbearable, I could not see and appreciate the paradisiacal beauty that surrounded me. All I could focus on was the miserable and unbearable pain. So I returned to the dentist. However, this time, I decided to have the tooth (which was one of my back teeth), pulled instead. And, although I lost a valuable, irreplaceable tooth, the amazing thing is that the moment the tooth was extracted, the pain instantly stopped. What a big relief this was! For not only was the pain completely gone but, now, I could finally see, smell, feel, and appreciate all of the beauty of the tropical paradise that surrounded me—something that I could not appreciate when I was in pain.

Well, the same can be true of those who suffer from an illness, such as clinical depression or bipolar disorder. Often, the mental and emotional pain that one feels is so intense that it makes it very hard to focus on the good, beautiful, and positive things around them. However, even though this may be the case, in spite of this, I personally have discovered that it can be done, even if it is to a limited degree. How? By feeding the mind positive things.

Feeding the mind positive things. One of the best things that we can do for our mind is to feed it valuable, good, positive, and uplifting things. This is vitally important to our emotional, mental, and physical health. Nevertheless, this is not always an easy thing to do. One reason why is due to human imperfection. Because we are all imperfect, we have an inborn tendency to gravitate towards bad things. The degree to which we do this may vary, depending on each individual. Some may have a lesser or greater craving to feed their mind bad and negative things. For example, some people have the bad habit of being nitpickers or faultfinders. Instead of looking for the good in things and others, they tend to focus on the imperfections and negative things. Some even take pride in being able to find and point out small imperfections or flaws in people or things that others don't seem to see or notice.

If we see ourselves being like this overly critical and negative person, then we need to stop doing this, because it can be harmful and damaging to both ourselves and others. On the other hand, life can be so much better when we look for the good in people and things (not the bad). For some people this may not be easy, especially if they have a habit or lifelong history of faultfinding and negative thinking, or if they suffer from depression. Because, when a person is down and depressed it's so easy to gravitate towards the negative. However, the good thing is that if we put forth genuine and real effort, we can change and train our minds to think positive.

One thing that can help us to be positive, is to think of ourselves as being a skilled artist or painter, and our minds as being a large, blank canvas on which to paint. Now, in regard to our own personal canvas (our mind), we have the choice to create and paint whatever images or scenes we want on it. So, what subjects and colors would you choose to paint? No doubt you would choose a most delightful and beautiful scene with warm and vibrant colors, especially if you intend on hanging your finished masterpiece or painting on the wall or in an area for you and all to see and enjoy. Well, the same can be true of our minds and what we allow or choose to feed and occupy it. We have the choice to fill it with whatever scenes and subject matter we want. Yes, we can make or create any kind of world that we wish on the ever changing and highly adaptable canvas of our mind. Fortunately, for us, the world and creation around us is full of many wonderful, delightful, beautiful, exciting, and inspiring muses and things to inspire us, and select from, so we don't have to travel or go too far to find them.

Unfortunately, for some people who suffer from an illness such as depression and bipolar disorder, thinking positive may not be an easy thing to do. Because they are experiencing and suffering from mental and emotional pain, it may be harder for them to see and appreciate the beauty in the things around them. However, they too, can be helped in this regard. True, it may take greater effort. But it can be done. So, what can help?

As it so happens, the world is not short on garbage and junk food that we can figuratively feed our minds on. It serves up a daily dose and endless supply of it, which can readily be found by simply turning on the TV, connecting to the internet, or playing certain video games, etc. So, if we want to be positive and mentally healthy, we need to be *selective* in what we choose to watch and be influenced by. In this regard, we may need to search for good and positive things.

Searching for good and positive things. It's been said: "You are what you eat." Although this may not always or entirely be true in all respects, to a certain degree having a good physical diet can be beneficial to our health. Well, the same is also true concerning what we choose to feed our minds.

Interestingly, it has been said that life is all about choices. So, with regards to the matter of choices, as to what we choose to consume and fill our minds with, what will you choose?

In regard to physical food, we (humans) often seem to crave and love to eat the things that may not be good for our health—things like fast-food, sweets, and junk foods. Sometimes we just can't seem to get enough of them. But, for our own good and overall health we have to exercise restraint when it comes to these things. The same can be true when it comes to the diet of mental food that we feed our minds. Correspondingly, like physical food, our minds also often crave what is not good and healthy for us. But, just like fighting the craving to eat physical foods that can be bad for our health, sometimes we have to get tuff with ourselves and fight the tendency to fill our minds with things that can be detrimental to having positive thinking and a good outlook on life. True, it's not that having a healthy mental diet is necessarily going to make us or our lives perfect, or that it's going to cure us of an illness such as depression, or bipolar, etc., but it can to a certain degree make our life a whole lot better.

When it comes to the thought process, it is only natural to have negative thoughts from time to time, that's only part of being human. But the key is to not allow ourselves to focus and dwell on them, so that we are overcome and controlled by them. Subsequently, in order to combat this, the best thing to do when we start to have negative thoughts, is to immediately dismiss them and put them out of our mind. And then, in turn, we need to key in on or focus on things that are positive, good, and healthy for us instead.

No doubt about it; fighting to be and stay positive can be a very hard and challenging thing to do at times, especially when we are undergoing difficult and challenging times. However, we have no choice but to fight, if we want to succeed and be better off. The truth is, negative thinking can feed and fuel discouragement and depression in us. And if we are not watchful and careful it can escalate to the degree where it can be like being in quicksand. For the more negative we are or become, the further we can sink deeper into the pit of misery and despair.

So, if we are fighting to stay positive, what things might we focus on or consider? Well, in the Bible at Philippians 4:8 it says: "Whatever things are true, whatever things are of serious concern, whatever things are righteous, whatever things are chaste, whatever things are lovable, whatever things are well-spoken-of, whatever things are virtuous, and whatever things are praiseworthy, continue considering these things." Why? Because these things are not only good and healthy, but they also serve as a protection for us.

Sometimes, because positive things may not seem to be readily visible, or apparent, or they don't happen to jump out at us so to speak, we may have to make a diligent search to find them.

214

Although, in fact, there are many beautiful, positive, and inspiring things all around us. Sometimes, all it takes is for us to be open, observant, and to look.

Find your joy. In observation, I've noticed that it is human tendency for a person — when they are feeling down or depressed — to look for, pursue, or do things that will make them feel better about themselves, a situation, or life. In particular, this seems to happen a lot with people who suffer from depression or some other type of mental or emotional pain. However, in a considerably large percentage of these cases, one usually winds up gravitating towards things that make matters worse, by filling or replacing the hurt or pain with alcohol, illicit drugs, binge eating, or some other harmful things. In the end, the person's misery or pain often becomes worse, because they are left with a bad addiction, or a troubling and guilty conscience, etc. If you happen to be one that this is happening to, why not try to find or pursue something that is good and healthy for you instead. In other words, find your true *joy* or passion in life— the one, positive, good, and healthy thing that will make you feel better about yourself and life—something that is going to add true value to your character and life—that will build you up, rather than discourage and tear you down.

What might you choose? Well, it could be virtually anything— from becoming a gourmet chef, a photographer, a writer, an artist such as a painter or sculpturist; a musician, or just learning to play an instrument. Undoubtedly, there are many things to choose from. The choice is totally up to you. The point is to fill the void or hurt in your life with something that is good and beneficial, something that can bring you a true measure of peace, satisfaction, joy, and happiness.

Keeping active. Another thing that can help us to stay positive is by keeping busy and active. It's been said: "An idle mind is the devil's playground." So, sometimes, in order to put or keep ourselves in a healthier and better frame of mind, we have to get up, move about, and keep active. Interestingly, I've often notice that in observing senior citizens, that the ones that seem to be the most joyful and healthy, are the ones that are always active and busy in one way or another.

Love and respect yourself. It is vitally important that we love and respect ourselves for who and what we are. Not to the point of excess of course (like being a narcissist), but, instead, to a healthy or balanced degree. So get to know yourself and accept yourself for who you are, which is a distinct and beautiful individual. Unfortunately, it took me some 60 years of my life before I finally figured this out. Sad to say, during the process I lost a lot of valuable time, because I allowed other things to sidetrack and distract me. But now, I am thoroughly enjoying life with the beautiful person that I found and discovered inside of me.

Unfortunately, we often don't see or appreciate ourselves for who and what we are (as being a distinct and beautiful individual). Because we often allow the distorted views or negative opinions of others and society get in the way and negatively influence us, which, if we are not watchful and careful, can lead to a sort of self-hatred, and self-destruction, that ends in us inflicting pain on ourselves by beating ourselves up mentally and emotionally. The truth is we can be our own worst enemy or critic. And, although it is good to examine and censure ourselves from time to time, an important thing is that we should never be too hard on ourselves, because this can lead to having a bruised or crushed spirit, which can cause and feed sadness and depression.

Sad to say, discontentment and self-hate can rob us of so many good and valuable things in life—things such as self-discovery, which can aid in helping us to learn many interesting and amazing things about ourselves, including discovering innate abilities, talents, and gifts that we didn't even realize we possessed. It can also rob us of development and growth, and being able to experience to the greatest extent possible the inner qualities of peace, joy, self-respect and love—good and healthy qualities and thinking that can add to our enjoyment and happiness in life. Because, by focusing and dwelling on negative and self-destructive things, we can stifle the growth of these things within us. But also, a self-destructive attitude and spirit can also be damaging to our personal health—mentally, emotionally, physically, and spiritually. So don't miss out on the good things of life, by sabotaging your own personal well-being and happiness—by being too overly critical and negative about yourself.

What are some things that can help one to come to appreciate, love, and respect themselves? Well, personally, I find that it is best when we don't live and judge ourselves by other people's opinions, standards, and ways. Fact is, no matter how hard we may try, we will never be able to please everyone. Another thing that helps is when we don't compare our self to others, because everybody is unique and different. Other people have their strengths and abilities, and we have ours.

An additional thing that can be helpful, is realizing that no one is perfect, including ourselves. Yes, no matter who we are, we all have both positive and negative things about us. However, a good and healthy practice is to focus primarily on the positive and not the negative.

Another thing that can help is by not taking ourselves and life too seriously. In other words, learn to relax, have a good time, and laugh. For laughter is good medicine for the soul.

And, lastly, and most importantly, view yourself as a beautiful and good person. Because that is what you are!

Weeding out bad and negative influences. Cultivating a positive attitude and spirit within us can be a lot like gardening. Now, I'm not claiming to be a skilled plantsman or garden expert, but when it comes to gardening, it is common knowledge to know that, along with planting, watering, and fertilizing, etc., also comes regular *weeding*. This is necessary because weeds can rob the soil and plants of healthy nutrients and water. And they can also choke out growth, thereby destroying a healthy flower garden, or crop of vegetables, etc., (depending on what it is that we are growing). Well, the same is true in regards to human beings, in that, *weeds*, or in this case, *negative influences*, can be harmful to our thinking, health, and growth. Yes, just like weeds in a literal garden, *negative influences* can sprout up and cause harm to us if we are not watchful and careful. How? By taking root in our mind and heart—choking out and destroying the potential or good in us, which can also wind up being harmful and detrimental to our health (mental and emotional). Therefore, it is vitally important that we guard our thinking, attitude, and outlook—making sure that they stay positive and healthy. How? By weeding out bad and negative influences. These weeds (negative influences) can come in many forms. They can be influences that we let in to our life and homes through television programs, movies, video games, computer websites, and even certain people that we choose to associate with. So, if we desire to have and maintain positive thinking and a healthy outlook, there may be certain things that we might need to be more selective about, or that we perhaps decide to avoid or remove from our life that have a negative and damaging influence on us personally.

Roll with life's punches. As we all well know, life is not all fun and games. As a matter of fact, sometimes it can throw us some pretty hard blows, so-to-speak. And, how we personally respond or react when this happens can make a big difference on how we fair when we are under fire or trial. For example, if we overreact to a situation it can make matters much worse. But when we handle matters calmly and rationally, we can often diffuse or lesson the magnitude or impact of a problem or situation that could so easily spiral out of control. How might this be done?

Well, when dealing with life's problems sometimes it is best to just roll with the punches. In other words, adapt to the changes. For example, our family car got hit twice; on two separate occasions, both within a matter of just a short time span. As a matter of fact, we had just gotten our vehicle repaired from being in its first accident, when only about a week or two later, someone ran into it again (in a store parking lot, while we were shopping). Both of these accidents of course were both costly and painful experiences. Also, to add insult to injury, both accidents were hit and run, where the other drivers fled the scene. This was indeed both irritating and frustrating, to say the least! However, after my wife and I thought about it, we reasoned that there is simply nothing that we can do about it. We can't change what happened. It's a done deal. It happened and now we must cope and deal with it. Either we can get all bent out of shape over it, allowing it to get the best of us, and knock us down, or we can say: "Oh well," get it repaired, and go on with our life. Well, we found that the latter was the best and healthiest choice. This way we minimized the drama, and we didn't prolong any possible mental and emotional pain. Yes, handling things this way is, by far, the best way to cope and deal with life's problems.

Reaping good from bad. Not every problem or negative situation that we go through in life is necessarily bad for us. Sometimes our problems or sufferings can yield positive results. For one, they can aid in helping us to develop good and valuable qualities that we did not have or possess before, which are things that can help, not only ourselves, but also others. For example, our personal sufferings and negative experiences can help us to become more sympathetic, understanding, and merciful to other people's situations, problems, sufferings, and pain. Having personally gone through similar things our self, helps us to be in a better position to relate and understand what other people are possibly going through. And therefore we can become a real source encouragement and comfort to them in their time of suffering and need.

Another thing that can be gained through sufferings and bad experiences, is that, sometimes they can help us to get to know ourselves better, in that, through the pain or grieving process, we begin to turn inward and reflect on things more deeply, and in the process, by means of performing a thorough examination of ourselves, we can discover interesting and amazing things about ourselves—things that were hidden—that we never knew existed prior to this—things such as innate talents, gifts, and abilities. Interestingly, this happened to me after my mom died from breast cancer. Surprisingly, during this most grievous of times, I discovered that I have a knack or ability for writing poetry. I even had a book of compiled poems published, entitled *"Poems That Touch Home."*

Well, thus far, in our discussion on coping with depression and bipolar disorder, I've touched on the importance of having *a positive social environment,* and also on cultivating *a positive attitude and healthy outlook.* Next, we will consider another important subject that can also be helpful, which is creating and having *a positive and uplifting home environment.*

A Positive and Uplifting Home Environment

Out of all places that we spend time at, for the most part, we generally spend the majority of our time at our home. Therefore, because of this, why not make or create a really warm, pleasant, refreshing, relaxing, and upbuilding home environment to live in, where we will enjoy it all the more. By doing this, we can add an even greater amount of peace and enjoyment to our lives, which can be beneficial to our overall health and happiness. So, what are some things that we might do to create a refreshing and relaxing home atmosphere?

Well, for one, we can make our home feel and be more relaxing and comfortable. And we can make it look more attractive too. We can also make it smell really good. In other words, it's a matter of constructing or setting up our home environment with things that will daily feed our five senses—the things that will be healthy for our mind, body, spirit, and soul. Good and valuable things that will create and stimulate peaceful, joyful, positive feelings and thoughts in us—things that will uplift our mood and spirit—things that will make us feel more peaceful, secure, relaxed, and happy. This is especially important for those who suffer from depression and bipolar disorder, for it can help them to better cope with their illness, which often goes hand in hand with feelings of anxiety and stress.

I'm not saying that we should go all out, spending a vast fortune to make our homes extravagant and plush. I don't know about you, but, like most people, I simply could not possibly afford it. However, if we are creative and thrifty, we can keep our needs modest, reasonable, affordable, and in good taste. So, what are some things that we can do to make our home environment more positive, uplifting, comfortable, and relaxing?

Use proper lighting. One thing that can help to make our home more comfortable and relaxing is by making sure that we use proper lighting, so that it is not too bright, and yet not too dim. Proper lighting is especially important for those who suffer from bipolar disorder, because their eyes are often highly sensitive to bright lights, which can make them feel irritable and uncomfortable.

Peace and quiet. It's been said: "Silence is golden." Yes, a certain amount of peace and quiet is important to humans, but, especially, is this essential for those who are bipolar, because their ears are often highly sensitive to noise. With this in mind, if possible, sometimes it's best to free ourselves from nerve rattling sounds, and disturbing chaos, by reducing or eliminating as much of the unnecessary noise and disturbances that we can.

Pleasant and soothing fragrances. Another thing that we can incorporate in to our home atmosphere is soothing and pleasant aroma fragrances, by utilizing aroma therapy, or scented candles, etc. This can help to calm one's nerves and put them in a better mood. However, for those who may be allergic to certain fragrances or smells, they may need to exercise caution when it comes to choosing the right ones, or perhaps they may wish to eliminate them entirely.

Listening to relaxing music. It has been said that "Music soothes the savage beast." True, music can have a calming and peaceful effect on many things, including humans. With this in mind, occasionally, we may want to have some soothing and refreshing music playing softly in the background, to create a relaxing atmosphere, and to help generate a pleasant mood.

Caution: When it comes to one's choice of music, it, of course, is a personal decision, as to what kind they may personally choose to listen to. However, sometimes, we may need to exercise caution when it comes to selecting certain types of music or songs, especially if we suffer from depression, because, depending on what the music is, some can leave us feeling melancholy and blue, which can end up triggering and feeding sadness and depression in us, making matters even worse.

Choosing comfortable furniture. Another thing that can help our home environment to be more relaxing, is by having comfortable furniture to sit on. With this in mind, you might decide to have a favorite, comfortable chair, lounge, or rocker available to sit on. Also, along with this, you may choose to have a soft and cozy, throw blanket nearby—something that you can wrap up in on a cool and crisp day—anything that will help you to feel relaxed, and that can aid in reducing stress.

A fireplace. A fireplace is not necessarily a necessity of life. However, personally, because of living in cold Minnesota winters, I thought that it would be nice to have one, because of the warmth and comfort that it can supply. Unfortunately, were I lived I didn't have one built into my home, so I decided to purchase an electric one. Surprisingly, it was relatively inexpensive, and also economically affordable to run. And, believe me, it was one of the best purchases that I've ever made. I absolutely love it! There's just something about it that puts me in a relaxed and cozy mood, especially on a cold and frigid, wintery day or night in good ole' Minnesnowta![66]

Choosing uplifting décor. It is truly amazing what a little home décor can bring to a lifeless room. It can transform a dull and boring setting into an uplifting, stimulating, fun, and exciting place. With this in mind, you might decide to add some joyful and stimulating décor to your home environment, such as: beautiful and interesting artwork; portraits or pictures of family, people, places, and things; or fun and pleasant knickknacks; or other refreshing and uplifting things—anything that will inspire you, make you smile and feel good about yourself, others, and life. In addition to this, you may want to paint your rooms soothing colors—refreshing hues that will have a calming effect on your mood and spirit—shades and tints that will help to relax your mind, heart, and soul.

Use of indoor plants. Indoor plants can bring natural beauty, life, and radiance to any room. Because of this, you may personally choose to incorporate some in to your indoor environment. Interestingly, plants not only give off valuable oxygen, and clean the

---

[66] Minnesnowta is a play on the word Minnesota. Due to its snowy winters.

air, but they can also be soothing, comforting, and therapeutic too. Besides this, there is just something good and special about nurturing, caring for, and helping other things to be vibrant and healthy. In the process, it can have sort of a reciprocal, good effect on us as well. It's like experiencing or having a healthy interchange of encouragement, the building of one another up.

Caution: There are some houseplants that some humans might be allergic to. So, you may have to be selective and careful in what plants you might choose.

Maintaining a clean and clutter free environment. An un-kept, cluttered, and dirty living environment, along with bad odors, can add discomfort and stress to just about anyone's life. It can even trigger and feed depression. Having this in mind, we may want to try to keep our home environment as clean and clutter free as possible. For this can, not only add peace, enjoyment, and comfort to our lives but, it can also be good for our overall health and wellness too.

No doubt, all of the things listed above will stimulate and feed our senses (sight, hearing, touch, and smell), positive and uplifting things that will be good for our overall health and well-being, including our emotional and mental health. However, these are just a few suggestions. The truth is, the sky is the limit as to what you might personally decide to incorporate in to your own personal home environment that will suit and satisfy your individual taste and needs. The important thing is to try to make your home a miniature, refreshing oasis; one that you can escape to and enjoy, especially in times of need—an environment that will produce a peaceful, relaxing, beautiful, and positive atmosphere that will uplift your spirits and make you think and feel better.

In addition to creating or making a positive and uplifting home environment for myself, there is something else that I did to help my depression and bipolar disorder; which was, having a *healthy diet and lifestyle.*

A Healthy Diet and Lifestyle

In many ways, having and maintaining a healthy diet and lifestyle is conducive to good health. It can make a big difference in how we feel and function on a daily basis. On the other hand, when we neglect our health, it can lead to various problems where we eventually feel and experience the negative effects. True, having and maintaining a healthy diet and lifestyle is no sure solution or guarantee that we won't ever get sick. However, when we do everything possible within our power and ability to be and stay healthy, we can, to a certain degree, lessen the chance.

When you think about it, our bodies are a lot like a house, in that it must be regularly and properly kept up and maintained, because if we neglect giving it the necessary attention and preventive maintenance that it regularly requires, it will eventually get rundown and fall apart. Having this in mind, what are some things that we might do or incorporate in our life that can promote good health within us? Well, one thing is by having a good diet.

A good and healthy diet. Having and maintaining a good and healthy diet is very important for everyone. Why? Because it is good for our overall health and well-being. Subsequently, if we eat good and nutritious foods, we will be properly nourishing our body with the right building blocks and things that it needs to refuel, energize, and restore its self. On the other hand, if we were to eat and subsist primarily on unhealthy junk food, we would be starving our bodies of the healthy nutrients that it needs to function properly. But, not only that, these bad things can be detrimental to our physical health. For example, we could become obese, which can lead to developing heart disease, high blood pressure, and a host of other serious health issues.

You might ask: What is a healthy diet? Well, according to the World Health Organization (WHO), a healthy, well-balanced and nutritious diet for an adult consists of eating: fruit, vegetables, legumes, nuts, whole grains, protein, dairy, and also good fats and sugars in proper proportions on a daily basis. If you personally happen to be one who needs help or assistance in this area, you might wish to consult your doctor or a local nutritionist, who will be more than happy to help you.

In addition to having a healthy nutritional diet, it is also imperative that we have a healthy lifestyle too. Because, what good is it, if we have a healthy diet but, we are living an unhealthy lifestyle?

What is a healthy lifestyle? Well, that depends on the individual, because, what may be a healthy lifestyle for one person, may not be healthy for someone else. The important thing, is to choose a lifestyle that is good and healthy for you personally; one that promotes good, overall health and well-being—a lifestyle that is free of harmful substances and things that are damaging to the mind and body.

Along with having a healthy diet and lifestyle, we also need to make sure that we are taking in an adequate amount of something else too, which is *water*.

Drink plenty of H^2O. Water is truly an amazing, life sustaining substance. Interestingly, it covers about 70% of the earth's surface. And it also makes up about 70% of the human body. The fact is, water is an essential and vital element to all life forms. It not only keeps us alive, but also, it's refreshing, it tastes good, and it is healthy for us too. For example, it helps our bodily organs to function properly. And it aids in proper blood circulation and digestion. It also, helps to flush harmful toxins from our bodies. Another amazing thing, is that, water has zero calories. Because of this, it can also aid in weight control and weight loss. Subsequently, with all of the good benefits that water supplies, it is wise to make sure that we keep properly hydrated. Personally, I drink about a gallon of water daily.[67]

---

[67] Caution: Because some people have medical conditions such as heart, and kidney issues, etc., that may limit their water intake needs, be sure to check with your doctor, and then follow his or her recommendations.

Note: If you exercise, you will need to factor this in to your water intake needs, so that you will be and stay properly hydrated, because exercise will naturally deplete water from your body through sweating. To help you to properly monitor your water intake levels, you might choose to use a water intake calculator to help you to calculate your personal, daily needs. Interestingly, some water intake calculators are available online for free. All you need to do is find one on an appropriate website; plug in your weight and your total daily workout time, and it will automatically calculate your targeted daily water intake for you. It's that simple!

Another thing that can aid in having good health is by ridding our bodies of harmful *toxins*.

Rid your mind and body of harmful toxins. Another thing that is good for one's health, and that can help us feel better, is to periodically detox our body of unhealthy toxins and other harmful substances. There are many ways that this can be done. One way is by periodically doing a weekend cleanse by eating natural detoxifying foods. Another way is by preparing certain green drinks that have a detoxifying effect.

Caution: Before consuming green drinks consult with your doctor to make sure it is safe and right for you.

Another way to detox, is by using a sauna to sweat out toxins. This can be an effective way of removing unwanted toxins from the body. Another good thing about saunas is that they can be very refreshing and relaxing.

Caution: Before using a sauna consult with your doctor to make sure it is safe and right for you.

Another way to help rid our bodies of unhealthy toxins, is by drinking plenty of freshwater. Because water is a natural way of helping our bodies to cleanse themselves, and flush impurities and toxins out of our system.

Another effective thing that can help to detox our bodies, is by eliminating unhealthy foods from our diet. Personally, one thing in particular that has helped me was by totally eliminating refined sugar from my diet. The truth is, refined sugar is not good for any of us, especially if we consume too much of it. For higher intakes of it can lead to health problems such as heart disease, diabetes, obesity, worsening memory, and also tooth decay.

Totally eliminating refined sugar from one's diet may seem a bit excessive to some people. And, of course, it is something that you don't have to personally do. However, the main reason why I personally decided to do it, is because I was consuming too much of it. Also, I just couldn't seem to gain control over it. So, for my own personal sake and immediate health, I decided that it was best for me to eliminate it entirely.

Prior to eliminating sugar from my diet, I had a huge sweet tooth. I pretty much loved any and everything that had sugar in it. You could say that I was a sugarholic, a true sugar junkie! There was a point when I was drinking anywhere from upwards to six or more cans of soda pop daily. And that was just soda, not to mention the cookies, donuts, cakes, ice cream, candy, and other items that contained sugar that I was also frequently consuming. The bad thing is, not only was this bad for my overall health, but it also put me in danger of being a borderline diabetic. In addition to this, it also caused me to put on a lot of unwanted weight. However, the good thing, is that, when I discontinued eating sugar, and started eating right, by implementing a good and healthy diet in to my life, along with exercise; my health quickly improved. Interestingly, within the first week of my diet, I lost 15 pounds, and within a total of four months, 32 pounds, which made me very happy, because I was able to fit back into my clothes and dress suits that I had grown out of in the past.

Another good and important thing that cutting sugar from my diet did, was that it helped my moods to become more stable, for I no longer had the sugar highs and lows. But the most important thing that I gained by giving up sugar, is that I am no longer a borderline diabetic!

True, eliminating sugar from one's diet is not an easy thing to do. It takes a lot of sacrifice and willpower. One reason why, is because there is sugar in practically everything! Another reason why, is because there are just too many temptations to deal with—like when we are out shopping at the local grocery stores. Interestingly, grocery stores are advertising experts. They know exactly what items are the *big sellers,* and what things will *attract* our attention. So, they conveniently locate and place these items where they are sure to catch our eye. Often, the moment we enter the grocery store, the first thing that we are greeted with at the entryway door is sugar products, such as: soda pop, freshly baked bakery items, chips, candies, etc. So that we will see and be tempted to buy them. The reason why, is because stores make a lot of money on these things. Unfortunately, because of this, a person that is on a special diet has to have strong willpower to say no to these things, which is not always an easy thing to do.

After I first started my sugar free diet, I vividly recall that after being without sugar for about five days, I suffered withdrawal symptoms, which left me feeling extremely irritable, crabby, and anxious. However, by the eighth day these symptoms went away for good. One thing that helped was that I replaced refined sugar with natural fruits, such as grapes, pineapple, oranges, watermelons, bananas, apples, plums, etc. Interestingly, now, after being off of sugar for so long, I find that fruits taste even better than they did in the past!

Another thing that helped in my resolve to stay off sugar, was that before I went on my sugar free diet, I prepared or conditioned my mind in advance (for a considerable length of time) to stick to my decision, so that once I started my diet, I would be determined to stay off of sugar. This way, if pastries and other sugar products were waved under my nose, or they were in the house for other family members to eat, they wouldn't tempt me to eat or consume them.

Refined sugar is just one thing that one may choose to eliminate, or reduce the amount of from their diet. There are many other foods and things that one can choose to either permanently or periodically eliminate from their diet that can help them to successfully detox their body.

In addition to detoxifying our bodies of harmful toxins, another important and beneficial thing that we can do to encourage and promote good health in us, is by incorporating *exercise* in to our lives.

Exercise regularly. When it comes to exercise, it is not only good for our physical health, but, also, it is very important to our emotional and mental health too. So, if you haven't already done so, why not try starting and maintaining a regular weekly exercise program. The truth is there are many health benefits associated with exercise. Some of them are: (1) It increases circulation of oxygen and blood flow to the body and brain, (2) It is an excellent stress reducer, (3) It helps rid our bodies of harmful chemicals and toxins, (4) It can boost our immune system, (5) It releases natural chemicals such as endorphins, dopamine, norepinephrine, and serotonin in the brain—things that will help us to be and feel better, (6) It can help us to sleep better at night, (7) It can aid in helping us to shed unwanted pounds, and lastly, (8) It can help us to feel more positive, confident, and better about ourselves.

Caution: Before exercising consult your doctor to make sure that it is safe and right for you.

Get plenty of sleep. Another important thing that is good for one's health and well-being, is to get an adequate amount of sleep—preferably eight hours per night. Because sleep helps our bodies to recover, be energized, and recharged for the next day. Without the adequate amount of sleep our mind and bodies cannot function properly, nor will we have the energy, focus, and stamina that we need to perform at our highest levels.

Purchase a good bed, and shoes. On average, we as humans spend about 8 hours per night sleeping, which basically amounts to about one third of our lives. Because of this, it is important to have a good and comfortable bed, so that we can get a good night's sleep. True, a good bed can be a very costly purchase. However, it's been said that there are two things in life that a person should never skimp on when it comes to cost or price, which is: (1) a good and comfortable bed and, (2) a good, supportive pair of shoes. The reason why, is because we spend the majority of our time in them. For if you think about it, if we are not in the one, we are in the other.

As respects beds, the reason why it is so vitally important to have a good, quality one, is that it can make a world of difference, as far as the *quality* of sleep that we get each night goes. Some good benefits of this is that it can truly refresh us, making us feel less stressful, more alert, energetic, alive, and ready to tackle another eventful and challenging day.

In regards to our feet, we can say that to a certain degree, and in many ways, that they are the pathways to good health. For example, if we weren't to take good care of our feet, it could cause us to develop various health issues, such as leg, or back problems, etc., which can wind up being very disruptive to our sleep, and also crippling, in our ability to be able to function and perform certain daily tasks, or to engage in many fun and enjoyable activities. Therefore, having this in mind, doesn't it make sense to protect and take good care of our feet the best way that we can, in particular, by wearing proper and comfortable shoes.

Take advantage of sunshine. The sun, which is located some 93 million miles away from planet earth, exerts a powerful influence on our lives. As a direct result, many people throughout history have become devoted sun worshipers. Today, there are the dedicated sunbathers, who regularly seek to acquire that all so appealing and fashionable Coppertone tan. Also, there's the annual vacationers that live in the northern states, who yearly migrate south during the cold winter months, to the highly attractive sunshine state of Florida, U.S.A, in order to enjoy the beautiful weather and bask in the rays of the warm sun. Truly, from all of this, we can undeniably see that the sun is very attractive and highly important and beneficial to us as humans.

Caution: Although the sun can have a positive and good effect on our moods, and so forth, on the flipside of things, it can also be harmful (causing skin cancer) if we don't take necessary precautions, such as wearing proper clothing, applying proper sunscreen lotion, etc., when being exposed to the sun's ultraviolet rays.

You might ask: Why are people so fascinated and attracted to the sun? Well, the reason why, is because in many ways it is good for our health and well-being. In what ways? Well, a couple of important and valuable things that the sun does for us, is that, it lifts us up emotionally, and it energizes us. Another thing is that, it provides valuable Vitamin D, which is something that our bodies require and that aids in keeping us feeling good and happy. Interestingly, there are many people who suffer from Seasonal Affective Disorder (SAD). This is due to experiencing a lack of sunshine during fall and winter seasons, when there are not as many sunny days, due to cloudy, overcast skies. From this, we can definitely see that the sun can exert a healthy and powerful influence on our lives, especially on our moods and mental health.

What might one personally do to combat SAD during gloomy, cloudy, overcast seasons? One thing that I personally did that seemed to help me, was by taking a Vitamin D supplement to compensate for a lack of sunshine. Another thing that I did, was that I used light therapy or a SAD lamp.

Light therapy uses artificial light that mimics natural sunlight. This can be an effective way to treat SAD and certain other conditions. True, light therapy lamps can be expensive. The good thing, is that, they are often paid for by one's medical insurance company. However, if medical insurance won't approve or pay for it, or you don't happen to have insurance, it can be purchased (depending on where you shop) for a somewhat reasonable price online. The important thing is that you do your research and shop around for both a good price and a good quality lamp (one that delivers the recommended 10,000 LUX light therapy), before you decide to purchase or buy.

Caution: Before taking Vitamin D supplements, or using a light therapy SAD lamp, be sure to check with your doctor beforehand to make sure that these things are safe and right for you personally. Also, he or she may want to monitor the dosage of Vitamin D, or the time and frequency of the use of a Light Therapy Lamp.

Personal cleanliness and proper grooming. It has been said that "Cleanliness is next to godliness." This includes not only the physical cleanliness of our homes, and cars, etc., but also, the personal cleanliness of our bodies. Yes, good personal hygiene and proper grooming are very important. They can have, not only a positive effect on how we look, or feel about ourselves, but they can also, give us a certain amount of dignity and self-respect. But more importantly, our personal hygiene is also good for our health and well-being. For example, just think about what could happen if we were to never brush our teeth. Eventually, they would rot and fall out. Also, if we were never to bathe and wash ourselves, it can lead to having body sores and infectious diseases. And just think of the bad odors all of this would produce. In the process we could lose a lot of friends, because nobody would want to be around us. How much better we and others are, when we give appropriate and proper attention to our personal cleanliness, and good grooming.

Learn to relax. Life can be stressful. Not only is this true, but it's probably a gross understatement. For many people have to daily cope with things such as, earning a living, rush hour traffic, pressures in school or on the job, the everyday hustle and bustle of life, and so forth. Because of these things, tensions and stress levels can so easily build and flare up in us, which, if we are not careful, can lead to serious health issues. Knowing this, it is absolutely vital for us to seek and find ways and things that can help us to relax and unwind. What kind of things might help? Well, there are a vast number of things that we can personally choose that can help us to relax and de-stress—things such as getting away and taking a needed break or vacation; or getting a body massage; or using a steam room or a sauna; or sitting in a whirlpool; or utilizing aromatherapy; or taking a peaceful and quiet stroll through nature's woodlands or a local park; or reading a good book; or gardening; or going fishing, etc.,—anything that we can utilize that will help us to relax and unwind.

Take Time to Breathe. From the very moment of birth, when we took our first breath of fresh air, it has been essential for us to breathe. This is both a necessary and vital function of life. For not only does it keep us alive, but it also serves other purposes as well, such as providing us with the oxygen that our bodies require to properly manage and regulate itself, so as to keep us healthy. For example, the oxygen that we take in flushes toxins, such as carbon dioxide out of our body. Oxygen also burns sugars and fatty acids in our cells to produce energy. These are just a couple of the valuable things that breathing does for us, there are more.

In addition to helping our physical bodies to stay alive and healthy, breathing can also play an important role in our emotional health too, especially, if we both learn how to and practice breathing right, which involves deep diaphragmatic breathing.[68] One of the benefits of doing this, is that, it can help to relieve stress and anxiety, which, in turn, can make us feel better mentally, emotionally, and physically.

Because breathing is so vitally important to our overall health and well-being, it would be advantageous for us individually, to set aside some personal time (even if it is only 5 minutes per day), to engage in breathing exercises. By doing this, we will feel so much better.

Take one day at a time. Often, it can be difficult for people with bipolar disorder to be able to function normally, on a daily basis, by performing simple daily tasks. In this regard, I personally found that it is best for me, not to get too worked up over worrying about what tomorrow or future days will bring, but instead, to learn to relax, by taking just one day at a time. This way, it helped me to avoid feeling too overwhelmed! Truth is, life has enough pressures and problems for us to have to deal with as it is, coupled with daily anxieties. A person doesn't need to add to this by putting too much of a load on themselves. So, just learn to relax, by taking one day at a time, by

---

[68] Note: For those of us that need help with breathing exercises and the techniques on how to breathe correctly, you can either consult a physician, or check out several good and helpful instructional videos online.

doing this, it can take a huge weight off of one's shoulders.

Help and Support from Family and Friends

As humans, we all need a good, positive, and loving support base—people that we can associate with, approach, have around, and seek advice from, etc.,—people who can encourage us, uplift our spirits, and make us feel good about ourselves and life. This is absolutely essential, especially, when we happen to be undergoing difficult, trying, and troubling times. This is where support from family and friends can come in real handy.

Personally, I can attest to how encouraging others have been to me, especially my family members. For example, when I was hospitalized in the past, for having severe depression, they were not only there for me, but also, they were very loving and supportive. Quickly rallying together, they came to my immediate aid, showing kindness, understanding, patience, and rendering helpful and positive assistance. And even though I was completely overwhelmed with sadness at the time, it made me feel good and secure having them in my corner and by my side.

Interestingly, encouraging words, whether they are written or spoken, can be extremely powerful and helpful! They can have a soothing, healing, and cheering affect upon one's mind, heart, and soul, thereby lifting and picking them up during difficult, discouraging, and hard times. On the other hand, negative speech, along with a lack of support and encouragement can cause and feed sadness, and even deep depression.

Often, when it comes to a person who is dealing with the distressing pain of depression and bipolar disorder, there are times when they may have the tendency to isolate themselves from others. Sometimes, this can go on for days, and weeks. Unfortunately, this happened to me, shortly after I had suffered a mental breakdown in 2011. Finally, my wife had to intervene and encourage me to seek immediate medical help, which I did. Fortunately for me, if it wasn't for her loving help, encouragement, and support, who knows how bad things might have gotten. Whatever the case, this shows how important it is for us not to completely isolate ourselves from others, especially from those who can give us encouragement and emotional support during times of need.

Setting Positive Goals

Having both short-term and long-term goals is important for everyone to have. The reason why, is because they help to keep us motivated, growing, and moving forward in life. Without goals, our lives can easily become stagnated and unfulfilled. Yes, goals are important for everybody, but especially, are they good and healthy for people who suffer from depression. Speaking from personal experience; it is so easy to become engulfed and weighed down in one's emotional pain and sorrows, that in the process we let life slip away or pass us by. So, if you personally don't have any goals that you are currently working on, why not start one today. It doesn't have to be anything huge or complicated. It could be the simple goal of going for a walk, or exercising for 10 minutes—three times a week. And then, after you get use to this, perhaps later, you might want to gradually increase the amount of your workout time, until you get to 30 minute workouts—three times per week.

When it comes to goals, sometimes it is best to keep them simple, realistic, and obtainable, rather than setting the bar too high, so to speak, only to fall short of reaching them, which in itself can be highly discouraging.

So, don't sit idle and let life pass you by. But, instead, be determined to make the most of it, by having and setting reachable and attainable goals that keep you, not only moving forward, but also, feeling proud and good about yourself, your personal achievements, and accomplishments in life.

Being Conscious of Your Spiritual Needs

As humans, we were created with a need, not only for physical food and things, but equally important, if not even more so, is the fact that we also have a spiritual need too. And by reaching out to fulfill and satisfy that need, it helps to contribute, not only to good spiritual health, but also, to good emotional, mental, and physical health too. The reason being, is because, all of these necessary factors and things happen to be interdependently connected or linked together. With that being said, what are some things that being spiritual can do for us?

Happiness. One important thing that being spiritual does for a person, is that, it promotes and contributes to their happiness. Interestingly, during his famous Sermon on the Mount speech, God's son, Jesus Christ, said: "Happy are those conscious of their spiritual need." (Matthew 5:3) Yes, by our recognizing the need for and seeking God's guidance, it contributes to real contentment; a sense of satisfaction; and fulfillment in life, which can bring us a good measure of personal joy and happiness.

Comfort during times of need. Another thing that being spiritual can do for us, is that, we can gain peace and comfort through prayer; especially, during times of need. At 2 Corinthians 1:3, 4 it says: "Praised be the God and Father of our Lord Jesus Christ, the Father of tender mercies and the God of all comfort…who comforts us in all our trials."

Valuable fruits of God's spirit. Some additional benefits that we can gain through spirituality, is that, the Holy Spirit, which we receive from God, can produce joy and other valuable qualities in us, qualities that can help us to endure trials and sufferings. At Galatians 5:22, 23 it says: "On the other hand, the fruitage of the spirit is love, joy, peace, patience, kindness, goodness, faith, mildness, and self-control."

Refreshment for our souls. God's son, Jesus Christ, invitingly encourages us at Matthew 11:28, 29, saying: "Come to me, all you who are toiling and loaded down, and I will *refresh* you… Take my yoke upon you and learn from me, for I am mild-tempered and lowly in heart, and you will find *refreshment* for yourselves… For my yoke is kindly, and my load is light."

Relief from burdens. Life is an amazing, wonderful, and beautiful thing. But it also has its share of troubles and problems too. However, fortunately, we are not alone in having to deal with them. For God willingly and generously offers to help carry our heavy burdens for us. At Psalm 55:22, we are encouraged: "Throw your burden on Jehovah, and he will sustain you. Never will he allow the righteous one to fall."

Positive hope for the future. In regard to those who may currently be suffering from a discouraging illness, the Bible gives positive encouragement, and hope. Concerning a future time, near at hand, God promises to cure all sicknesses and diseases. Isaiah 33:24 says about that coming time period: "And no resident will say: I am sick. The people dwelling in the land will be pardoned for their error." What a truly amazing time this will be, when people are no longer sick!

Yes, as we can see from the above examples, there are many helpful and wonderful things that we can gain from being conscious of our spiritual need.

In conclusion, from all of the information and things that we just considered, we can clearly see that there are many things that one can personally take advantage of and do that can aid in helping them to successfully cope with depression and bipolar disorder. For a condensed list of some of these things, as well as, additional, helpful things, see the information *"A Recipe for a Healthy Mind,"* on pages 238-239. And also, *"Things That Can Help Fight Added Depression,"* on pages 240-243.

A Recipe for a Healthy Mind

1. View yourself as a beautiful and good person.

2. Stay positive, by feeding your mind positive and up-building things.

3. Don't completely isolate yourself from others.

4. Associate with optimistic, encouraging, helpful, and happy people.

5. Be forgiving.

6. Always look for the good in people and things, even when it doesn't seem to be there.

7. Get plenty of rest and sleep.

8. Have and maintain a good and healthy nutritious diet.

9. Drink plenty of water. Because water promotes good health, and helps to flush harmful toxins out of our system.

10. Avoid consuming too much refined sugar. This can be bad for one's overall health.

11. Exercise regularly. It's important to have a consistent, weekly exercise program in place. Caution: Be sure to check with your doctor first before starting an exercise program, and then, follow his or her suggestions and recommendations.

12. Get plenty of sunshine; or during cloudy seasons, such as wintertime, when the sun doesn't come out as much, you may want to take a Vitamin D supplement. Or, if possible, use Light Therapy (a SAD lamp). Caution: Be sure to use appropriate sunscreen when exposed to the sun. Also, when it comes to Vitamin D supplements or Light Therapy, be sure to consult your doctor to determine what is best for you.

13. Have and set good and healthy obtainable goals.

14. Set limitations. It's important to know your limitations, and to set boundaries. This way you won't be spreading yourself too thin or be biting off more than you can personally handle or

chew, which can result in inflicting unnecessary stress and anxiety on ourselves.

15. Practice giving. The Bible says: "There is more happiness in giving than there is in receiving." (Acts 20:35)

16. Make time for recreation and play.

17. Don't vegetate mainly on TV or surfing the internet. Instead, you might want to find a good book to read. Or do some other fun and creative things.

18. Release daily stress. You can do this by using and having stress reducers in place. There are many options to choose from. Find what works best for you.

19. Learn to relax and breathe.

20. Take one day at a time.

The things listed above may seem like a lot to do and apply at first. But don't worry. Don't let this overwhelm you. Instead, you might want to incorporate just one thing at a time in to your daily routine. And then, when you become comfortable with it, you might want to slowly and progressively add more. Keep in mind that even if you do just a little, it is more beneficial than not doing anything at all.[69]

---

[69] Note: This is not to say that if a person applies these things, that they, as a result will have a perfectly healthy mind. However, it can to a certain degree be beneficial and helpful when we personally do all that we can to lead good and healthy lives.

Things That Can Help Fight Added Depression

Do's & Don'ts: Listed below in no specific order:

- Don't become a product of negative thought. But instead, fight it! This is important because often our thinking has the power to dictate who we are or what we become.

- Do not expect or look to receive approval from everyone. It may never happen!

- Don't blame yourself for having bipolar disorder. It is not your fault. It's a disease, like cancer or any other illness. Nor is it due to your being mentally or spiritually weak as some ignorant or highly uninformed people might imply. It is just a malady or illness that people happened to get. So, don't punish yourself. Also, you are not a bad person because you suffer from depression or bipolar disorder. It can happen to anybody.

- Don't expect or wait for anybody to help you with your mental health condition. The balls in your court. So, take the initiative to seek and get the medical help and any other assistance that you may need.

- Don't stop taking your prescribed medications, unless it is recommended by your doctor; otherwise, this can cause a mental relapse.

- Do not place yourself in an overly negative and critical environment that aggravates and feeds your depression.

- Do not completely isolate yourself from others. As humans, we were created or made to be social creatures that both need and can positively feed off of others.

- Don't hold grudges by keeping account of the injury or pain that others may have inflicted upon you. It is better to forgive, even if the wrongs that people commit against us seem intentional. Why? Because resentment and hate can be harmful and damaging to our emotional, mental, and physical health.

- "Do not let yourself be conquered by the evil, but keep conquering the evil with the good." (Romans 12:21)

- Don't be overly negative and critical of others. Fact is, we can find faults and weaknesses in everyone, including ourselves. We all have them. The reason being, is because, we are all sinful, imperfect creatures. The better thing to do, is to look for and focus on the good in people and things. If we practice doing this, it will be good for us and others, including our own health.

- Don't let depression control you. Take control of the steering wheel so-to-speak, and guide and steer yourself in a positive and uplifting direction.

- Don't expect perfection or too much from others. Also, don't put anyone on too high of a pedestal. Have reasonable expectations and opinions of people. This way, you won't be too devastated or let down if they should happen to disappoint you.

- Don't let your shortcomings discourage and crush you. But rather, view your mistakes and negative experiences as valuable stepping stones of positive learning experiences that: (1) Will help to improve your outlook on life, and (2) Will aid in improving and strengthening your value and character, and (3) Will help to prepare you for a better future; rather than viewing them as stumbling blocks of hurt and pain, which can cripple your growth, development, forward momentum, and progress, as well as rob you of inner peace, joy, and happiness.

- Don't let others dictate or decide your personal value or self-worth. Instead, accept and appreciate yourself for the beautiful and valuable person that you are.

- Don't beat yourself up over past mistakes. True, it is normal to feel bad about the shortcomings and errors that we have made in life, especially, big ones. But too much guilt can crush one's spirit. It can also rob us of our inner peace, joy, and happiness. The truth is, we cannot correct or change our past. But we can; however, learn from our mistakes and move forward. You will feel so much better for doing this.

- Don't let others keep punishing you for your past mistakes. I call this type of finger pointing and fault-finding, which is often accompanied by nasty, verbal assaults, the *"You did this. And you did that, syndrome."* This type of fault-finding or finger pointing is when someone never lets you forget the past. But rather, they keep bringing it up, over and over again, constantly throwing it in your face; causing you to re-live the pain over and over again. The fact is, for the overall health, well-being, and benefit of both us and them, they need to get over it, and so do we. For finger pointing can be highly crippling and damaging to both the recipient and their friendship or relationship with others. But it can also make life truly miserable!

- Do not allow your mind free reign to think as it wants. But instead, exercise self-control and discipline. Like driving a moving vehicle, we must take and maintain control of the wheel so to speak, by guiding and steering our minds in a positive direction to where we want it to go.

- Don't let *bad* feelings or emotions get the best of you. The fact is, bad feelings and emotions can drown or bury us if we allow them to. But also, they can make us sick (emotionally, mentally, and physically). So, don't let them overwhelm you. Instead, take and keep control over them.

- Don't over-think things. Sometimes, if we dig too deep, especially, in regard to negative things, it can create unnecessary problems, which can lead us into a sinkhole of misery and despair.

- Don't let the hypocrisy of others discourage you.

- Don't keep or pursue hurtful, discouraging, or worthless, so-called "friends." They will only pull you down. So, cut them off and let them go. And then, move on to seeking positive associates that will love, encourage, support, and build you up.

- Don't sit idle for too long. Try to stay busy. For it's been said "An idle mind is the devil's playground." Also, inactivity can be harmful to us to a certain degree, in that, it can zap us of our energy, causing us to become more sluggish, and even depressed. On the other hand, being active in good pursuits can energize us—giving us even more energy! Also, it can aid in helping us to have a more positive viewpoint and outlook about ourselves! So try to stay busy if you can.

- Don't feel sorry for yourself. Too much self-pity can be self-destructive and damaging.

- Don't let the overly negative and critical opinions and viewpoints of others discourage and tear you down. The truth is, there are much better and more uplifting things in life to concentrate and focus your valuable time, energy, and attention on.

- Don't let others emotionally abuse you. Unfortunately, there are some sick people in the world who get their kicks out of verbally crushing and abusing others. However, for your own emotional and mental health, and overall well-being, get away from them ASAP, and avoid them like the plague!

- Don't let others judge or determine your personal standing with God. The truth is, sometimes people can be overly negative and critical, self-righteous, and condemning. But ultimately, the decision lies with God. It is up to him to judge and decide your fate and standing with him.

- Do not self-medicate. Unfortunately, some people try to drown their sorrows and pain in alcohol, or illicit drug use, etc. But in the end these crippling and self-damaging pursuits wind up leaving them feeling empty and even more depressed.

- Don't give up. As difficult as life can sometimes seem, it is still worth living. And often, circumstances or things that at present may seem completely lost and hopeless, oftentimes, they can and do change for the better. So, keep hope alive. For hope, is like a bright beacon that brightens our path and enlightens our way!

Story 1

FINDING THE LOST MAN
THAT LIES WITHIN — ME

I walked the lonely streets alone for many a year, searching to find the lost man that lies within—me. Not having any help, sure direction or guide, and not knowing exactly where to look, I soon became disheartened, and confused. Because no matter where and how hard I searched, I just couldn't seem to find, the lost man that lies within—me.

So, I turned to living a debauched life of sin and crime. And I indulged myself in pleasures of various kinds; anything, to help ease the pain, to wipe away the blues from my heart and mind. But these vices and pursuits only made matters worse. Because I still couldn't find, the lost man that lies within—me.

One day, a certain man happened to pass my way. He had gray hair and a beard, and a timeworn face. And so, I stopped him to ask for his help, hoping that he could perhaps provide direction, or shed some valuable light, on how I might find the lost man that lies within—me. I reasoned that, surely, this well seasoned old man, with the knowledge, wisdom, and experience that he has gained throughout his lifelong years, would easily be able to provide the direction I need, even if it be just a small crumb or a kernel of truth that would be useful to me to find, the lost man that lies within—me.

After clearly explaining my dilemma, and expressing to him my desperate and urgent need, the old man, without uttering one single word, leaned forward. And he peered into my misty eyes. Then, he shrugged his shoulders, and shook his head. Afterwards, he turned around, and continued moving on ahead, down a long and twisted road, in his own fixed path. I guess he just didn't have much to say or share?

Sadly, the discouraging encounter with the old man only left me feeling more baffled, exasperated, and lost. You see, I've always had such a strong yearning, an eager desire to find that poor ole soul that I'm so desperately seeking to find, the lost man that lies within—me.

Not satisfied with the present, or settling for anything less; not wanting to live just any ole life, I continued on my steadfast and arduous journey, still hoping; still seeking to find, the lost man that lies within—me. Then, suddenly, the night turned pitch-black. And the air became bitterly cold. But I didn't have a sweater or anything, to comfort and warm my freezing soul.

After the darkness and coldness roughly set in, it became ever more soberly clear to me, just how deeply I was lost. That's when a horrible fear grabbed hold of me. And I began to further question, and even doubt, that I might find the lost man that lies within—me.

Following fear; came further frustration, anger, increasing sorrow and pain. The kind of things, all working together in unison, can torment a soul, and totally rob one of peace. And I started to lose all hope, that I would truly ever find the lost man that lies within—me.

As days and years passed by, I verbally lashed out at people that I rubbed shoulders with. Because, nobody; not a single soul, didn't seem to understand or even care, about the miserable plight that I was in. Sadly, the insensitivity of their cold hearts left me feeling lonelier, down, and depressed. And I began to despise them for this, and avoid them. Because they made the hurt I feel a whole lot worse.

Later, one day, as I walked along the city streets, with my head hanging low, and in sober thought; just out of the blue, I looked up, and when I did, I caught sight of my reflection in a sheet of glass. It appeared in a hazy storefront window as I passed. But the image I saw didn't seem to match the vision of the man in my head, the one I was hoping to find; the lost man that lies within—me. Perhaps the tears in my eyes got in the way, and prevented me from being able to clearly see. Whatever the case, I left brokenhearted and down. However, still onward bound, and determined, to find the lost man that lies within—me.

As I continued to travel through life, I looked for landmarks, signs, and clues; anything, that might help to lead me to, the lost man that lies within—me. But the sights and sounds that I was seeing and hearing, were not inherently familiar to my soul. They only left me feeling more puzzled, disoriented, and lost.

Often, in life, there are many obstacles that get in one's way, when they are pursuing a vision, a goal, or a dream. Like the things that were impeding my efforts to find the lost man that lies within—me.

Finally, one day, when I was about to give up on my search; completely concede defeat; throw in the towel; suddenly, the heavy grey clouds that forever loom above my head, broke open in the sky. And a thick callus fell from my eyes. Afterwards, the sun came out, and it began to shine, ever so bright! So brightly, that it illuminated my heart, mind, and darkened soul. Then, it happened. At a time that I would have least expected it to occur. He appeared! The man I thought was forever lost within—me. The person I've always longed to see and know. He miraculously arrived and stood before my very soul! The experience was so touching and moving that I could barely believe my eyes! Now, for the very first time in my life, my face began to light up and glow. And immediately, I broke down and started to cry. Because of the sheer joy I was feeling inside. For he took away all the anger, frustration, and loneliness I used to feel. And the pain I felt for so long; finally began to heal. No, this was no imaginative dream that I was having; it was all so genuine, and ever so real!

Now, because of him; the man within—me, who was once lost, but now is found, I'm seeing life anew and in a completely different way. Because the tormented and lost soul that I became in the past, has finally been set free at last. For upon his arrival, he bestowed upon me a very special gift; something that not too many people in life come to possess; an important element that's absolutely vital to one's soul; their peace, happiness, and well-being, and that is, a love of self.

The strange thing is, now, I've also come to have love for other people too. But this is a good thing, a true blessing. Because this new outlook, along with finding the lost man that lies within—me, helps me to keep anger in control and pain at bay. And it prevents the troublesome, ugly things of my past, from resurfacing to re-plague my mind, heart, and soul, the way that they used to.

This wonderful and drastic change of mind and heart, along with the most important thing, which is, finding the man that was lost within—me; I owe, not to anything in particular that I personally did. However, I guess it does help when you start to accept people and things for the way they are. It also helps when you finally let go of your past; the things that left you bitter, angry, and scarred.

It's not that things are totally rosy now, for this is no made up fairytale, some imagined *"Cinderella Dream."* I still have to face the daily realities of life, and any challenges that come my way. But at least I've found an inner peace, joy, happiness, and contentment that I had never known and experienced before. Precious and priceless qualities, that are by far more valuable than any diamonds, gold, or material possessions that one can possess. Because the man within—me, the person who was once lost, has now been found, and he is free!

True, many years were lost in my search, looking to find the lost man that lies within—me. For through the process, I've grown old and gray. But, although the journey was both long and painful, it was well worth all the time and effort spent. For it brings much joy to my heart and soul to know, that the man within—me, is no longer lost, but that he is finally here!

Now, I'm as free as a bird, that is no longer kept down, for I can now see, hear, feel, and discover many things; things that were hidden from and eluded me in the past; amazing things that are far above and beyond this world. But the most important and rewarding thing of all is, I'm now able to spend the exciting and valuable time left, with the beautiful man that lies within—Me!

Story 2

NO VACANCY HERE

I recently met some new friends. They came to me in my hour of need. You see, my whole world had fallen apart; I was down in the dumps; and my heart had begun to bleed.

One day, I awoke to a loud knocking and rapping at my door. As I lay there in bed, thoroughly agitated and annoyed, by the unexpected sound and disturbance, I yelled out: "Who is it?" But, there was no response; just a steady knocking and rapping at my door.

"Go away! Let me be! Can't you see that I am trying to sleep?" I angrily shouted. But, still no response, just a knocking and rapping at my door.

I grumbled and muttered to myself: "Who can this be, at this early hour of the day? Why don't they just go away, and leave me alone to stay?"

Knock, knock, knock... rap, rap, rap... goes the annoying and disturbing sound again.

So, I forcefully and painfully pulled myself out of bed, and stumbled to the door. Then, I flung the door open, and yelled: "What do you want?"

The person on the other side of the door; dressed in a long, white overcoat, and clutching a traveling pack in his hand, respectfully and calmly said: "Hello, I'm sorry to wake you, Sir. Sorry to trouble you, indeed I am. My name is Peace. I'm just a traveler passing through, looking for a place to rest."

In response, I said to Peace (hoping that he would just turn around and leave soon); "I don't think I have the space? You see, this place is small, and a little cramped for room!"

Peace replied: "That's quite okay with me, Sir. I don't need much room; just a place to rest my head. Also, from the visual signs above, the way things are looking in the dark and cloudy sky— shelter from the coming storm!"

With that being said; what could I say? So, I opened up and invited Peace inside.

Later that night, as Peace and I sat together by the fireplace and talked, I told him my sad story, about how everything fell apart, and how it completely broke my heart.

Peace sat and listened patiently until I was done speaking. Then he reached into his travel pack and pulled out a fiddle, and he started to play and sing. He played a very charming tune, and sang with an angel's voice. It was the most beautiful and soothing thing I have ever heard! It made me feel restful, cozy, and warm. And, before you knew it, I dosed off and fell sound asleep.

The next day, once again, I awoke to a loud knock at my door.

So, I rose up to see who it was. It was a stranger; someone named, Love. He said: "I'm but a traveler passing through, looking for a place to stay."

In response, I replied to Love: "Peace is already here. I don't know if I have the room for one more soul to lay?"

Love, entreatingly remarked: "I traveled a long way, from a distant land afar. I won't take up much space. I'm just looking for shelter, before daylight turns to dark!"

So, I gave in, and opened up, and let Love inside, for he possessed a true sincerity, that I just could not deny.

Later, in the evening, as Love and I sat together and talked, I told him my sad story about how everything fell apart; how it broke my heart; and how bad I felt. All the while, Love sat patiently, listening till I was done speaking. Then, Love told me a story about a man he used to know. He said: "There is a man that I once knew, who, initially, had a very good and tender heart. But then, in time, he had undergone some very difficult problems and things that caused him a lot of pain and sorrow—horrible things that brought him to his knees and that made his heart break and bleed. As a result, the man eventually wound up moving far away, completely isolating himself from the cold and cruel world. And, unfortunately, he turned bitter and sad. For, from day to day, things only got worse for him, and increasingly bad!"

Apparently, the man's story that Love was relating, was so sad to tell, that it brought Love to tears! At one point, he even paused, the lump in his throat to clear.

Interestingly, the man's story (Love was relating), seemed so similar to mine. It was like I was peering into a mirror and seeing myself for the very first time. Then, suddenly, bewildering things that seemed so puzzling to me in the past, now, finally started to come together and make perfect sense—as sunlight began to rise and flood into the dark shadows of my mind and heart. And, as my vision began to clear and un-fog, I also began to hear the sound of my heart and feel its rhythmic beat and feelings once again. And, before you knew it, I dosed off and fell into a deep and wonderful, blissful sleep.

The next day, again, I awoke to a knock at my door. When I answered, it was another stranger. His name was, Joy—with the heart of a boy. He said: "I'm a traveler passing through, looking for a place to lodge."

In response, I said to Joy: "I don't think I have the room, since I now have Peace, and Love."

Joy replied: "I won't take up too much space. I just need a place to reside. So, please dear, Sir, if you will, please let me come inside!"

"Alright then, come on in," I finally said.

Later that night, as Joy and I sat around and talked, I told him my sad story about what had happened to me; but then, how Peace and Love came and knocked at my door, and how they both moved in. In response, Joy said: "I'm glad to hear that things for you have positively turned around! The last thing you need in life is to be lying with your face buried in the ground! You know, I think this calls for a celebration, a time to laugh and cheer!" At this, Joy quickly sprung to his feet, and started to move and dance, as his face lit up and shined with a joyful radiance!

What an amazing sight to behold, as I watched Joy, pirouette, tap, jump high into the air and spin, and lay his soft shoes down so gently upon the ground. Immediately, Peace joined in and began to play his fiddle, and Love began to sing along.

The spectacle was so joyful and delightful to watch and hear, that I just couldn't help, but to get up and join in the dance, to move myself to the rhythm of the beat; to hop, boogie, and prance.

Peace played his fiddle, and Love sang along, while Joy and I danced to the delightful song! We danced and played the night away, right up to the early morning dawn. Then, afterwards, the four of us sat together and watched the sun rise. It was the most amazing and beautiful sight I had ever beheld, since I opened up and let Peace, Love, and Joy in to my life!

The next day, I heard a knock at my door. I answered it. It was someone named, Get-Me-Down. He said: "I'm a traveler passing through, looking for a place to crash."

In response, I said to him, before I closed the door: "No Vacancy Here!" Finally, at last!

Story 3

OLD MAN ZUCKERMAN

AND

HIS NOISY OLE CANE

He walks with an itty-bitty gimp, a hitch, and a giddy up too; wielding a cane in his hand, with a mighty firm grip; dressed in a faded, tattered suit, and scuffed up, bent over shoes; sportin a dusty, secondhand, Stetson hat, with a cocked down brim; movin like a snail, as he slowly inches himself along, down a long, city sidewalk street, while he whistles to the tune of his favorite song.

A rap, a tap, tap… a rap, a tap, tap… goes his noisy ole cane, as he gingerly passes by; whistling that all so familiar refrain off key. Suddenly, he stops and pauses, but, only for a moment, to wipe his sweaty brow, with a dingy, white, monogram handkerchief that bears a stranger's mark. Then, he continues on his way, without notably missing a beat… a rap, a tap, tap… a rap, a tap, tap… goes his noisy ole cane, as it forcefully strikes hard against the ground, while he whistles to the sound of the beat.

Old man, Zuckerman, is his name; the man from Okoboji, with his noisy ole cane. A rap, a tap, tap… a rap, a tap, tap… goes that annoying, disturbing, and irritating sound — like the blasts of a jackhammer worker pounding on the street, or a big ole woodpecker steadily drumming on a tree!

A rap, a tap, tap… a rap, a tap, tap… "Here he comes! Here comes old man, Zuckerman! He's right on time today; the same as all other previous days!" many curious onlookers confirm and say. "Day after day, like clockwork, he passes by our way, along this same ole path, no later than ten o eight. Strolling pass the barbershop… pass the hardware store… and then, finally, down and around the corner drugstore at the end of the street. He's traveled this way for so long a time that he's even worn a path in the cement! A rap, a tap, tap… a rap, a tap, tap… goes the sound of his noisy ole cane, as it forcefully strikes hard against the ground, while he whistles to the tune of his favorite song, with an occasional shrill, shriek, and squeal! Old man, Zuckerman, is his name, the man from Okoboji, with his noisy ole cane!" A rap, a tap, tap… a rap, a tap, tap!

He has no special skills or hidden talents; no good looks; no higher education. He's got little credit to his name, and even less cash. He's just an ordinary, everyday guy, with worn out knees and spindly legs; sportin a crooked smile, with two spaced teeth in the middle, wide enough to place three stacked quarters between.

He's sure to stir up a giggle, illicit a smile, or inspire a joke or two, from onlookers, as they watch him pass through. For he walks with an itty-bitty gimp, a hitch, and a giddy up too; wielding a cane in his hand, with a mighty firm grip; dressed in a faded, tattered suit, and scuffed up, bent over shoes; sportin a dusty, secondhand, Stetson hat, with a cocked down brim; movin like a

255

snail, as he slowly inches himself along, down a long, city sidewalk street, while he whistles to the tune of his favorite song.

A rap, a tap, tap… a rap, a tap, tap… goes the sound of the cane.

"Look at old man, Zuckerman," people stop, and look, and say. "Every single day, he passes along our way; no later than ten o eight. Strolling pass the barbershop… pass the hardware store… and then, finally, down and around the corner drugstore at the end of the street. He's traveled this way for so long a time that he's even worn a path in the cement! A rap, a tap, tap… a rap, a tap, tap… goes his annoying cane! The sound of it is almost enough to drive you to go insane!"

As the people and curious onlookers chatter amongst themselves, about old man, Zuckerman, and his noisy ole cane, he eventually reaches the end of the block. And then, he turns the corner, and disappears from sight. Afterwards, daylight gradually falls, and it turns to night.

~

It is now the next day, for yesterday has come and gone. The time is ten after ten in the morning. So, one man at the Barbershop turns to those present, and he says: "It is now ten minutes after ten, according to my watch. Has anyone seen old man, Zuckerman? I wonder what's keeping him today, and why he's so late! Like clockwork, he always walks along this street, at the same time, each and every day, with his noisy ole cane."

"Oh, haven't you heard," the Barber sadly replies. "He died last night and went to heaven. I have to admit, the street's feeling a little empty and quiet, and the sky's a little blue, without old man, Zuckerman, and his noisy ole cane strollin through, with a rap, a tap, tap… a rap, a tap, tap… as he joyfully whistled along, to his favorite tune!"

"We have to agree," the inquiring man, and all the other people present reply to the Barber. And then, continuing, with one harmonious voice, they all say: "This Street will never ever be quite the same; from this day going forward on, now that Old Man, Zuckerman, and his Noisy Ole Cane are gone!"

Story 4

THE PIT OF DOOM

"Help!... Help!... Help!... Somebody help me! Help!... Help! I've fallin into a trap! Please help me! Please!" I yelled and cried out loud, as I sat there, waist deep, suspended upright in the deadly pit of doom.

"Help me!... Help me!... I've fallen in quicksand, and I can't get out! Help!... Help!... Help!" I continued to yell and frantically shout about.

Pausing for a moment, I stopped to listen, to see if someone was near, someone who might have heard my cries for help, who perhaps could come and rescue me. But, sad to say, no one was there. No one around to hear my pleas, as I sat there helplessly, slowly sinking into the ground.

~

Narrator:

Poor, Everest Hothmyer! Never in his wildest dreams would he had ever imagined to be in this frightening mess and gloom;

sitting in a deadly pool of earth, water, and sand—this colloid of liquefied soil. The thirsty swallower and hungry destroyer of souls, that lies quietly, secretly, patiently in wait, for the unwary to blindly happen upon and fall into its trap, this unimaginable fate and nightmare in the horrifying "Pit of Doom!"

~

Everest Hothmyer:

Angry and upset, I thought to myself: *"How could I let this happen? Why wasn't I alert to the possible dangers that might lie hidden in my path? Why did I allow myself to fall into the horrible and sad situation of this death dealing trap? Dropping... sinking... descending... slowly plummeting downward into the pit of misery and despair — the large, highly inescapable, deadly pothole that in one huge, big gulp, can swallow a man whole!"*

~

Narrator:

Unfortunately, the crazy, but yet, scientifically truthful thing about quicksand, is that, the more that a person wiggles, squirms or moves, or tries to fight it, the faster they sink.

Initially, when Mr. Hothmyer first stepped into the pit, he was knee deep in quicksand. But then, he slowly and gradually began to sink up to his waist, where he now unfortunately stands.

Frantically looking and searching for a way out, Everest proceeds to quickly assess the situation, as he scans the area with his eyes, looking for something that he can perhaps reach, something that can possibly be used to help pull him up and out of the open pit. However, sad to say, to his misfortune and dismay, he finds absolutely nothing, not a single thing that might help to save him from this overwhelmingly frightful state—this most awful and horrifying fate! All he can do now is to wait, hope, and see if someone, who might be traveling nearby, will happen to come his way before it's too late!

~

Everest Hothmyer:

I'm slowly sinking, dropping, descending further and deeper into the bottomless pit of despair — the cold, callus, insensitive, heartless and cruel, death dealing chasm — the camouflaged, open grave, that secretly lays its trap for the unsuspecting and unwary victim to fall into. I can't help but to panic and scream, knowing that this horrible predicament that I've gotten myself into, for a certainty, spells my ultimate doom!

"Help me!... Help me!... Help!... Help!... Help!" once again I proceeded to scream at the top of my lungs. But sadly, to no avail. For there is no one anywhere around to pull me up and out of this incarcerating pit of doom, this tormenting place of hell!

"This is crazy!" I screamed with a loud and angry voice.

"Man… I am dumb! I'm nothing but a big, stupid idiot! How in the world could I have let this happen—to fall into this awful mess?" Everest, angrily says to himself, with a lump in his throat, a whimper in his voice, and tears in his eyes, as he finally breaks down and starts to weep, with a painful cry.

~

Narrator:

Unfortunately, with the passing of time, with the ticking away of each and every moment on the clock, Everest proceeds to slowly descend further into the pit of agony and despair. For he is now up to his chest in quicksand.

As he lies there contemplating the inevitable truth of his extremely bad situation and plight, he begins to panic even more! Then, suddenly, his whole life begins to quickly flash before his eyes.

Moving at the speed of light, Everest's mind begins quickly thumbing through every page in the extensive library of memories that are conveniently stored and tucked away in the small compartments, crevices, and recesses of his extremely complex, human mind.

Truth is, because the agonizing pangs of facing possible death has no censure or off switch — at a time that you do not wish or want it to — it will blurt out any and everything about you, concerning things that have happened in your entire life, even things that you may not have been fully aware of or conscience of in the past; or about the things that you deliberately tried to hide and bury away in the back of your mind—things that you are not proud of, or perhaps you're ashamed of, or that you are too cowardly to accept and face.

The reason why, is because fear of death holds no secrets; it tells no lies. It is a revealer of secrets. It leaves nothing uncovered and unspoken, no stone unturned. It reveals all and everything about you (from your idiosyncrasies, down to your tiniest of faults), any and everything that you may have willfully or unconsciously put or stashed away deep in your psyche or locked away within the chambers and vaults of your mind and heart. Interestingly, during this amazing unveiling process, people often view or see life in a completely different and much clearer way than they ever did in the past. However, unfortunately, it is also a time when extreme guilt and shame can surface to plague your mind, heart, and soul—about the things that you should have done or tried, or even failed to do, when you had the opportunity and time (while you were still alive).

~

Everest Hothmyer:

Suddenly, my whole life began to flash before my eyes. It candidly told me the complete truth about present days, and times of distant past. It reminded me about everything—about the things I've seen; and places I've been; and also about the things I've done; failed to do; and the things that I've said.

"I should have hugged my mom and dad, and told them how much I love them. I should've gone out to lunch or for a cup of coffee or tea with my sister. I should have found and married the girl of my dreams, settled down and had children, a nice family. I should have traveled and seen the *Seven Wonders of the World*: (1) the "Great Pyramid of Giza," (2) the "Great Wall of China," (3) "Petra," (4) the "Coliseum in Rome," (5) "Chichen Itza," (6) "Machu Picchu," and (7) the "Taj Mahal." I should have learned to play a musical instrument. And I should've written a book. I should have done something special, good, and important to be remembered for—to leave behind my indelible mark for doing something to make a difference in the world or in someone's life, instead of foolishly squandering and wasting my time away, from year to year, and from day to day. Now, here I am, about to die this shameful and humiliating death in a stupid hole; sinking into oblivion, disappearing forever from sight, into the depths of darkness, within the cold and lifeless bowels of the earth—an incredibly sad and miserable fate that no one on earth deserves to suffer and die. Never in my wildest imagination or dreams would I have ever thought that the earth would open its mouth and swallow me alive!

~

Narrator:

As time progresses, Everest sinks further and deeper into the pit of doom. He is now up to his neck in quicksand. It is just below his Adams apple.

~

Everest Hothmyer:

Suddenly, as I looked up and in to the far distance, beyond natures natural door or opening (a gap in the forest of trees); a wide-open doorway that's located within the tall trees that outline the dense woodland and forest, that forms both a gateway entryway into the woods, and also an exit that leads to a spacious, open clearing, carpeted in a grassy field of overgrown blades, I happened to spot and see the image of a person, who appears to be in the shape of a woman, with long, flowing, golden hair.

"Wait a minute," I thought to myself, as I zoomed in and closely focused in on the image: *"Is that my friend, Joy? Could it be that she came to look for and find me, as she has so often done in the past? Especially during difficult and stressful times, when I'm feeling ever so down and blue; when things are just not going well; during times when I need to get away for a while—to try to make rhyme and sense out of it all?"*

"Joy!... Joy! I'm over here! Joy!... Joy! It's me, Everest! Help me!... Help me!... Help me, Joy!" I shouted as loud as I could.

In response, Joy turned and looked at me—but, as though she didn't hear or even care. And then, she turned away, and quickly vanished into thin air.

With tears in my eyes, and a whimper in my voice, I yelled: "Joy, come back! Joy, please come and rescue me! Come and lend me your helping hand! Come and pull me up and out of this death dealing mixture of water and sand. So, I can once again stand upon solid ground; the place where I used to walk; the happy place where I used to reside, on the clouds of heaven, to where the sun reaches out and greets the sky! Can't you see that I'm lying here in trouble, distress, sadness, and pain? Help me!" I yelled at the top of my voice. "Help me, Joy! Oh Joy, please hear my cries for help! Come and save me from this awful predicament and horrible mess that I've gotten myself into—this miserable fate of impending doom!"

~

Narrator:

The quicksand has now reached higher—all the way up to

Everest's mouth. He is trying his hardest to keep it up and out of the pit. But, unfortunately, he is fighting a losing battle. Finally, after taking his last breath of fresh air, his mouth falls beneath the surface, and then his eyes.

With his head now fully submersed beneath the surface, in sheer desperation, Everest proceeds to raise his hands up and out of the quicksand towards the sky. And then, all of the sudden, he feels a strong hand clasp around and tug on his wrist. Then he feels his body start to rise. It rises up and up, until it is completely out of the pit. And it keeps on climbing and ascending, way up high, clear over darkened clouds, and the bluest of skies; straight on up to the happy place, to where the sun greets the sky!

~

As soon as Everest reaches the destination above, a place called: *"The Resplendent City of Silver and Gold,"*— to his surprise, he sees that Joy is there, standing by his side. However, for some reason, Joy has a much different appearance than she used to have in the past. For her face glows with a glowing brightness, radiance, and splendor that Everest has never before seen; a brightness of true effervescent beauty that could never be surpassed!

~

Everest Hothmyer:

"Joy, you did it!" Everest happily exclaims. "You came to my rescue and aid after all—at both a time and in way that I would never have imagined. You saved me once again! Thank you for your assistance; for lending me a helping hand, and for being my friend!"

In response, Joy says: "Overwhelming sadness is like being in quicksand. It can consume and swallow a person whole. It can sink them into a pit of misery and despair, and even take away their life and soul. You see, in life, there are many uncertainties— you never know what tomorrow will bring. One day, you can be on top of the world. And then, the next day, you can fall into a dark hole or pit. If or whenever that happens, the best advice is to get back up, and never, ever quit!"

In happy reply, Everest turns to Joy and says: "Thanks to you, Joy, I have nothing to fear anymore. For nothing can get and pull me down again into the depths of darkness, despair, and gloom, that lay deep beneath the surface, where true pain and misery lie. Because, I am determined to never again leave your loving, upbuilding, and most encouraging side! For you, Joy, have the ability and strength needed to keep me upon solid and stable ground, and the power to pull me up and out of anything, even the very scary, seemingly insurmountable, and overwhelming, 'Pit of Doom!'[70]

---

[70] Summary: *"The Pit of Doom"* story may seem a little dark and gloomy at first, but as you can see, it has a bright and happy ending! The premise of the story shows the strong influence and effects that depression can exert and have on a person. But, more importantly, the beautiful thing, is that, eventually, Everest discovered what it would take, and help, to pull him up and out of it, which was finding and latching on to the encouraging and uplifting quality of *joy*.

The Importance of Love

As human beings, there is one highly important thing that each and every individual requires, and that is *love*. It is a natural, innate need that is built into all of us. But not only this, it is absolutely necessary and vital to our overall peace, joy, happiness, and well-being. Without it, we don't fare very well. In this regard, I once heard an interesting story that conveys the importance of this.

In the story, there happened to be a hospital nursery, where the doctors were puzzled as to why many of the newborn babies were medically and physically not faring well; that is, except for one child in particular, which was the baby who was situated at the far end of the nursery, by the entry/exit door. For some unexplained reason, this child seemed to be happy, thriving, and healthier than all the rest. It was a complete mystery!

So, one day, the doctors decided that for several nights they would secretly and quietly hide, monitor, and closely watch the area to see what they could possibly learn. Interestingly, to their complete surprise, they found that the cleaning lady, who worked at the hospital — who regularly cleaned the nursery, each and every night — would, after she finished cleaning and mopping the nursery floor; she would stop and wait at the end of the nursery by the entry/exit door until the floor was completely dried. And, while she stood there patiently waiting, she would always pick up the baby that was nearest her, and cradle and gently rock it in her arms. And then, after the floor was dry, she would then put the baby back in its crib, and then leave.

The conclusion of the story was;— the reason why the baby at the far end of the nursery, by the entry/exit door, was happier and healthier than all of the other babies, is because of the love and attention that it was regularly being shown by the old, cleaning woman. What a beautiful and wonderful story! It's an excellent example that shows both the importance and difference that being loved and appreciated makes in people's lives.

Constructive Criticism?

Over the years, I've noticed that society in general has become increasingly negative, critical, and even cynical in their thinking about everyone and anything. Personally, I believe that this mindset, to a large degree, has to do with the false teaching of "constructive criticism."

Constructive criticism is the process of people noting the faults and weaknesses of others, and then offering their opinions on how they can improve in some fashion or form—in regards to their work performance, attitude, behavior, etc. The truth is, so-called *"Constructive Criticism"* can, and has been offered, or given, to a person in regard to pretty much anything and everything in life. However, the thing that is most intriguing about this, is that, it has been taught that this tool (constructive criticism) is a good thing, in that it can potentially help a person in a positive way. However, from both personal experience, and also observation of the negative and harmful effects that it has on others, I have noticed that it often has the exact opposite effect.

What is interesting, is that, although warranted or solicited suggestions for improvement can sometimes be helpful in life; many wield this tool "constructive criticism" like a sledgehammer to bash, destroy, and crush others, which often leaves a devastating aftermath. In the end, the feigned disguise of being a helpful, building, and improvement tool, winds up being what it truthfully is instead, which is *destructive* criticism.

The interesting and crazy thing is, in reality there is no such thing as *"constructive* criticism." For according to Merriam Webster's Dictionary, *criticism* means: "The act of expressing disapproval and noting the problems or faults of a person or thing."

Another source, Dictionary.com defines criticism as: "The act of passing severe judgment; censure; faultfinding."

So, from the definitions above, we can clearly see that *criticism* has a *negative* connotation, not a positive one. There is nothing constructive about it! It is meant to tear down—not to build up. To simply place the word *constructive* in front of the word criticism doesn't make it good or beneficial.

Interestingly, a poem that I wrote, entitled, *"Criticism's Path,"* so aptly notes the negative and bad effects that criticism can and often has on a person. It reads:

It can slay the largest of giants,

Suppress the littlest of growth

Destroy even a glimmer or ray of hope

It can cause anxiety, frustration, and internal pain,

Produce sadden tears that fall like copious rain

It knows no compassion,

It will consume everything in its path

Criticism can leave an ugly aftermath.

∼

So, when it comes to receiving "constructive criticism," you may want to be careful or cautious. Sure, it's one thing to ask for help or to solicit one's honest advice or opinion about a matter or something, but to give or allow them open or free reign to completely bash and crush you and your accomplishments is an entirely different thing! So, take peoples so-called "constructive criticism" in stride. Don't allow it to swallow you up and destroy you.

Growing in a Negative Environment

Below are some valuable tips on how to continue to develop, grow, and remain emotionally and mentally healthy in an overly critical and negative environment. Listed in no particular order, they are:

- Cultivate and maintain a positive attitude or spirit.

- Have and maintain control over your feelings and emotions. Do not let them get the best of you.

- Focus mainly on the positive and good in people and things, and not on the bad.

- Have a regular reading and feeding program that nourishes your *mind* and *heart* with good, healthy, positive, and uplifting things. Things that will generate feelings of love, joy, peace, goodness, kindness, and so forth.

- Don't get too worked up about overly negative and critical situations or people. However, depending on the severity of the situation, if possible, you may need to avoid or steer clear of certain harmful people or things.

- Don't get discouraged by the lack of maturity, development, and growth in others.

- Work hard to encourage and buildup your family members and friends. For this will create a strong inner circle of strength that will help to support and encourage you and one another, especially during times of need.

- Regularly pray to God for strength, help, and support.

- Never give up hope.

Cause of Bipolar Disorder

(A New Theory)

In my previous book *"Bipolar Disorder, A Patient's Story,"* I stated that it was my personal belief that *environment* was the thing that caused my bipolar disorder illness. However, now that I have had time and circumstance to delve deeper into and consider this subject and matter even closer, I wish to amend my theory. Now, I believe that, although *environment* was the *primary* factor that caused my illness, I have come to discover through thorough examination of myself and personal experiences that other factors and things were also involved—that it took more than just environment alone to cause my mental illness. Fact is, I now believe that there was, not just *one* thing alone, but rather, that there were *six* things in total — all working together and feeding off each other — that contributed to and led to my having bipolar disorder illness. See the chart and information below:

CAUSE OF BIPOLAR DISORDER (Six Things)			
#	Factor	Source	Product of
1	Environment	Primary	Society's structure, thinking, behavior, and actions.
2	Personal experiences	Secondary	- Environment. - Random happenings and personal choices.
3	Personality	Secondary	- Environment. - Genetics (possibly?). - Personal experiences. - Thinking. - Feelings and emotions.
4	Thinking	Secondary	- Environment. - Personal experiences. - Personal beliefs and

			viewpoints.
			- Feelings and emotions.
5	Feelings & emotions	Secondary	- Environment.
			- Personal experiences.
			- Personality.
			- Thinking.
6	Emotional trauma or stress	Secondary	- Environment.
			- Personal experiences.
			- Personality.
			- Thinking.
			- Feelings and emotions.

Note: *"Environment"* Meaning: society's structure, thinking, behavior, and actions (inside and outside of home).

Yes, as you can see from observing the chart above, according to the listed items, there was, not just *one* thing alone, but instead, there were *six* things in total that caused my bipolar disorder illness. They were (1) *environment,* (2) my *personal experiences*, (3) my *personality*, (4) my *thinking*, (5) my *feelings and emotions,* and lastly, (6) *emotional trauma or stress*. Note: This is a new theory that I personally discovered, conceived or came up with.

In the past, during Step #5 *"Finding the Root Cause of My Illness,"* of the bipolar disorder healing process (back when I was initially searching to find the root cause or source of my bipolar disorder), I discovered that *environment* was the culprit that caused my illness. However, now, by means of further, thorough, self-examination, and personal experiences, I've come to discover, realize, and believe that environment was not the single factor or thing, acting alone, that caused my disease, for along the road to recovery and being cured of my bipolar disorder, I discovered five (5) additional factors or things that played significant, *secondary* roles in contributing to my mental illness as well. Under the following six subheadings, note the way that each of these individual, 6 factors (which are also listed in the above chart), contributed to my developing and having bipolar disorder.

Environment

*In what way did my **environment** contribute to my mental illness?* Whether we realize it or not, our *environment* that we live and function in, can have a powerful influence and effect on us (for good or bad). Unfortunately, the bad environment that I was in (prior to being cured of my bipolar disorder illness) was unjust, unloving, and overly critical and negative towards me (and yet, at the same time, it was accepting, encouraging, and loving to others). Among other things, it viewed and treated me as though I had little to no importance or value. The result of this cold and unjust treatment had a detrimental effect on my mind, heart, and soul, thereby resulting in anxiety, stress, and depression, which later led to bipolar disorder.

Interestingly, if this bad environment would have been different or if it had eventually changed for the better—by turning around and viewing and treating me justly—with love, respect, and kindness, etc., rather than the unjust an unloving way that it did, I believe that I would not have come down sick with depression and bipolar disorder in the first place. The reason being, is because, there would not have been anything there (in the environment) to cause me mental and emotional anguish, anxiety, suffering, and pain.

Another interesting thing, is that, if I were the type of person who had a callous and insensitive heart—a person that didn't really care about how others or society viewed and treated me—the environment would possibly, not have had any negative effects on me whatsoever. In other words, the horrible way that I was being viewed and treated would not have been penetrable, in that, it would not have had any impact or influence on me. It would have been like water off a duck's back—thereby, possibly protecting me from certain harm. But, in reality, possessing a callous and insensitive heart would not be the way to be, for this would have been unhealthy for me too. But not only that, it would also make me no better or different than the emotionally insensitive, cold climate and environment that I was in. However, because I am a caring, loving, and appreciative person with a big heart, it bothered me when I was being viewed and treated unjustly, disrespectfully, and as though I was of little to no value (something that took place pretty much on a daily basis). The end result was that this bad environment produced feelings of frustration, anxiety, hurt, and pain, etc., in me, which triggered and fed depression, and later on, led to bipolar disorder illness.

Could environment *alone* have caused my depression and bipolar disorder illness? The answer is *no*. I believe that although *environment* was the *primary* factor or cause, that also, in addition to this, other factors — secondary things — were also needed to cause my mental illness. Because in order for the bad environment to harm and affect me negatively, (1) my *personal experiences*, (2) my *personality*, (3) my *thinking*, (4) my *feelings and emotions*, and lastly, (5) *emotional trauma or stress* would also have been involved. For more on the 'environment' that I was in (prior to being cured of my bipolar disorder), see Step #6 *"Finding the Right Environment,"* on pages 44-54; and also my book *"Bipolar Disorder, A Patient's Story."*[71]

Personal Experiences

*In what way did my **personal experiences** contribute to my mental illness?* As it turned out, I've had many personal experiences in life—a lot of them were good, and others were bad. Unfortunately, the negative or bad things that I experienced and was exposed to eventually outweighed the good, in that, they had a greater influence and impact upon my health. The end result was that these harmful things ended up taking a negative toll upon my mental and emotional well-being.

Today, in looking back at and examining my past, and the harmful and detrimental effects that my bad experiences had on me, I was wondering if there was perhaps something that could have been done to stop or prevent these things from having had such a harmful and negative effect on me and my health. In other words, if I could travel back in time, what could I possibly have done to

---

[71] My book *"BIPOLAR DISORDER, A PATIENT'S STORY,"* can be purchased at www.amazon.com

change things, so that my bad experiences would not have hurt and harmed me?

Perhaps, one possible solution, would be to take away all of the bad experiences that I went through, so that I didn't have to go through and experience them. Sure, this sounds good in theory. However, in reality, this would be totally unrealistic, because it is a normal part of life and the imperfect structure of both society and human beings for everyone to be exposed to both positive and negative experiences. You cannot shield and protect someone from these things. And yet, although this may be true, life's experiences can be different and harder for some people, than they are for others—based upon the subject matter, degree of difficulty, and the trying issues and circumstances that they have to personally face and go through.

Another possibility to consider—that perhaps could have prevented, or at least served to lessen the impact or degree of mental and emotional harm that I experienced, would be for me to change the way that I personally viewed or looked at the issues or problems that I was undergoing—so as to avoid or lessen the harm, hurt, and pain. In other words, change the personal interpretation or meaning of how I viewed or perceived these things, so as to soften the blow, so to speak. Of course, this is easier said than done. But also, changing the personal interpretation or meaning of an issue, or something, still doesn't take away the true, actual, underlying situation or problem. It only masks or covers it over.

Perhaps, another possible way to handle things, so that my bad experiences would not have harmed or hurt me, would be for me to completely ignore the problems all together—acting like they never happened or hoping that they would eventually go away. However, this too would not work either, because it would be like putting a Band-Aid over an open sore or injury. True, you can't see the sore or injury, because it is covered over. But, it's still there. Yes, in reality, although you may try to ignore the issue or problem that you are experiencing (by covering it over, so to speak), it is still entering and affecting your subconscious mind, and also your heart and soul, which, in time, will eventually resurface, to perhaps inflict even greater injury or harm. Fact is, this and the other scenario above is what happened to me personally.

Note: When it comes to truly understanding what another person might be going through in life, in regard to situations, problems, and trials, etc., often, as an onlooker, it is hard for us to understand or even begin to imagine what they are really going through. One reason why, is because, each of us are separate individuals with a unique internal make up and personality that is different from anyone else. Another reason why, is because, each of us has our own set of problems that are often unique to us and our individual circumstances alone. In other words, no other person is necessarily going to have or go through the exact, same problems or situations that we personally are going through—thereby limiting their scope of understanding when it comes to truly relating and understanding what we are experiencing or going through. That is why these things are called: *"personal"* experiences. Sometimes, we, as observers and onlookers, may think or say that we understand. But, in reality, we really don't.

Could my personal experiences *alone* have caused my depression and bipolar disorder? The answer is *no*. I believe that they were only a *secondary* factor, and that additional factors and things were also needed as well. The reason why, is because, our personal experiences are a product of and are influenced and effected by, (1) *environment*, (2) our *personality*, (3) our *thinking* and, (4) our *feelings and emotions*. For more on my 'personal experiences' see my book *"Bipolar Disorder, A Patient's Story."*

Personality

*In what way did my **personality** contribute to my mental illness?*[72]

---

[72] ***Personalities—what makes them?*** There are a number of contributing factors that go into shaping our individual personality. Among them are: our social status, our economic situation, our environment, our culture, our parents, our friends and associates, and also our religious background. Even the television programs and movies we watch, as well as other forms of entertainment, leave their impression and mark. And lastly, although not proven, possibly our genes.

Well, in order to understand how my personality contributed to my mental illness, you first have to know and understand what my environment was like. As I mentioned earlier, it was an environment that was oppressive, unjust, unloving, and overly critical and negative towards me, personally—an environment that viewed and treated me as being of little to no importance or value. Okay, now that we have gotten that out of the way, let me go on to explain how my *personality* contributed to my illness.

After taking a closer look at myself, and also the structure and circumstances of my environment (the previous environment that I was in prior to being cured of my bipolar disorder), I came to discover that environment was not the only cause of my mental illness, but also, in addition to this, there were also certain aspects or things about my personality—certain *qualities* or *traits* that I possessed, that were also to blame. How or in what way? In that, these qualities were stirring up anxiety, depression, hurt, and pain, etc., in me — bad feelings and emotions that my overly critical and negative, past environment was directly responsible for creating and feeding. Unfortunately, these things ended up creating serious problems for me, in that, they had a direct effect on my health (mental and emotional), which eventually led to me suffering from depression, and later on, having bipolar disorder.

The strange thing, is that, as far as my *personality* goes, it wasn't necessarily anything bad about me that was causing problems, but rather, it was some of the *good* qualities that I possessed that were causing issues for me. How could this be remedied or fixed? Truth is, the primary or main source of the problem — my past, bad *environment* — which I had to reenter at times (after I had left it and replaced it with a new and good environment), was not going to change for the better. Therefore, I had no other alternative or choice but to alter or change things about myself instead, that is, if I wanted my mental and emotional health to recover, improve, and to eventually be healed and cured of my depression and bipolar disorder illness.

What was it that I needed to alter or change about myself or my personality? I needed to change, not my entire personality, but rather, I had to alter and balance out some of the good traits or qualities that I possess. For example, such as the attribute or quality of being *nice* (overly nice in my case), which was causing people to either take advantage of or attack me mentally and emotionally in some fashion or form.

Another thing that I needed to change or balance out was my innate trait or ability to *think deeply*, which I unwisely was allowing my negative environment to influence and direct in a bad and negative way. In essence, the bad environment was diverting my thinking away from being positive, by influencing it to go in to negative areas— down the wrong path— into areas that were stirring up bad feelings and emotions in me. How was it doing this? It was by means of the bad environment unjustly attacking my character, image, and value, which I believe, for some reason, it was envious and jealous of. The end result, was that this highly caustic, negative environment diverted my mind and attention away from positive thinking and thoughts, towards unhealthy and negative ones, thereby causing me to inflict mental and emotional harm and pain on myself. In other words, it was a matter of *negative* feeding *negative!*

Interestingly, if I was the sort of person that had an insensitive or callous heart, or if I just didn't care about how people and society viewed and treated me, the bad environment would possibly not have had any negative and harmful effects and influence on me whatsoever. In other words, it would not have been penetrable. However, because I am a good, caring, appreciative, and loving person with a big heart — that wanted to be viewed and treated in a humane, just, and kind way — the same way that other people within my environment were being viewed and treated, it bothered me that I wasn't. The end result, was that it produced feelings of frustration, anxiety, and depression in me, which eventually led to bipolar disorder.

So, from the above information we can see, that, along with my bad *environment,* that also my *personality* contributed to my illness. However, on the other hand, if my environment would have been different, by being positive, caring, loving, and supportive, rather than being unjust, unloving, overly critical and negative, it would not have triggered and produced bad feelings and emotions in me in the first place. And therefore, I would not have come down sick. In other words, if you take away the bad and negative environment, you, in effect, take away the harmful source, structure, and conditions that affected and influenced my personality in a negative and harmful way, by triggering and feeding depression and other bad feelings and emotions in me. So from this we can see that environment was the *primary* cause of my mental illness, and that my personality was *secondary*. For more information on my 'personality' see Step #7 *"Putting On A New Personality,"* on pages 55-69.

Thinking

In what way did my **thinking** *contribute to my mental illness?* It contributed, in that, I had the habit of thinking about and dwelling on (consciously and unconsciously) negative things within my environment that were disturbing to me, in particular, ugly things that were being directed and thrown (intentionally and unintentionally) at me, personally, by my negative environment. It's not that I selected or chose to think about and dwell on these unhealthy and negative things, but rather, it was the overly critical and negative environment, which was unjustly attacking my character, image, and value, that was triggering, fueling and feeding my mind to think and dwell on negative things. In other words, by attacking me, personally, it was influencing the subject matter that I think and dwell on. Also, because, by nature, I am a person that is a *deep thinker* anyways (one that often has the tendency to over think things), this didn't help matters either. The end result, was that these disturbing things wound up causing me a lot of frustration, anxiety, hurt, and pain, which led to depression, and eventually bipolar disorder.

How could this problem have been remedied or solved so that my thinking didn't have detrimental effects on me and my mental health? Well, upon pondering and thinking about it, I came up with three possible solutions or scenarios.

Scenario #1: Take away the bad environment that was triggering and feeding negative thoughts and thinking in me, and replace it with a good and positive environment that is encouraging, loving, and supportive—an environment that is interested in my overall health, welfare, and well-being. Would this work? Perhaps, that is, if you could find such an environment.

Interestingly, if the bad environment that was triggering and feeding negative thoughts, thinking, and emotions in me was removed or replaced with a positive, loving, and caring environment, I believe that I would not have come down sick with bipolar disorder in the first place, because there would not have been anything there to trigger, fuel, stir up, and feed negative thoughts and thinking in me—things that caused mental anguish, suffering, depression, and pain.

Scenario #2: Change my thinking from negative to positive. This is something that I had tried. However, in my personal case, this was often not an option, because the ugly things that were being directed at me, personally (pretty much on a daily basis), by my bad environment, were up close and personal, and in my face, so to speak—making them virtually impossible to avoid or escape.

Scenario #3: Harden my heart — making it insensitive, callous, and oblivious to pain — so that the negative, harmful, and hurtful things that were being directed and thrown at me by the bad environment would not bother and affect me. Would this work? The answer is *no.* Because desensitizing and hardening my heart would only serve to rob me of the beautiful qualities of peace, joy, happiness, kindness, and love, etc. But also, it would make me insensitive, uncaring, and unsympathetic to other people's problems, sufferings, and pain as well.

Out of the three scenarios above, I found that scenario #1 was the best choice for me, personally. The amazing thing, is that, it worked! For after I replaced my unhealthy, overly negative, bad environment with a good, positive, and healthy one instead, the negative and harmful thoughts and thinking that were feeding depression in me, in the past, eventually disappeared, and my mental and emotional health greatly improved!

Could my thinking *alone* have caused my depression and bipolar disorder? The answer is *no*. It was a *secondary* factor only. For other factors and things were also needed to cause my mental illness. Because my thinking was influenced, triggered, and fed by the following things: (1) my *environment*, (2) my *personal experiences*, (3) my *personality,* and as the next factor will go on to show, (4) my *feelings and emotions*. For more information on my 'thinking' see Step #7 *"Putting On A New Personality,"* on pages 55-69.

Feelings and Emotions

In what way did my ***feelings & emotions*** *contribute to my mental illness?* As was mentioned earlier in Step #8 *"Controlling Your Feelings and Emotions,"* (one of the 15 healing stages that were leading to me being cured of my bipolar disorder), our *bad* feelings and emotions (depending on what they are) can be harmful to our physical health (possibly causing such things as: heart problems, high blood pressure, strokes, respiratory issues, digestive troubles, skin diseases, hives, ulcers, and a host of other physical health problems). But also, our *bad* feelings and emotions can also be harmful and detrimental to our mental health as well.

As I mentioned earlier, in regard to my personal case of bipolar disorder, the overly critical and negative environment that I was in was creating, triggering, and feeding negative thinking in me. Unfortunately, this negative thinking also gave rise to and stirred up *bad* feelings and emotions in me as well, which led to anxiety, depression, and later to bipolar disorder.

Once again; using the same, simple, hypothetical thinking — and yet effective — reasoning and example as I did previously. If I could somehow travel back in time, to try to correct or change my past, how could things have possibly been changed, so that my *feelings and emotions* would not have had a harmful and negative effect on me and my mental and emotional health? One way, is by replacing the bad environment with a good and positive one. This way the negative sources and triggers that were in the bad environment—that were giving rise to bad and hurtful feelings and emotions in me—would have been eliminated—thereby sparing and preventing me from getting ill.

Another possible thing that could have been done to detour or stop bad feelings and emotions from developing in me and ruining my health (mental and emotional), is by becoming insensitive and callous to the injustices and hurtful things that I was experiencing and going through—thereby shielding and protecting me from any mental and emotional harm. However, handling things this way would not be healthy. Because, for someone to not be fazed or affected in some way by serious issues and things that are being directed and thrown at them personally, would not be normal. By becoming insensitive and callous, it would make them less than human.

True, there is the other extreme way of looking at and handling issues too — where some people are too *overly sensitive* about things that people say and do to them — being offended by just about anything and everything that is said or done. But, when you think about it, what possibly made them that way in the first place? Could it be that they were picked on and beat up mentally and emotionally when they were younger and, now, later in life, it's hard for them to suffer anymore abuse? Who knows? Whatever the case, if the environment that they were exposed to in their past was a more positive, better, and healthier one; perhaps they may not be as overly sensitive as they are today.

Could my feelings and emotions *alone* have caused my depression and bipolar disorder? The answer is *no.* I believe that although they played a significant role, that they were only a *secondary* factor, for it took other things as well to cause my mental illness. Because my feelings and emotions were generated and triggered by (1) my *environment,* (2) my *personal experiences,* (3) my *personality* and, (4) my *thinking.* For more on 'feelings and emotions' see Step #8 *"Controlling Your Feelings and Emotions,"* on pages 70-77.

Emotional Trauma and Stress

*In what way did **emotional trauma or stress** contribute to my mental illness?* The emotional trauma or stress that I was subjected to, which I spoke about in my previous book *"Bipolar Disorder, A Patient's Story,"* was brought on by job related issues, etc.,— extremely stressful, personal experiences and things that I went through—that ended with me suffering a mental breakdown, which I personally believe was the final step or factor in the bipolar producing process that triggered bipolar disorder.

Interestingly, if you were to take away the bad, negative, and stressful environmental conditions, and the harmful, personal experiences and things that I was being subjected to on the job, I believe that I would not have come down sick. Because there would not have been anything there to create and trigger emotional trauma or stress—that opened the way for me to contract bipolar disorder illness.

Could emotional trauma or stress *alone* have caused my depression and bipolar disorder illness? The answer is *no.* I believe that it was a *secondary* factor only, and that other factors and things were also needed as well to cause my mental illness. Because my emotional trauma or stress was created, triggered, and fed by (1) my *environment*, (2) my *personal experiences*, (3) my *personality*, (4) my *thinking,* and lastly (5) my *feelings and emotions.* For more information on the emotional trauma or stress that I experienced, see my book *"Bipolar Disorder, A Patient's Story."*

As you can see from all of the information above, there were a lot of contributing factors and things that were involved in my getting or developing bipolar disorder—at least, as far as my individual case was concerned. But it also, shows that for some people (like myself)—that the process causing mental illness, doesn't necessarily happen overnight, so to speak. Instead, it is a progressive process of various stages and numerous factors that happens over a period of time.[73]

At this time, in light of my recent discoveries and experiences, and all of the factors and things that were needed to cause my depression and bipolar disorder illness, I would like to present or propose a *new theory* as to how bipolar disorder is possibly contracted by some, if not by all people. In light of the foregoing information, it is now my understanding and belief that it is not just *environment* alone, nor is it just *emotional trauma or stress* alone, nor any of the other above factors working alone (independently by themselves), that causes bipolar disorder, but rather, that *all* of the six (6) factors that I discovered and listed above, are needed for someone to contract or have bipolar disorder.[74] In other words, in looking at and closely examining the example of my personal case, none of these individual factors *alone* (by itself) could have caused my bipolar disorder illness—not 'environment' alone, not 'personal experiences' alone, nor my 'thinking' alone, etc. Nor could only just two or three of these factors happening simultaneously, could have caused my illness. But rather, it took a perfect storm of *all* six (6) of these factors and things working together, simultaneously, to make it happen. Why? Because all of these factors are interconnected—meaning that they are closely linked or interrelated to one another.

---

[73] Note: I wish to make known the practice and purpose of my using the same illustrations repeatedly for several of the 6 subjects above. Although it may seem somewhat repetitive and redundant to the reader, frequent use of the same illustrations was both deliberate and necessary to prove how closely related and connected each of the six, individual subjects are to each other. Also, due to their close, relative relationships, it shows how *all* of these related, six things, were needed and had to happen for me to contract bipolar disorder. In other words, I believe that all of these individual things working together, simultaneously, are what caused my mental illness. But, not only this, these simple illustrations easily explain and drive home the thoughts and points for comprehension and clarity.

[74] This is a completely new theory—my own, personal theory—that it takes a total of six (6) factors working together, simultaneously, to cause bipolar disorder. The six factors are: (1) *environment*, (2) *personal experiences*, (3) *personality*, (4) *thinking*, (5) *feelings and emotions*, and lastly, (6) *emotional trauma or stress.* This is my understanding and belief of what causes bipolar disorder in people—which is a brand-new theory that I solely came up with or discovered on my own. No one else helped me with it, nor contributed or added anything to it in any way, shape or form.

They do not act alone or by themselves!

In closing, I would like to say that it has been extremely helpful and gratifying to me to have personally figured out all of the important and valuable things above. For me to have discovered the 6 factors that caused my bipolar disorder was an amazing thing—to say the least! For not only am I absolutely thrilled that I could do something valuable to contribute to the advancements of health and science, by finding both the cause and cure for my bipolar disorder illness, but also, most importantly, I was able to use the acquired knowledge that I've gained through my discoveries and findings, as I traveled along the road to recovery from my mental illness (during the 15 steps that I went through, as I discussed and highlighted earlier in this book), to benefit personally from these things. For by working hard to eliminate or change the 6 factors above, that I discovered and believe contributed to and caused my mental illness, I finally was able to get better, heal, and successfully reverse the damage that was done in the past, and thereafter, to totally cure myself of depression and bipolar disorder—an incredible feat and outcome that has, not only proved my new theory — that it takes a total of the 6 factors or things that I highlighted above to cause bipolar disorder — to be true, but also, it has greatly enhanced and improved my health (mental and emotional), and overall life for good! For the amazing results that I have gained has brought me an enormous amount of lasting peace, joy, and happiness!

Today, it is my hope that my findings, discoveries, and amazing, personal story, will go on to inspire and encourage others for many days, months, and years to come!

Vitamins and Minerals

The chart below contains a list of vitamins, minerals, herbal and amino acid supplements, and what they are good for:

Vitamins and Minerals Chart		
Item	Source	Value
Beta-carotene	Provitamin A Carotenoid	Good for eye and skin health, and improves memory and cognitive function. Some natural sources of Vitamin A are: carrots, sweet potatoes, butternut squash, kale, spinach, broccoli, apricots, cantaloupe, red and yellow peppers, and peas. The body converts Beta-carotene into Vitamin A (retinol). Caution: large doses of Vitamin A can cause serious health issues, including death.
Biotin (vitamin B7)	Vitamin	Good for healthy hair, skin, nails, and brain function. Some natural sources of biotin are: eggs, milk, bananas, nuts, soybeans, organ meats, whole grains, cauliflower, and mushrooms.
Calcium	Mineral	Is good for tooth and bone health. Some natural sources of calcium are: dairy products, yogurt, cheese, tofu, collard greens, spinach, kale, rhubarb, salmon, sardines, beans, lentils, edamame, almonds, figs, whey protein, and seeds. Note: Vitamin D is needed to absorb calcium.
Choline	Nutrient	Is good for improving memory and cognition. It is also good

		for DNA synthesis. In other words, it induces cells to make new genetic material (DNA) and to divide. Some natural sources of choline are: eggs, cottage cheese, cauliflower, broccoli, Brussels sprouts, shiitake mushrooms, salmon, tuna, cod, chicken, turkey, beef, beef liver, almonds, lima beans, soybeans, kidney beans, red potatoes, quinoa, and wheat germ.
Chloride	Mineral	Chloride helps keep our body fluids properly balanced. Natural sources of chloride are table salt or sea salt.
Cobalt	Trace Mineral	It maintains the nervous system. Some natural sources of Cobalt are: cabbage, lettuce, spinach, kale, figs, raisins, apricots, prunes, dates, oysters, mussel, liver, and beef. Note: the intake of too much cobalt can cause various health issues, including cognitive decline.
Copper	Mineral	Is good for maintaining the immune system, healthy bones, blood vessels, and nerves. It helps the body to absorb iron. It also turns sugar into energy. Some natural sources of Copper are: Swiss chard, spinach, kale, liver, oysters, lobster, shiitake mushrooms, almonds, cashews, sesame seeds, and dark chocolate.
Fiber	Nutrient	Is good for normalizing bowel function and preventing constipation. Lowers cholesterol levels. Helps control blood sugar levels. Some natural sources are: fruits, vegetables, sweet

		potatoes, lentils, beans, whole grains, chickpeas, quinoa, chia seeds, oats, popcorn, almonds, and nuts.
Folate (Vitamin B-9)	Vitamin	Folate is necessary for producing red and white blood cells, producing DNA and RNA, and transforming carbohydrates into energy. Good for memory, thinking, and depression. Some natural sources of Folate are: Dark green leafy vegetables, broccoli, Brussels sprouts, asparagus, eggs, legumes, beets, citrus fruits, bananas, avocado, papaya, nuts and seeds, beef liver, fortified grains, and wheat germ.
Fluoride	Mineral	Good for healthy teeth. Source of Fluoride is fluoridated water.
Iodine	Mineral	Good for proper thyroid function. Some natural sources of Iodine are: eggs, seaweed, dairy, cod, shrimp, tuna, prunes, lima beans, and iodized table salt.
Iron	Mineral	Improves cognition, boots immunity, helps to reduce fatigue, promotes increased energy, and improves athletic performance. Some natural sources of iron are: spinach, broccoli, red meat, turkey, fish, shellfish, liver, legumes, pumpkin seeds, quinoa, tofu, and dark chocolate.
Magnesium	Mineral	Promotes bone and heart health, it reduces blood pressure, and improves sleep and mood. Some natural sources of magnesium are: leafy greens, okra, avocados, bananas, tamarind, milk, yogurt, salmon, halibut,

		mackerel, oysters, raisins, nuts, legumes, seeds, whole grains, beans, tofu, baked potatoes with the skin, and dark chocolate.
Manganese	Mineral	Promotes bone health; it is an antioxidant; lowers blood sugars; promotes thyroid health; improves brain function; and helps to reduce weight. Some natural sources of manganese are: kale, spinach, romaine lettuce, asparagus, acorn squash, apple, blueberries, pineapple, blue mussels, oysters, clams, oatmeal, hazelnuts, pecans, soybeans, lima beans, kidney beans, chickpeas, legumes, lentils, brown rice, sesame seeds, peanuts, and dark chocolate.
Molybdenum	Mineral	The body uses it to process protein and DNA. It also prevents toxin build up. However, too much molybdenum can cause a buildup of uric acid in the body, producing gout like symptoms. Some natural sources of molybdenum are: Black-eyed peas, beef, chicken, lima beans, yogurt, cheese, beans, lentils, bananas, whole grains, and eggs.
Niacin (Vitamin B3)	Vitamin	Promotes good HDL, LDL, and triglycerides levels. It boosts brain function. And it promotes skin health. Some natural sources of niacin are: plain yogurt, tofu, broccoli, spinach, tomatoes, milk 1%, bananas, apple, salmon, light tuna, turkey breast, chicken breast, ground beef, beef liver, brown rice, sunflower seeds,

		pumpkin seeds, cashews, chickpeas, edamame, lentils, raisins, whole wheat bread, and marinara sauce.
Omega-3 fatty acids: EPA/DHA	Nutrient	Good for the heart, brain, eyes, skin, bone and joint heath, and reducing risk of certain cancers. It can also fight depression and anxiety. Some natural sources of Omega-3 are: salmon, mackerel, tuna, sardines, herring, flax seeds, Chia seeds, walnuts, flaxseed oil, soybean oil, canola oil, and fortified foods such as milk, eggs, yogurt, and juices.
Phosphorus	Mineral	Good for healthy teeth and bones. Helps produce DNA and RNA. Also filters out waste in kidneys. Some natural sources of phosphorus are: milk 2%, plain yogurt, mozzarella cheese, eggs, apple, Clementine, asparagus, lentils, tomatoes, cauliflower, peas, russet potatoes, lean ground beef, chicken breast, scallops, salmon, kidney beans, cashews, sesame seeds, cooked oatmeal, brown rice, whole wheat bread, pita bread, and tortillas.
Potassium	Mineral	Good for the heart and nervous system. It also helps to regulate fluid balance. Some natural sources of potassium are: eggs, milk 1%, soymilk, yogurt, mozzarella cheese, bananas, apple, apricots, cantaloupe, orange juice, prunes, raisins, spinach, broccoli, tomato, asparagus, iceberg lettuce, acorn squash, lentils, salmon, light tuna, turkey breast, beef top sirloin,

		white beard, white rice, brown rice, peanut butter, cashews, flaxseed, black tea, brewed coffee, and molasses.
Protein	Nutrient	It boosts metabolism, it helps to build muscle mass and strength, it aids in recovery after exercise or injury, it reduces appetite, increases fat burning, and lowers blood pressure. Some natural sources of protein are: eggs, milk, cottage cheese, Greek yogurt, tofu, chicken and turkey breast, lean beef or pork, shrimp, oysters, clams, scallops, salmon, herring, lentils, quinoa, pumpkin seeds, peanuts, peanut butter, almonds. And protein powers.
Selenium	Mineral	It acts as an antioxidant, it boots immune system, promotes thyroid health, and helps prevent mental decline. Some natural sources of selenium are: eggs, shiitake mushrooms, oysters, yellowfin tuna, sardines, halibut, sunflower seed, brazil nuts, and chicken breast.
Sodium	Mineral	Sodium, commonly referred to as salt, helps to maintain balanced fluid levels in the body. It is necessary for health. But too much or not enough of it can cause health issues.
Sulfur	Mineral	It builds and repairs DNA, and protects cells from damage. Some natural sources of sulfur are: eggs, cheddar cheese, parmesan cheese, milk, broccoli, asparagus, red cabbage, onions, radishes, Brussels sprouts, leeks, turkey, chicken, beef, ham, liver,

		shrimp, mussels, scallops, almonds, Brazil nuts, peanuts, walnuts, pumpkin seeds, sesame seeds, legumes, lentils, chickpeas, oats, wheat, whole grains, and cider.
Ubiquinol (Co-Q10)	Vitamin	CoQ10 is good for energy, and DNA replication and repair. It is also good for heart health. Some natural sources of Ubiquinol are: eggs, nuts, whole grains, cabbage, broccoli, oysters, avocados, and oranges.
Vitamin A	Vitamin	Good for healthy eyes and immune system. Reduces risk of acne. Supports bone health. Some natural sources of Vitamin A are: eggs, skim milk, ricotta cheese, yogurt, spinach, broccoli, carrots, sweet potatoes, summer squash, red sweet pepper, cantaloupe, apricots, mangos, beef liver, chicken breast, sockeye salmon, Atlantic herring, light tuna, black-eyed peas, baked beans, and pistachio nut. Caution: Because Vitamin A is stored in the body, too much can lead to toxic levels.
Vitamin B1 (thiamin)	Vitamin	It helps the body turn food into energy. Some natural sources of Vitamin B1 are: yogurt, acorn squash, black beans, corn, white rice, egg noodles, pork, trout, and sunflower seeds.
Vitamin B2 (riboflavin)	Vitamin	It helps the body build red blood cells. It aides in producing energy. Some natural sources of Vitamin B2 are: eggs, beef, beef liver, clams, mushrooms, and almonds.

Vitamin B5 (pantothenic acid)	Vitamin	It promotes healthy skin, hair, eyes. It helps the nervous system, and liver to function properly. It turns food into energy. Some natural sources of Vitamin B5 are: milk, yogurt, egg yolk, kale, broccoli, sweet potatoes, mushrooms, cauliflower, corn, avocado, tomatoes, pork, chicken, beef, salmon, lobster, shellfish, whole grain breads and cereals, lentils, split peas, and soybeans.
Vitamin B6 (pyridoxine)	Vitamin	It aides in healthy brain function and nervous system and metabolism. It also helps turn food into energy. Some natural sources of Vitamin B6 are: cottage cheese, tofu, spinach, onions, carrots, winter squash, potatoes, chickpeas, bananas, watermelon, sockeye salmon, yellowfin tuna, chicken breast, turkey, beef liver, raisins, and marinara (spaghetti) sauce.
Vitamin B12 (cobalamin)	Vitamin	Supports healthy, hair, skin, and nails. It is good for boosting energy, and improving memory. May improve mood and systems of depression. Some natural sources of Vitamin B12 are: eggs, yogurt, cheese, liver, clams, sardines, beef, tuna, trout, and salmon.
Vitamin C	Vitamin	Good for growth and repair of body tissue. Some natural sources of Vitamin C are: oranges, red and green peppers, broccoli, tomatoes, Brussels sprouts, spinach, turnip greens, cabbage, cauliflower, potatoes, watermelon, raspberries,

		blueberries, cranberries, pineapple, papaya, grapefruit, cantaloupe, strawberries, mango, and kiwi.
Vitamin D	Vitamin	Good for healthy bones. It can help boost mood, and reduce pain. Some natural sources of Vitamin D are: Fortified milk, salmon, mackerel, and sardines. And also the Sun.
Vitamin D3	Vitamin	Is strengthens bones and immune system. It boost mood. It can improve cognitive function. Some natural sources of Vitamin D3are: eggs, cheddar cheese, milk 2%, sockeye salmon, rainbow trout, light tuna fish, Atlantic sardines, cod liver oil, chicken breast, beef liver, portabella mushrooms, and white mushrooms. Note: too much of these things can cause high cholesterol.
Vitamin E	Vitamin	It's an antioxidant; it's good for eye health, and enhances immune function. Some natural sources of Vitamin E are: spinach, broccoli, tomato, kiwifruit. Mango, wheat germ oil, sunflower oil, safflower oil, soybean oil, hazelnuts, almonds, sunflower seeds, peanuts, and peanut butter.
Vitamin K1 and K2	Vitamin	Promotes blood clotting. Also good for bone and heart health. Some natural sources of Vitamin K are: Natto, eggs, milk 2%, mozzarella cheese, kale, spinach, iceberg lettuce, broccoli, turnip greens, collards, carrots, carrot juice, okra, soy beans, edamame, grapes, blueberries, sockeye salmon, shrimp, chicken breast, chicken liver, roasted

		ham, ground beef, pomegranate juice, Caesar salad dressing, olive oil, canola oil, pine nuts, cashews, and figs. Note: K2 remains in the blood longer.
Zinc	Mineral	It boosts immune system helping to fight off bacteria and viruses. It helps the body to make proteins and DNA. And it helps wounds to heal. Some natural sources of zinc are: low-fat milk, yogurt, Swiss cheese, cheddar cheese, mozzarella cheese, green peas, lobster, oysters, Alaska king crab, flounder, chicken breast, chicken dark meat, beef chuck roast, beef patty, loin pork chops, kidney beans, baked beans, chickpeas, almonds, pumpkin seeds, cashews, and instant oatmeal.
L-Tyrosine	Amino acid	It is an amino acid that supports brain function, and mental alertness. And it also helps to alleviate stress. L-Tyrosine can be naturally found in eggs, cottage cheese, soy, avocado, bananas, fish, chicken, turkey, oats, wheat, peanuts, sesame seeds, pumpkin seeds, and beans.
Ginkgo Biloba	Herbal supplement	It is an extract from the leaves of the ginkgo tree. It improves brain function and well-being by increasing blood circulation to the brain. Caution: It is said that people who are older, or if you have a condition that causes bleeding, or if you have seizures or epilepsy, or if you're pregnant, or if you have diabetes, you should not take Ginkgo Biloba.

References:

Beta-Carotene (last updated August 2020) Retrieved from
https://www.healthline.com/health/beta-carotene-benefits#foods-sources.

Biotin (Last updated March 2019) Retrieved from
https://www.healthline.com/nutrition/biotin-rich-foods.

Calcium (Last updated August 2018) Retrieved from
https://www.healthline.com/health/8-fast-facts-about-calcium. (Last updated
November 2021) Retrieved from https://www.healthline.com/nutrition/15-
calcium-rich-foods#TOC_TITLE_HDR_2.

Choline (Last updated November 2019) Retrieved from
https://www.medicalnewstoday.com/articles/327117. (Last updated April 2021)
Retrieved from https://www.healthline.com/nutrition/foods-with-choline.

Molybdenum (Last updated May 2017) Retrieved
from https://www.healthline.com/nutrition/molybdenum#TOC_TITLE_HDR_6
Retrieved July 4, 2022; https://ods.od.nih.gov/factsheets/Molybdenum-
HealthProfessional/ Retrieved July 4, 2022.Copper. (Last updated July 2021)
Retrieved from https://www.healthline.com/nutrition/foods-high-in copper
#TOC _TITLE _HDR_2

Ubiquinol (Co-Q10) (Last updated July 2022) Retrieved
from https://ubiquinol.org/blog/six-incredible-ways-get-ubiquinol-coq10-food.
(Last updated December 2019) Retrieved
from https://www.medicalnewstoday.com/articles/327209

Chloride (Last updated March 2021) Retrieved from
https://www.mountsinai.org/health-library/nutrition/chloride-in-diet.

 Cobalt (last updated November 2020) Retrieved from
https://www.netmeds.com/health-library/post/cobalt-functions-food-sources-
deficiency-and-toxicity

Copper (Last updated October 2017) Retrieved from
https://www.medicalnewstoday.com/articles/288165#:~:text=Copper%20is%20
an%20essential%20nutrient,cardiovascular%20disease%20and%20osteoporosis
%2C%20too. (Last updated October 2018) Retrieved from
https://www.healthline.com/nutrition/foods-high-in-copper.

Fiber (Last updated January 2021) Retrieved from
https://www.mayoclinic.org/healthy-lifestyle/nutrition-and-healthy-eating/in-
depth/fiber/art-20043983. (Last updated October 2020) Retrieved from
https://www.healthline.com/nutrition/22-high-fiber-

foods#TOC_TITLE_HDR_10.

Folate (Vitamin B-9) (Last updated December 2021) Retrieved from https://www.medicalnewstoday.com/articles/287677. (Last updated April 2022) Retrieved from https://www.healthline.com/nutrition/folic-acid#benefits-uses. (Last updated February 2020) Retrieved from https://www.healthline.com/nutrition/foods-high-in-folate-folic-acid.

Fluoride (Last updated April 2022) Retrieved from https://ods.od.nih.gov/factsheets/Fluoride-HealthProfessional/

Iodine (Last updated November 2020) Retrieved from https://www.webmd.com/diet/health-benefits-iodine#1. (Last updated February 2018) Retrieved from https://www.healthline.com/nutrition/iodine-rich-foods

Iron (Last updated February 2018) Retrieved from https://www.medicalnewstoday.com/articles/287228#benefits.   (Last updated May 2022) Retrieved from https://www.verywellhealth.com/iron-supplements-benefits-4178814. (Last updated January 2020) Retrieved from https://www.healthline.com/nutrition/healthy-iron-rich-foods#1.-Shellfish.

Magnesium (Last updated January 2020) Retrieved from https://www.medicalnewstoday.com/articles/286839. (Last updated January 2020) Retrieved from https://www.healthline.com/nutrition/magnesium-supplements#benefits. (Last updated March 2022) Retrieved from https://facty.com/food/nutrition/10-foods-rich-in-magnesium/?style=quick&utm_source=adwords&adid=460303997732&ad_group_id=73726056362&utm_medium=c-search&utm_term=magnesium%20foods&utm_campaign=FH-USA-Search-10-Foods-Rich-in-Magnesium-Desktop&gclid=EAIaIQobChMI8OPTx6SA-QIVFozICh3whwP0EAMYASAAEgKhxvD_BwE.

Manganese (Last updated August 2018) Retrieved from https://www.healthline.com/nutrition/manganese-benefits. (Last updated March 2021) Retrieved from https://ods.od.nih.gov/factsheets/Manganese-HealthProfessional/.

Molybdenum (Updated May 2017) Retrieved from https://www.healthline.com/nutrition/molybdenum#TOC_TITLE_HDR_4. (Updated March 2021) Retrieved from https://ods.od.nih.gov/factsheets/Molybdenum-Consumer/

Niacin (Updated July 2021) Retrieved from https://www.healthline.com/nutrition/niacin-benefits#TOC_TITLE_HDR_5. (Updated March 2021) Retrieved from https://ods.od.nih.gov/factsheets/Niacin-HealthProfessional/.

2 2 2

3 3

Omega-3 fatty acids: EPA/DHA (Last updated October 2018) Retrieved from http://www.healthline.com/nutrition/17-health-benefits-of-omega-3. (Last updated August 2021) Retrieved from http://ods.od.nih.gov/factsheets/Omega3FattyAcids-Consumer/

Phosphorus (Last updated July 2020) Retrieved from http://www.healthline.com/health/phosphorus-in-diet. (Last updated July 2020) Retrieved from http://ods.od.nih.gov/factsheets/Phorus-healthProfessionals/

Potassium (Last updated September 2017) Retrieved from http://www.healthline.com/nutrition/what-does-potassium-do. (Last updated June 2022) Retrieved from http://ods.od.nih.gov/factsheets/Potassium-HealthProfessional/

Protein (Last updated March 2019) Retrieved from http://www.healthline.com/nutrition/10-reasons-to-eat-more-protein#TOC_TITLE_HDR_5. (Last updated January 2022) Retrieved from http://www.healthline.com/nutrition/high-protein-foods.

Selenium (Last updated August 2019) Retrieved from http://www.healthline.com/nutrition/selenium-benefits

Sodium (Last updated July 2022) Retrieved from https://newsinhealth.nih.gov/special-issues/eating/salty-stuff

Sulfur (Last updated February 2020) Retrieved from http://www.healthline.com/nutrition/foods-with-sulfur

Vitamin A (Last updated August 2018) Retrieved from -benefits#Food-Fix:-Immune-System-Boost. (Last updated June 2022) Retrieved from http://ods.od.nih.gov/factsheets/VitaminA-HealthProfessional/

Vitamin B1 (thiamin) (Last updated December 2021) Retrieved from https://www.healthline.com/nutrition/thiamine-deficiency-symptoms#basics

Vitamin B2 (riboflavin) (Last updated July 2022) Retrieved from https://www.webmd.com/diet/foods-high-in-riboflavin#2

Vitamin B5 (pantothenic acid) (Last updated April 2017) Retrieved from https://www.medicalnewstoday.com/articles/219601#why_do_we_need_vitamin_b5

Vitamin B6 (pyridoxine) (Last updated December 2020) Retrieved from http://www.medicanewstoday.com/articles/219662. (Last updated June 2022) Retrieved from http://ods.od.nih.gov/factsheets/VitaminB6-HealthProfessional/

Vitamin B12 (cobalamin) (Last updated June 2018) Retrieved
from https://www.healthline.com/nutrition/vitamin-b12-benefits; (Last updated
January 2022) Retrieved from https://www.healthline.com/nutrition/vitamin-
b12-foods#foods-list

Vitamin C (Last updated July 2022) Retrieved
from https://www.verywellhealth.com/the-benefits-of-vitamin-c-supplements-
89083; (Last updated July 2022) Retrieved
from https://www.mountsinai.org/health-library/supplement/vitamin-c-ascorbic-
acid

Vitamin D (Last updated February 2021) Retrieved
from https://www.webmd.com/vitamins-and-supplements/ss/slideshow-low-
vitamin-d

Vitamin D3 (Last updated April 2022) Retrieved from
https://www.discovermagazine.com/lifestyle/17-vitamin-d3-benefits-everyone-
should-know. (Last updated April 2022) Retrieved from
http://ods.od.nih.gov/factsheets/VitaminD-HealthProfessional/

Vitamin E (Last updated March 2021) Retrieved from
http://ods.od.nih.gov/factsheets/VitaminE-HealthProfessional/

Vitamin K1 and K2 (Last updated March 2021) Retrieved
fromhttp://ods.od.nih.gov/factsheets/VitaminK-HealthProfessional/

Zinc (Last updated December 2021) Retrieved from
http://ods.od.nih.gov/factsheets/Zinc-Consumer. (Last updated December 2021)
Retrieved from http://ods.od.nih.gov/factsheets/Zinc-HealthProfessional

L-Tyrosine (Last updated October 2021) Retrieved from
http://www.webmd.com/diet/health-benefits-l-tyrosine#2

Ginkgo Biloba (Last updated March 20222) Retrieved from
http://www.webmd.com/vitamins-and-supplements/benefits-ginkgo-biloba

Disclaimer: I do not endorse or recommend that anyone take vitamin, mineral, herbal, or amino acid supplements, nor do I endorse or recommend the vitamins, minerals, herbal or amino acid supplements in the chart above. These things are provided for educational purposes only. Before starting or taking vitamins, minerals, herbal or amino acid supplements, consult with your doctor or other professional health officials to make sure that they are safe and right for you.

References

Listed by Page Number

Page 29

1. Eleanor Roosevelt, the diplomat and former first lady, once said: "No one can make you feel inferior without your consent." (July 2022) Retrieved from https://quoteinvestigator.com/2011/03/30/not-inferior/.

Pages 75, 212

2. According to World Health Organization (WHO), a healthy diet for an adult. (29 April 2020) Retrieved from https://www.who.int/news-room/fact-sheets/detail/healthy - diet.

Page 174

3. National Institute of Mental Health (NIMH). (November 2017). Prevalence of Bipolar Disorder Among Adults. Retrieved from https://www.nimh. nih.gov/health/statistics/bipolar-disorder.shtml.

4. The World Health Organization (WHO) says that worldwide: "In 2019, 40 million people experienced bipolar disorder." (8 June 2022). Retrieved from https://www.who.int/news-room/fact-sheets/detail/mental-disorders.

Sources

(Famous Bipolar People)

Vincent Van Gogh, artist. Perry, I. 'Vincent van Gogh's illness a case record' in Bulletin of the History of Medicine, 1947, Volume 21, pp. 145-172.

Edgar Allan Poe, poet and writer, "Poe certainly had manic and depressive periods". Life and Letters and the London Mercury: An International Monthly of Living, Published by Brendin Pub. Co., 1929 (v.2 1929 Jan–Jun, p.171)

Ernest Hemingway, American journalist. He was diagnosed with bipolar disorder and insomnia in his later years. He committed suicide in 1961. Being Ernest: John Walsh unravels the mystery behind Hemingway's suicide." Independent.co.uk. 10 June 2011. Retrieved 18 November 2016.

Charles Dickens (2017, May 28) Retrieved from https://allthatsinteresting.com/historical-figures-mental-disorders.

Abraham Lincoln, Researchers believe he suffered from major depressive disorder [manic depression]. In a letter to his first law partner. Lincoln writes: "I am now the most miserable man living. If what I feel were equally distributed to the whole human family, there would not be one cheerful face on the earth. To remain as I am is impossible; I must die or be better, it appears to me." Retrieved from bphope.com. (July 2022)

Florence Nightingale, suffered from bipolar disorder. CBC News. (Updated May 2003) Retrieved from http://www.cbc.ca/news/world/Florence-nightingale-suffered-from-bipolar-disorder-1.366460.

Mark Twain (2017, March 4) Retrieved from https://medium.com/@michellemonet/twelve-famous-people-who-were-highly-successful-in-spite-of-their-mental-illness-36793055f41b.

Vivian Leigh, Holden, Anthony (1988). Laurence Olivier. New York: Atheneum. p. 183. ISBN 978-0-689-11536-3. "At these moments Vivien turned into a stranger, whom he was seemingly incapable of helping. It was the beginning of a long and tortured series of such attacks, to be diagnosed some years later as manic depression."

Kim Novak — Rebecca Keegan (13 April 2012). "Kim Novak says she's bipolar, regrets leaving Hollywood". Los Angeles Times.

Marilyn Monroe: The Final Days, a 2001 documentary, shed some light on her drug use and mental health. "We knew that she was a manic depressive," Monroe's physician, Hyman Engelberg, MD, says in the film. "That always meant that there were emotional problems and that she could have big swings in her moods."

Phyllis Hyman, American R&B singer-songwriter. Michael, Jason (2007). Strength of a Woman: The Phyllis Hyman Story. Jam Books. ISBN 978-0979489006.

Amy Winehouse, English singer-songwriter. Salahi, Lara (25 July 2011). "Amy Winehouse: Career Shadowed by Addiction". ABC News. Retrieved 24 July 2011.

Jimmy Piersall, Goldstein, Richard (4 June 2017). "Jimmy Piersall, Whose Mental Illness Was Portrayed in 'Fear Strikes Out,' Dies at 87". The New York Times. Retrieved 4 June 2017.

Delonte West. Ken Berger (22 November 2010). "West deals with bipolar disorder, gets back on track". CBS Sports. Archived from the original on 23 November 2010.

Mel Gibson "Mel opens up, but ever so fleetingly." The Sydney Morning Herald. (15 May 2008)

Richard Dreyfuss, actor, appeared in a BBC documentary to talk about his experience with the disorder. Entertainment | Comedian Fry reveals suicide bid". BBC News. 21 July 2006. Retrieved 30 August 2015.

Robert Downy Jr, "Robert Downy Jr health: Actor's health battle revealed by family member – the symptoms." (January 2020)

Judy Garland, according to The Sage Encyclopedia of Intellectual and Developmental Disorders, Judy Garland may have suffered from bipolar disorder. Retrieved from thelist.com (July 2022)

Patty Duke, actress, author, and mental health advocate. Duke, Patty (1992). A Brilliant Madness: Living with Manic Depressive Illness. New York: Bantam Books. ISBN 978-0-553-56072-5.

Rosemary Clooney, (1977). This Is For Remembrance. Playboy Press. ISBN 978-0671169763.

Jim Carrey, "Mariah Carey reveals bipolar disorder." BBC News. April 2018.

Maria Bamford , David Burger (22 June 2011). "Comic Maria Bamford will cross personal boundaries at Utah show". The Salt Lake Tribune. "I was re-diagnosed (after a three-day stay at the hospital) as Bipolar II". II" Maria

Bamford, American comedian, stated in an interview with The Salt Lake Tribune that she has been diagnosed with bipolar II disorder.

Linda Hamilton, "Linda Hamilton says she has bipolar disorder". MSNBC. 14 September 2004. Archived from the original on 16 September 2004. Retrieved 30 August 2015

Carrie Fisher, "Entertainment | Comedian Fry reveals suicide bid". BBC News. 21 July 2006. Retrieved 30 August 2015. "Carrie Fisher 'strikes back' at mental illness". Usatoday.Com. 30 May 2002. Retrieved 30 August 2015.

Catherine Zeta-Jones, Welsh actress, has Bipolar II disorder. Fleeman, Mike (13 April 2011). "Catherine Zeta-Jones Treated for Bipolar Disorder". People. Time, Inc. Retrieved 13 April 2011.

Jean-Claude Van Damme (2012, May 2) Retrieved from http://www.howibeatdepression.com/how-jean-claude-van-damme-beats-bipolar.

Connie Francis. Robert Sokol (1 March 2007). "Lipstick on your collar?" Bay Area Reporter.

Nina Simone. Higgins, Ria (24 June 2007). "Best of Times Worst of Times Simone". The Times. London. Retrieved 8 May 2010. "Interview with her daughter."

Frank Sinatra, American singer and actor. "Being an 18-karat manic depressive, and having lived a life of violent emotional contradictions, I have an over-acute capacity for sadness as well as elation."Summers, Anthony; Swan, Robbyn (2005). Sinatra: The Life. New York: Alfred A. Knopf. ISBN 978-0-375-41400-8.

Charlie Sheen, American actor. Charlie Sheen reveals bipolar diagnosis on Dr Oz". Evening Standard. 19 January 2016. Retrieved 3 August 2020.

Jimi Hendrix, wrote a song about his own life and experience entitled: "Manic-Depression."

Charlie Pride, Pride, Charley (May 1995). Pride: The Charley Pride Story. Quill. "Pride discusses business ventures that succeeded and those that failed, as well as his bouts with manic depression. He tells his story with no bitterness but lots of homespun advice and humor."

Kurt Cobain, "What Nirvana's Lithium says about religion and mental health."

Britney Spears opens up on bipolar disorder: 'I turn into a different person' Caitlin McBride in Irish Independent, 23 Dec 2013, visited 24 Jul 2020.

Sinead O'Connor, Today.com: "Sinead O' Connor opens up about mental illness struggle in emotional video."

Dusty Springfield, English pop singer. Eliscu, Jenny. (14 June 2007), "The Diva and Her Demons." Rolling Stone. (1028):58–69. Retrieved 23 July 2011. Annie J. Randall (2009). Dusty!: Queen of the Postmods. Oxford University Press. p. 128. ISBN 978-0199887040.

Rene Russo, American actress, producer, and former model. Christie D'Zurilla (15 October 2014). "Rene Russo didn't expect to reveal her bipolar disorder – but she did". Los Angeles Times.

Chris Brown, American singer, songwriter, rapper, dancer, and actor, Brown has been diagnosed with Bipolar II disorder. Miriam Coleman (1 March 2014). "Chris Brown Suffers From Bipolar Disorder, PTSD, Says Court Report". Rolling Stone.

Selena Gomez, American singer-songwriter and actress. Revealed her bipolar diagnosis in April 2020 in an Instagram livestream with Miley Cyrus.

Demi Lovato: Bipolar but staying strong. (2015). Retrieved from treatmentadvocacycenter.org/about-us/our-blog/69/2036.

Mariah Carey, American singer-songwriter. Diagnosed with Bipolar II disorder in 2001. Mariah Carey reveals bipolar disorder". BBC News. 1 April 2018. Retrieved 11 April 2018.

Dick Cavett, "CNN.com – Transcripts". Transcripts.cnn.com. 12 June 2005. Retrieved 30 August 2015.

Jane Pauley, TV presenter and journalist. The former Today and Dateline host describes being diagnosed with bipolar disorder in her 2004 autobiography Skywriting: A Life Out of the Blue, as well as on her short-lived talk show.

Jesse Jackson, Jr., former member of the United States House of Representatives, has stated he's been diagnosed with bipolar II disorder. Szalavitz, Maia (16 August 2012). "Jesse Jackson Jr.'s Bipolar 2: A Diagnosis Muddled by the Market". Time. Time Inc. Retrieved 16 August 2012.

Jonathan Winters. Pat Dowell (30 July 2011). "Jonathan Winters Reflects On A Lifetime Of Laughs." Weekend Edition Saturday. NPR.

Ted Turner, American Media businessman. Founder of CNN. At Long Last, He's Citizen Ted." Forbes. Retrieved 30 August 2015.

Ben Stiller, Quote of the Day: Ben Stiller on depression". 20 August 2001.

Burgess Meredith, "Burgess Meredith dies at 89 – 10 September 1997". CNN.

10 September 1997. Retrieved 30 August 2015.

Jaco Pastorius, jazz musician. "Jaco was diagnosed with this clinical bipolar condition in the fall of 1982. The events which led up to it were considered "uncontrolled and reckless" incidents.

Francis Ford Coppola, American film director, producer, and screenwriter, was diagnosed by a psychiatrist as having bipolar disorder. Phillips, Gene D. (2013). Godfather: The Intimate Francis Ford Coppola. University Press of Kentucky. p. 157. ISBN 978-0-8131-4671-3.

Winston Churchill, Ye, R. (2015). International Bipolar Foundation, "Winston Churchill and mental illness."

Theodore Roosevelt, psychologist Kay Redfield Jamison said she characterized Theodore Roosevelt as: "hypomanic on a mild day. He wrote 40 books, and read a book a day, even as president. He also went into an extended depression that saw him reinvent himself as a cowboy." Retrieved from bphope.com (July 2022).

Ludwig van Beethoven (2012, September 12) Retrieved from https://www.theatlantic.com/health/archive/2012/09/historical-geniuses-and-their-psychiatric-conditions/262249/ (2017, May 28) Retrieved from https://allthatsinteresting.com/historical-figures-mental-disorders.

Wolfgang Amadeus Mozart (2017, April 11) Retrieved from https://graduateway.com/mozart-and-bipolar-disorder/.

Earnest Hemingway, "Being Ernest: John Walsh unravels the mystery behind Hemingway's suicide". Independent.co.uk. 10 June 2011. Retrieved 18 November 2016. Thakkar, Vatsal; Collins, Christine Elaine (2006). Depression and Bipolar Disorder. Infobase Publishing. p. 15. ISBN 978-1-4381-1836-9. Hemingway family mental illness explored in new film". Retrieved 18 November 2016.

Virginia Woolf. Dalsimer, Katherine (May 2004). "Virginia Woolf (1882–1941)". American Journal of Psychiatry. 161 (5): 809. doi:10.1176/appi.ajp.161.5.809. PMID 15121644.

Rembrandt van Rijn (2007, January) Retrieved from https://pubmed.ncbi.nlm.nih.gov/17220733/.

Pablo Picasso, Irregular: Bipolar Picasso. (2016, October 10). Retrieved September 25, 2020 from https://centmagazine.co.uk/art-bipolar-picasso/

Sir Isaac Newton, "The Madness of Sir Isaac Newton." (2012, September 12)

Retrieved from https://www.theatlantic.com/health/archive/2012/09/historical-geniuses-and-their-psychiatric-conditions/262249/ (2017, May 28) Retrieved from https://allthatsinteresting.com/historical-figures-mental-disorders.

ABOUT THE AUTHOR

Author, Charles Shelton, is a graduate of Northwestern Electronics College of Technology. He lives in the state of Minnesota. He enjoys reading, writing, the arts, drawing and painting, composing music, exploring and learning new things, going on nature walks, vacationing in Florida, California, and other beautiful and fun places, and spending time with family and friends.

Other books written by Charles are: *"Bipolar Disorder, A Patient's Story,"* and *"Emerald Green,"* and *"Poems That Touch Home,"* and *"Short Stories by Charles Shelton,"* and *"The Kingdom of Colors, Words, and Sounds."*

The books above can be purchased at www.amazon.com

NOTE TO READER

Concerning the four *Short Stories* in this book that I personally wrote (titles listed below) — any reference to historical events, real people or places are used fictitiously. Other names, characters, places, and events are products of the author's imagination, and any resemblance to actual events or places or persons, living or dead, is entirely coincidental.

Story 1: *"Finding The Lost Man That Lies Within—Me"*

Story 2: *"No Vacancy Here"*

Story 3: *"Old Man Zuckerman And His Noisy Ole Cane"*

Story 4: *"The Pit of Doom"*

DISCLAIMER

This book is not a medical book that is intended to provide medical advice or to take the place of medical advice and treatment from your personal Healthcare professional, physician, etc. Readers are advised to consult their own doctors or other qualified health professionals regarding the treatment of medical conditions such as depression and bipolar disorder. The author shall not be held liable or responsible for any misunderstanding or misuse of the information contained in this book or for any loss, damage, or injury caused, or alleged to be caused, directly or indirectly by any treatment, action, or application of any lifestyles, exercises, actions, treatments, vitamins, herbs, minerals, amino acid supplements, or any food or food source discussed in this book. The U.S. Food and Drug Administration have not evaluated the statements in this book. The information is not intended to diagnose, threat, cure, or prevent any disease.

www.ingramcontent.com/pod-product-compliance
Lightning Source LLC
Chambersburg PA
CBHW060003100426
42740CB00010B/1377